15 February 2013

Dear Stanley,

Thanks for the inspiration and the fresh ideas. I hope you find the ideas in this book, which are heretical both in the mainstream and on the left, fresh as well.

In Solidarity,

Brian

The Middle Class Fights Back

The Middle Class Fights Back

How Progressive Movements Can Restore Democracy in America

BRIAN D'AGOSTINO

New Trends and Ideas in American Politics

Raymond A. Smith and Jon Rynn, Series Editors

 PRAEGER

AN IMPRINT OF ABC-CLIO, LLC
Santa Barbara, California • Denver, Colorado • Oxford, England

Library of Congress Cataloging-in-Publication Data

D'Agostino, Brian.
  The middle class fights back : how progressive movements can restore democracy in America / Brian D'Agostino.
    p. cm. — (New trends and ideas in American politics)
  Includes bibliographical references and index.
  ISBN 978–1–4408–0273–7 (hard copy : alk. paper) — ISBN 978–1–4408–0274–4 (ebook) 1. Middle class—Political activity—United States. 2. Middle class—United States—Economic conditions. 3. Income distribution—United States. 4. Political corruption—United States. 5. United States—Economic policy. 6. United States—Social policy. I. Title.
HT690.U6D34   2012
305.5′50973—dc23   2012010984

ISBN: 978–1–4408–0273–7
EISBN: 978–1–4408–0274–4

16 15 14 13 12   1 2 3 4 5

This book is also available on the World Wide Web as an eBook.
Visit www.abc-clio.com for details.

Praeger
An Imprint of ABC-CLIO, LLC

ABC-CLIO, LLC
130 Cremona Drive, P.O. Box 1911
Santa Barbara, California 93116-1911

This book is printed on acid-free paper ∞

Manufactured in the United States of America

I dedicate this book to the Wisconsin and Occupy protestors, who restored hope for the future of American democracy.

Contents

Series Foreword

Change is perennial within the American system of politics and government: the electoral calendar, the ebb and flow of presidential administrations, shifts along generational lines, and long-term patterns of partisan realignment—to name a few of the rhythms and cycles to be found in the political sphere. And so, one year's innovative thinking can become the next year's conventional wisdom, and then the following year's stale orthodoxy. This book series, *New Trends and Ideas in American Politics*, focuses on the most important new currents that are shaping, and are shaped by, U.S. politics and government.

The early 21st century is a particularly important time to focus on a proactive approach to the participatory processes, governmental institutions, socioeconomic forces, and global contexts that determine the conduct of politics and the creation of public policy in the United States. The long demographic dominance of the Baby Boom generation has begun to recede as the Boomers age, even as society becomes ever more open and diverse along lines of race, ethnicity, gender, and sexuality. From the waning of the worship of "the market," to the disasters of the Bush era, to the unprecedented presidential election of 2008, to the steady emergence of a more multipolar and ever-less-certain global context, Americans are faced with new challenges that demand not simply new policies and procedures, but entirely new paradigms. At the same time, emerging vistas in biotechnology and information technology promise to reshape human society, the global ecological system, and even humankind itself.

New Trends and Ideas in American Politics casts a wide net, with volumes in the series unified mostly by novel, sometimes even counterintuitive, perspectives that propose new policies and approaches for Americans to govern themselves, to relate to the rest of the world, and to safeguard the future for posterity. This is no small task, yet throughout its history, the United States has proven itself capable of initiating creative, productive periods of reform and renewal. Indeed, in one of the most strikingly regular and recurrent features of American history, intense periods of political change have occurred about every 30 to 40 years, including the founding in the 1790s, the Jacksonian age of the 1830s, Reconstruction in the 1860s and 1870s, the Progressive Era of the early 20th century, the New Deal of the 1930s, and the upheavals of the 1960s. By this reckoning, the United States is overdue for another such fertile period of political reform; indeed all the elements of a major political realignment are already in place: the Reagan Revolution has run its course, its political coalition fragmented beyond recognition; government is proving itself unable to tackle issues from health care to the environment to globalization, yet seems frozen in place; and citizen engagement is on the rise, as seen in such measures as exceptionally high voter turnout in 2004 and 2008 and proliferation of citizen discussion in political blogs and at "tea parties" tinged with near-revolutionary zeal. Finally, the occupy movement is an encouraging sign that political participation and commitment are increasing. Discerning the patterns in this welter of change will be among the chief tasks of *New Trends and Ideas in American Politics*.

In this volume, *The Middle Class Fights Back*, Brian D'Agostino both analyzes the roots of the decline of the middle class in the United States, and points the way to a brighter future for the 99%. Building on the efforts of the Occupy movements, he shows how the national security state, free market ideology, and the scapegoating of various parts of the middle class, such as teachers, has formed the foundation for the attack on the middle class. In addition, various scare tactics such as worries about the public debt have been used to immobilize progressive movements.

But D'Agostino shows that there is reason for hope. We can pursue a green New Deal to restart the economy, and we can envision a society in which employees own the firms they work for. He sketches the outline of a first-rate educational system, and finally, he discusses how progressives can move from here to a better there.

Raymond A. Smith
Jon Rynn
Series Editors

Acknowledgments

No book is a solitary accomplishment, and this one benefitted enormously from exchanges of ideas with many intelligent people, only a few of whom can be mentioned here. Kelly Feighan, Thomas Giblin, Olivier Mathey, David Orlikoff, and Paul Roochnik read parts of the manuscript and provided valuable feedback. My thinking on worker ownership and control of enterprises is indebted to Carl Davidson and Olivier Mathey. A physicist and financial professional, Dr. Mathey wrote a rigorous and sophisticated appendix on this subject for Chapter 6, and contributed to my thinking in many other areas ranging from international finance to military and energy policy.

Conversations with Moshe Adler, Andre Burgstaller, Jonathan Feldman, Thomas Giblin, Seymour Melman and Richard Wolff gave me important insights into political economy. Saul Mendlovitz emboldened me to imagine a world without war and how to get there. John Burroughs, Alice Slater, Peter Weiss and my other friends at the Lawyers Committee on Nuclear Policy shaped my thinking about international security and environmental issues. Julie Cavanagh, Norm Scott, and others in the Grassroots Education Movement provided important insights on public education and trade unionism, as did Lois Weiner and Constance L. Benson.

I value the ongoing friendship and advice of Robert Y. Shapiro, my doctoral mentor in the Columbia University Political Science Department, who encouraged me to proceed with this project. Cornel West deserves a special acknowledgement for inspiring me and supporting my work. My understanding of political psychology has benefitted from conversations with Jerrold Atlas, Lloyd deMause, Richard Morrock and other members of the International Psychohistorical Association, as well as Myriam Miedzian, Charles Strozier, and Louise Taylor.

It has been a pleasure interacting with the publishing professionals at ABC-CLIO and PreMediaGlobal. Before working with my editors at Praeger—Steve Catalano, Jonathan Rynn, Raymond Smith, and Valentina Tursini—I could not have imagined how much a publisher could contribute to the substance of my thinking. Jon, Ray, and Valentina saw the potential in my book proposal when it wasn't obvious, and provided support and guidance that were indispensable in launching this project. Valentina brought the same grasp of essentials and vision of possibilities to my initial proposal for the book and to the Praeger editorial committee's response to it. As a result of the committee's feedback and her intellectual and communication skills, this book is vastly better than the one I first had in mind.

I owe my biggest debt of all to Jonathan Rynn, whose idea it was that I write this book and who nurtured it from start to finish. I reality-tested many of the ideas herein over breakfast conversations with Jon, and came away with my head buzzing with new ideas. Dr. Rynn read the entire manuscript and provided astute suggestions for improvement. The usual author's disclaimer of course applies here; none of the good people I've mentioned had anything to do with my mistakes, and few will agree with everything I've written.

I gratefully acknowledge the financial assistance and moral support of my parents Nicholas and Marion D'Agostino, and my sister Terry LaRocca. Passionate and intelligent political conversations with my brother Joseph D'Agostino and other conservatives, including some of my students over the years, stimulated my thinking and provided valuable insight into belief systems different from my own. Many of my progressive students made comments and posed questions that were no less helpful. My Episcopalian pastor Victoria Sirota and the Order of Urban Missioners helped me discern that it was my mission to undertake and complete this project. Finally, this book draws from a lifelong and ongoing exchange of ideas with my spouse Constance L. Benson—a scholar, author and teacher with an unfailing commitment to social and economic justice—who also provided invaluable personal encouragement and support for my work.

Introduction

On September 27, 2011, several thousand middle-class protestors descended on Wall Street to express their outrage at the widening economic gulf between ordinary Americans—99 percent of the country's population—and the rich 1 percent that owns more than a third of the country's wealth. While I refer in this book to "the middle class," rather than "the 99 percent," like the Occupy movement I am concerned more broadly with the common good, which encompasses the poor in the United States, people beyond the borders of the country, and the earth's ecology, on which human survival itself depends. I focus on the American middle class, defined in Chapter 1 in terms of income, because it is playing a pivotal role in an emerging coalition that can uphold that common good.[1] This coalition—which encompasses a majority of the poor and a small minority of the rich—is part of an ongoing, international political uprising against the militarism and corporate domination that are undermining the prosperity and security of ordinary people everywhere.

While the American middle class faces rising tuition and student loan debt, increasing health care costs, attacks on their unions, joblessness, and home foreclosure, the 1 percent—epitomized by a corrupt and arrogant financial elite—continues to profit from a political-economic system rigged in their favor, amassing vast personal fortunes at the

---

1. Similarly, middle classes were at the core of the revolutions that established parliamentary democracy in England in the 17th century, achieved American independence in 1776, and that toppled the Old Regime in France in 1789.

xiv   Introduction

expense of ordinary people.[2] Over a hundred activists pitched tents in the financial district's Zuccotti Park and vowed to occupy the site until fundamental reforms were enacted. The Occupy movement captured the political imagination of middle-class people everywhere, inspiring similar encampments in dozens of American cities.

Conservatives—both in the Tea Party scene and in mainstream corporate America—depicted the Occupy protestors as immature and "not serious," a lazy, dirty, and irresponsible mob having no coherent political agenda.[3] A more aggressive counterattack came from elected officials in Oakland, Portland, New York, and some other cities with Occupy encampments. To justify police actions to clear the sites, they condemned them as unsafe and unsanitary, ignoring the hundreds of hardly safer or more sanitary places in their cities—like high-crime neighborhoods, rat-infested public parks, and badly maintained public schools and housing for the poor—which these same officials had somehow managed to overlook for decades. In Oakland, the chief of police reportedly lied about an increase in crime in order to justify using tear gas to disperse the protestors (Daily Kos 2012).

As ridiculous as these claims were, they gained plausibility from frequent repetition by "serious" media pundits, giving mayors the legitimacy to use force against the protestors. New York's Mayor Michael Bloomberg dispersed the original Wall Street encampment at Zuccotti Park with riot police in a surprise raid in the middle of the night on November 15 (Smith 2011). Meanwhile, the *New York Times* tried to dismiss the movement by ignoring it. When thousands of Occupy Wall Street protestors marched in New York City two days later, the *Times* buried the story in the local news section of the paper (Newman 2011). By contrast, it had covered the police action against the encampment in a lead, front-page story bearing huge headlines.

This combination of repression and manipulation of information did not diminish the movement. The repression only made visible the authoritarian way that America's state capitalist elite deals with legitimate dissent. To be sure, repression and police brutality have been familiar facts of life for political radicals, the poor, and minorities for much of American

---

2. I frequently refer to this system as "state capitalism," following usage by Seymour Melman (1983, 2001) and others. Robert Heilbroner (1985) discusses the increasingly important role of the state in the evolution of capitalism and the symbiotic but sometimes strained relationship between the political and corporate elites.

3. In November 2011, Republican presidential candidate Newt Gingrich, then facing public scrutiny for accepting millions of dollars in "consulting" fees as a de facto Washington lobbyist, commented about the Occupy protestors that they should "get a job after you take a bath" (Lupica 2011).

history, acts of violence that generally go unreported and unnoticed in the mainstream. What was different about the Occupy movement, however, was the participation of thousands of ordinary middle class Americans in major protest, their personal experience of this ugly side of the state, and the publicizing of this ugliness in the media and on the Internet.

Historically, the American middle class has tended to identify its interests with those of the rich, believing that anyone who works hard can prosper and only the lazy and irresponsible end up poor or on the wrong side of the law. It is another matter, however, when middle class white folks see images in the media and on the Internet of the police pepper spraying unarmed protestors who look like them and their mothers. Such images are accelerating a shift in the political identity of the middle class, driven by felt economic grievances, from one that encompasses the rich to an identity that encompasses the poor. The Occupy movement's 1 percent / 99 percent way of defining class both reflects and contributes to this revolutionary development.

These recent events are part of a well-established pattern of revolt and repression going back to Shays' Rebellion in 1786, a pattern that includes the movements for abolition of slavery, women's suffrage, the rights of labor, civil rights and social equality, peace and disarmament, environmental protection, and other mobilizations of ordinary Americans to democratize power and craft a just and sustainable future (Zinn 2003). When I use the term "progressive movements," I am referring to mobilizations that are taking one form at the present time but have taken all these other forms in the past and will take new forms in the future as long as power holders continue to run roughshod over the needs of the people.

As for the control of information by state capitalist elites, that is breaking down even as you are reading this book. I read the *New York Times* online on a regular basis, and I am struck by the outpouring of powerful, learned, and deftly written comments from readers who routinely demolish David Brooks and the paper's other conservative pundits.[4] The *Times* is now competing with thousands of news and opinion sites on the Internet. It *must* publish its readers' comments, even if they repeatedly embarrass its regular columnists, or those readers will go elsewhere for more interesting information.

---

4. The *Times* also hires a few critical thinkers, most notably Paul Krugman, who elicits positive comments of equally high quality. My point, however, is that the power elite's monopoly of information and one-way channels of communication is becoming a thing of the past in the age of the Internet.

Indeed, if the corporate-controlled media was until recently what the Church establishment was in the Middle Ages—the authoritative custodian of culture and legitimizer of political and economic power—then the Internet today is what the printing press was in the fifteenth century. When I try to envision a humane and sustainable future beyond state capitalism, I am inspired by the way that the widespread availability and uncontrollable dissemination of printed texts democratized culture in the past, paving the way for the democratic revolutions of the modern period. As discussed in Chapter 8, the progressive movement in America today can use Internet and mobile communication—combined with networks of face-to-face relationships—to bypass America's media establishment and moribund political institutions and institute a "government for the people" through national direct democracy.

Unlike existing parties, the kind of political formation I have in mind would not compete for elected office in the state, but would institute fundamental policy and institutional reforms through national referenda.[5] This book outlines an agenda of such reforms that has two characteristics. First, it is carefully designed to transform the country's power structure and usher in new policies—such as demilitarization, worker ownership and control of enterprises, a green New Deal, and an infusion of resources into neglected public schools—that can actually achieve the goals of the Occupy movement for a peaceful, sustainable, and just society. Second, the agenda I outline can gain the support of a majority of the Occupy movement and of the American people generally.

In order to participate in government in a meaningful way, ordinary people need to understand both the existing system and a program of policy and institutional reforms that can create their preferred future. The first part of this book addresses the existing system, the ways it loots middle-class Americans, and the ideologies that conceal what is happening. Chapter 1 shows how the national security state redistributes income from middle-class taxpayers to the rich even as it fails in its supposed mission to protect the American people. Chapter 2 discusses the

---

5. As discussed in Chapter 8, this would not abolish America's constitution but would alter it by superimposing a component of direct democracy on the existing machinery of government, which would execute and adjudicate such directly enacted legislation just as it does laws passed by Congress. The latter would also continue its work, but could be superceded at any time by the people legislating directly. National direct democracy does not require a constitutional amendment if a large majority of the population, acting on the principle of popular sovereignty, demands it. That principle is what Thomas Jefferson invoked when he wrote, in the Declaration of Independence, that "the People" have the right to alter any form of government that becomes destructive of the ends for which it was established.

economic regimes of capital flight and deindustrialization, legitimized by free market ideology, that are undermining middle-class livelihoods and incomes while corporate profits continue to soar. Chapter 3 dismantles the ideologies that scapegoat public school teachers, union members, and other middle-class workers for the national decline that the state capitalist elites themselves have engineered. Chapter 4 explodes the myths about America's public debt and the supposed evils of taxing the rich that support the current right-wing attack on government.

The second part of the book is a manifesto of the policy and institutional reforms that can achieve the goals of America's progressive movement. Chapter 5 presents the elements of a green New Deal and related initiatives in the areas of energy, taxes, and foreign policy. Chapter 6 outlines local and national initiatives that can transform a corporate capitalist economy that enriches the few into an economy of worker-owned and - controlled enterprises capable of creating general prosperity. Chapter 7 discusses what a first-rate public education system would look like and how to create it. Chapter 8 concludes the book with a road map for building the progressive movement, bypassing the dysfunctional institutions in Washington and on Wall Street, and enacting the progressive agenda outlined in this book into law and public policy.

I want to conclude this introduction with some thoughts on the subject of "class warfare," a term that will certainly be deployed by conservatives in an attempt to discredit the ideas in this book. It will be helpful to begin by stepping back to get some historical perspective on the fierce political polarization in America today. In the 1950s, under the fiscally conservative Republican administration of Dwight Eisenhower, the top marginal tax rate on the rich was 90 percent, and the country was building the interstate highway system—the largest public infrastructure project in its history. None of this was framed as stealing from the rich in support of a "tax-and-spend" agenda.

Some half a century later, Republican leaders were excoriating President Barack Obama as a "big-government" liberal for infrastructure spending in a 2009 stimulus package that was trivial by comparison. The next year, he was accused of "class warfare" for wanting to allow the Bush tax cuts to expire, which would allow the highest marginal rate to go from 35 percent back up to 38.6 percent. If the charges against Obama are justified, then Eisenhower was a big-government politician on steroids and a communist promoting class warfare. That is complete nonsense, of course, but it is a measure of the irrationality that prevails among American conservatives today.

How did the Republican Party get from Eisenhower to its current degraded state? The main protagonist of that transformation was President Ronald Reagan, who, with a genial persona and ebullient optimism about "America," launched what truly can and should be called a class war, one waged by politicians, pundits, and CEOs on behalf of the country's richest 1 percent. Reagan's agenda consisted of massive tax reductions for the rich combined with an attack on unions, middle-class jobs, and social services for the poor. This class war on behalf of the rich has continued for more than thirty years, but it was never called by its proper name. It is only when corrective action is being taken on behalf of the 99 percent that anyone is talking about "class war," and it is apologists for the rich who are deploying that term against progressives.

While the progressive movement can and should protect the interests of the middle class from this onslaught, there is much more at stake. In serving the interests of the rich, state capitalism is neglecting the common good, destroying not only the prosperity of ordinary people today but also the ecological stability on which the future security and prosperity of all depends.[6] The mission of the progressive movement is precisely to uphold that common good, taking actions that will create a just and benign future not only for middle-class Americans but for all. This book is intended as an intellectual tool kit for leaders and ordinary people who want to participate in that revolution.

---

6. The most immediate threat to ecological stability arises from climate change and its worldwide destruction of agriculture, which is already becoming evident in the recent epidemic of extreme floods, droughts, and windstorms. Climate change is caused by excessive carbon fuel use, which occurs because the free market does not impose future environmental costs on those who buy, sell, and use carbon fuels in the present. Reversing climate change will require a carbon tax or similar government intervention (see Chapter 5).

PART I
HOW THE RICH RULE

CHAPTER 1

The National Security Scam

INTRODUCTION

Some coincidences seem laden with meaning. Two events that have profoundly shaped our world occurred in the same year on opposite sides of the Atlantic. British philosopher Adam Smith published *The Wealth of Nations*, marking the birth of modern industrial capitalism. Under that rising economic star, British colonists in North America simultaneously launched a bold political experiment in republican democracy. The year, of course, was 1776.

This historical perspective lends context to the meanings of "free market" and "national security," phrases that corporate and political leaders use today in ways that deceive and confuse ordinary people. To most Americans, a free market system is one in which competition among businesses results in the goods and services that consumers want at the lowest possible cost. This is also the kind of thing Adam Smith meant by the "invisible hand."

Economists now know that to work in this benign way, a market must be comprised of many enterprises, each of which is too small to influence the market price. But conservative politicians and pundits today routinely use the term "free market," which has these positive connotations, to legitimize the power of corporations big enough to dominate not only markets but entire governments as well. Adam Smith detested this kind of concentrated and corrupt power, evident in the British East India Company of his own day (Micklethwait and Wooldridge 2005).

Similarly, to ordinary people, national security means the use of troops and weapons to protect the land and its people from would-be conquerors and oppressors. This is also what the colonial militias meant to the founding fathers in 1776 when they came to view Britain as an alien and oppressive power. By contrast, conservative politicians and pundits today use the term "national security"—which connotes protection and freedom—to legitimize a trillion-dollar-per-year plunder of U.S. taxpayers by defense contractors and Pentagon bureaucrats for government programs that have little to do with protection and freedom.[1]

Conservatives tend to make icons of the founding fathers and the Constitution, while the left is so inclined to smash icons as to forget what was distinctive and new in the United States. Yes, it was deeply marred by the enslavement of Africans and the genocidal displacement of Native Americans. Women and propertyless white males could not vote. But the ideals of popular sovereignty and civil liberties embodied in the American Revolution and the U.S. Constitution were at the time a force for liberation in the world. If 13 underdeveloped and sparsely populated colonies could break free from the mighty British Empire (albeit with crucial French assistance) and govern themselves without a king, why should other peoples tolerate the oppression of kings and emperors? And the American Republic, prodded by grassroots activists, became more democratic over time, abolishing slavery in 1865, granting women's suffrage in 1920, expanding the rights of labor in the 1930s, and abolishing racial segregation in 1964.

Along with these democratic developments, however, the United States was also becoming the epicenter of world capitalism, a place where independent family farmers were being displaced by big agriculture, where great industrial cities were marred by squalid slums, and where big corporations hired thugs to break unions, advertising firms to manipulate consumer wants, and lobbyists to bend government to their purposes. This struggle between democracy and capitalism continues today. After World War II, the United States replaced the British Empire as the dominant world power, and beginning in 1980, the country's ruling elite launched a neoliberal class war at home and abroad that continues to this day.[2]

---

1. All categories of national security spending in the president's 2011 budget request, according to the nonpartisan Center for Defense Information, amounted to $1.049 trillion (Wheeler 2011).
2. The term "neoliberal" is confusing for many people. It refers to policies that free the rich and corporate elite to pursue their goals with the least possible interference from government, which is really the opposite of what is generally meant by "liberal." The term is based on an older usage of "liberal" to mean anything that promotes freedom. By "neoliberal," I mean the policy agenda of reducing taxes, downsizing government (except national security and other corporate welfare), deregulating markets, dismantling unions and permanent jobs, and creating an unregulated global market economy. These policies have been associated with massive job loss in the United States— 30 million full-time positions eliminated from the early 1980s through 2006, according to Louis Uchitelle (2006)—positions lost mostly to global outsourcing and the use of temporary, part-time, and prison labor. For the effects of neoliberal policies abroad, see Stiglitz (2003, 2007).

Self-serving power is always legitimized in terms of "liberty," "justice," or some other noble rhetoric. In the name of freedom and free markets, conservative leaders today—both Republicans and "centrist" Democrats—are dismantling the private sector jobs and government and union benefits of ordinary Americans (Hawthorne 2008; Laursen 2010; Uchitelle 2006). In the name of national security, human bodies are sacrificed on the altar of geopolitical power, and corporations loot not only the U.S. taxpayer but also the resources of our entire planet. In the name of the Constitution, right-wing activists are subordinating democracy itself to corporate and plutocratic power.

The American people now face stark choices. Doing nothing is the same as waiting and watching as the country's self-absorbed and irresponsible power elite plunges the nation and the world into a new dark ages of poverty, violence, and environmental collapse. But there is an alternative, glimpses of which were the March 2011 Wisconsin uprising in support of the state's embattled public employees (King 2011) and the Occupy movement that began at Wall Street six months later. That alternative is the awakening of a sleeping giant—America's middle class.[3] This book aims to enlist that giant in toppling the plutocratic order and demanding economic and political reconstruction on just and sustainable foundations.

THE IRRATIONALITY OF NATIONAL SECURITY IDEOLOGY

In the innermost sanctum of America's national security state—complete with its own priesthood and elaborate theology—stands the nuclear weapons arsenal. The holy of holies enshrines unimaginable power—not

---

3. For purposes of this book, "middle class" can be defined economically as households that are above the poverty line but not "rich." In 2011, the poverty line was set at $22,350 for a family of four (U.S. Department of Health and Human Services 2011). The income level separating "middle class" and "rich" is more subjective. In 2010, political debates about whether to extend the Bush tax cuts for "the rich" referred to a cutoff of $250,000 for joint tax returns and $200,000 for individuals (Calmes 2010). The Occupy movement's definition of the rich as the top 1 percent of the population would encompass all with incomes over $350,000 in recent years (Luhby 2011).

In order to calculate tax burden—the factor most relevant for this book—I am constrained to use income intervals for which tax data are available. On this basis, I define "middle class" as households with adjusted gross income between $20,000 and $200,000 (see the Appendix 1). This income interval accounts for about 60 percent of U.S. households who file tax returns and also happens to be the segment of the U.S. population that provides about 60 percent of "federal funds" tax revenues. While the households in my chosen interval include some that are below the poverty line, these were excluded from my calculation of tax burden, which was based only on households that paid federal income tax (see Appendix 1.1). My definition is broad, encompassing what is generally called the "lower middle class" and the "upper middle class."

just military power on steroids but the ultimate power of the universe. The worship of these weapons and the theological nature of nuclear doctrines have been studied intensively by Robert Jay Lifton and other scholars (Chernus 1989; Lifton 1979; Lifton and Falk 1982; Lifton and Markusen 1990). This veneration helps explain policies that in mundane terms make absolutely no sense.

America's vast and variegated nuclear arsenal is now being reduced to "only" 1,550 weapons under the New START treaty (U.S. Department of State 2010). The arsenal was designed to fight (and thereby deter) a nuclear war against the Soviet Union, which went out of existence more than 20 years ago. Whether or not that Cold War rationale ever made sense, there can be no such justification today. A few dozen nuclear weapons—a "minimum deterrent" in Pentagon jargon—would be more than sufficient to "deter" North Korea, Iran, China or any other state (Beljac 2011; Lewis 2008).

This assumes, of course, that it is morally acceptable to base national security on a technology that would incinerate millions of human beings and make radioactive wastelands of entire cities. I do not accept this assumption, but that is another discussion. Suffice it to say here that there is no conceivable *military* justification for maintaining hundreds of nuclear weapons.

Those who insist on maintaining such absurd levels of overkill—led by Republican Senator Jon Kyl of Arizona (Bennett 2011)—never discuss the country's nuclear policy in such concrete terms, nor do mainstream journalists or Democratic politicians ever challenge them to do so. The need for such discussion is waved aside, as if with a magic wand, by merely invoking the sacred words "national security." After shaking down the Obama administration for $10 billion in additional nuclear weapons expenditures as a condition for approving New START (Young-Smith 2010), Kyl still wanted to delay ratification, which proceeded in December 2010 over his objections (Baker 2010).

It merits some reflection how such a clearly dysfunctional use of tax revenues as seen in U.S. nuclear policy can persist, especially in a time of extreme fiscal austerity. There would appear to be two factors. In addition to the previously mentioned veneration, massive economic inertia prevents a rapid phasing out of the nuclear weapons arsenal. Tens of thousands of scientists, engineers, managers, and workers have developed skill sets and built their careers around building and maintaining nuclear weapons. Billions in annual corporate revenues are at issue. The Livermore, Los Alamos, and other weapons labs; General Electric, Boeing, and other corporations that manufacture nuclear weapons and their delivery vehicles; and the government bureaucracies and workers that plan, manage, and operationally deploy nuclear forces constitute formidable special interests.

It is a truism of political science that such specialized groups are much more highly organized in the promotion of their interests than the general public (Olson 1971). The Lawyers Committee on Nuclear Policy, Abolition 2000, and other public interest organizations promoting nuclear disarmament employ only a few dozen staff, funded precariously by even fewer foundations. By contrast, the labs, defense contractors, and military agencies, such as DARPA, field a well-funded propaganda machine that enlists thousands of think-tank personnel, university professors, government officials, and corporate lobbyists (Hartung 2002; Cabasso 2007a). The contractors also funnel tens of millions of dollars in political contributions to Senator Kyl and other members of Congress of both parties, money on which politicians depend to pay for the television advertising and other campaign costs that get them or keep them in office (Hartung 2002).

The economic and political inertia of such interests, however, only partially explains their grip on government policy. School reform advocates also point to special interests—mainly teachers, their unions, school district bureaucracies, and colleges of education—to explain the shape of public school systems (Hess 2006). Yet the claim of educators on tax revenues is not nearly as large or secure as that of military interests. One measure of this is compensation. A weapons engineer earns 75 percent more than a teacher with the same level of education, and the chief executive officer of a medium-sized defense contractor earns over 18 times as much.[4] And yet it is not considered outrageous for state politicians and conservative pundits to attack teachers' modest pension plans as a misuse of tax revenues (Greenhut 2009), even as a Republican Congress declares obscenely overfunded national security programs exempt from significant federal budget cuts. This double standard requires something more than an economic explanation. We must return to the veneration of nuclear weapons—and of military power generally—the missing factor in any rational picture.[5]

---

4. In 2011, the median total compensation for these three occupations in the Los Angeles area were as follows: public school teacher—$78,703; senior aerospace engineer—$137,680; and aerospace chief executive officer—$1,452,105 (Salary.com 2011). All these occupations require a master's degree. This raises the question of why so many taxpayers can feel ripped off by teachers' unions while having no such feelings about more highly paid defense personnel. To be sure, the compensation of the latter is comparable to that of similar job titles in civilian industry. But my point is that defense personnel, like teachers, are paid out of tax revenues.
5. Some of the psychological sources of this veneration are explored in Appendix I.

The irrationality of conservative discourse is nowhere more apparent than in its double standard for using the term "government." This dirty word is reserved for public services that meet human needs or for the regulation of markets in the public interest. Along with unions and public schools, government has become a scapegoat for the country's declining economic performance. "Tax-and-spend" politicians are allegedly feeding a ravenous and unproductive public sector with the hard-earned wealth of the middle class. In this picture, capital is being siphoned from the engines of economic growth into a dysfunctional, corrupt, and bloated world of earmarks; out-of-control red tape; and entitlement programs that sap ordinary people of their personal responsibility (Armey and Kibbe 2010; Beck 2010).

Yet somehow, hundreds of billions of tax dollars spent on unnecessary weapons systems and military bases and massive Pentagon waste are considered not government but something else—"national security." The sacred-cow status of the latter was on display in April 2011, when House Budget Committee Chair Paul Ryan unveiled an alternative budget that would essentially dismantle Medicare while leaving America's defense budget virtually unchanged (Preble 2011). And neither journalists, nor mainstream progressive pundits, nor the Obama administration were willing to challenge the military sacred cow by proposing deep spending cuts.[6]

I would argue that attacks on government in general are misguided. Yet productive citizens *are* being looted, and their wealth *is* being squandered on unproductive activities and redistributed unjustly. It is just that military-related programs are more guilty of these sins than any other category of government spending (Melman 1983). And the nature of the redistribution is just the opposite of what conservatives imagine.

In fiscal year 2010, national security accounted for two-thirds of federal discretionary spending.[7] According to the nonpartisan Center

---

6. In a bipartisan agreement in the summer of 2011, across-the-board federal budget cuts were scheduled to go into effect in 2013 if the government did not enact more targeted deficit reduction plans by later in the year. As part of that agreement, national security spending would be cut by $450 billion over 10 years (Cassata 2011). While Republican politicians and Defense Secretary Leon Panetta issued shrill warnings that such cuts would be draconian and would imperil national security, in fact they would amount to less than 5 percent of national security spending, and that is on the unrealistically conservative assumption that the latter would otherwise level off at its current amount of about $1 trillion per year.

7. According to the Office of Management and Budget (2011, table S-11), total fiscal year 2010 discretionary spending was $1.26 trillion, of which appropriations for the combined Security Agencies and Overseas Contingency Operations (mostly the wars in Afghanistan and Iraq) were $.85 trillion.

for Defense Information (Wheeler 2011), this understates total national security spending, which now exceeds $1 trillion per year, nearly four times what is spent on Medicaid (U.S. Office of Management and Budget 2011, table S-4). This is more than eight times the military spending of China (Stockholm International Peace Research Institute 2011), the only country that Pentagon planners think might eventually challenge the United States militarily. As this imbalance suggests, the vast bulk of America's national security spending has nothing to do with protecting the U.S. population or ensuring a democratic world order. Rather, as I will show in the following pages, it serves to enrich the already rich investors in defense and other corporations while imposing the tax burden primarily on the middle class. The effect is to redistribute income upward—not to the allegedly idle poor—and to concentrate power in the most bloated of power centers: the national security state.

THE NATIONAL SECURITY STATE IS NOT DESIGNED TO PROTECT THE U.S. POPULATION FROM ATTACK

Whatever else Americans may think about national security, few would consider total world domination by Pentagon bureaucrats and corporate CEOs as a legitimate use of their hard-earned tax dollars. Yet this is precisely the *stated* national security policy of the United States today, albeit expressed in jargon that is less ominous sounding. According to *Joint Vision 2020* (U.S. Department of Defense 2000), which presents official U.S. policy at the time of this writing, the overall goal of U.S. military power is "full spectrum dominance." In this context, "full spectrum" means all the earth's environments—land, sea, air, space, the electromagnetic spectrum, and cyberspace—in other words, the entire world. "Dominance" is defined as the capacity to do whatever they want in these environments and to prevent anyone else from doing what *they* want, in other words, total domination. Thus, "full-spectrum dominance" is Pentagon language for "total world domination." As will be shown later in this chapter, the "national interests" that supposedly justify such total power turn out to be, in reality, *corporate* interests.

Once this is understood, it becomes comprehensible why our national security system costs the taxpayer a trillion dollars per year. Even were the country to forgo extravagant excesses like a 1,550-weapon nuclear arsenal, the proverbial $2,000 toilet seats, and other notorious waste and overbilling (Fitzgerald 1989; O'Boyle 1998), world domination would be expensive. Perhaps it should cost "only" half a trillion, and the taxpayer is being ripped off for the other half. This would be bad enough. But the question would still remain as to why the United States needs total world domination.

Here we encounter the same rhetorical sleight of hand that enables Senator Kyl to legitimize absurd levels of nuclear overkill. Pentagon planners and their accomplices in Congress justify full spectrum dominance by invoking the familiar mantra "national security." Such vast military power, the argument goes, is the only way to protect the American people from terrorists, "rogue states" like Iran and North Korea, potential future adversaries such as China, and other threats to the security of ordinary Americans that we cannot even imagine at present (U.S. Department of Defense 2000). As with nuclear policy, however, this legitimation of the county's defense policy as a whole only works as long as rational discussion is waved aside with the magic wand of "national security."

If rationality is permitted to count for anything, it is a simple matter to dispose of the claim that full-spectrum dominance is intended or able to protect the American people from harm. Human populations are vulnerable to attack from two sources, what are called "state actors" (e.g., Iran and China) and "nonstate actors" (e.g., al-Qaeda). Pentagon planners believe that state actors can be deterred from using weapons of mass destruction by the threat of nuclear retaliation (U.S. Department of Defense 2000). Indeed, this is one reason they are unwilling to relinquish nuclear weapons. (As explained previously, a few dozen weapons are more than sufficient for this purpose.) Note that the United States would continue to have this deterrence capability were Iran to acquire nuclear weapons. Although using the specter of a nuclear armed rogue state to frighten ordinary people, policymakers know very well that this is a bogeyman.[8]

No dictator, however evil and irresponsible, would use weapons of mass destruction against a nuclear armed state. The probability of retaliation would be high, and annihilation of the attacker's state would destroy the very thing its dictator cares most about—his own power (Jervis 2005).[9] It follows from this that a nuclear-armed Iran would pose no

---

8. Jervis (2005) explains why the classical theory of nuclear deterrence applies to rogue states. This is undoubtedly common knowledge among Defense Department officials responsible for nuclear policy and among politicians who have studied nuclear policy or been briefed on it.

9. In acknowledging that nuclear deterrence "works" under most circumstances, I do not mean to imply that it is a safe and reliable path to security, much less a morally acceptable one. In fact, I see no role for nuclear weapons in achieving human security (see Chapter 5). But here I am addressing only the question of whether full-spectrum dominance is needed to protect populations from weapons of mass destruction. Under prevailing military assumptions, it is not.

threat to Israel—which is armed to the teeth with nuclear weapons— much less a threat to the United States.

The reason Pentagon planners do not want Iran and North Korea to have nuclear weapons has nothing to do with the security of Israelis or Americans. It is because nuclear-armed states are able to dominate non-nuclear states, a power advantage that disappears when both sides are nuclear armed (Jervis 2005). But maintaining the power of political elites is not the kind of reason that would persuade ordinary Americans to fork over their hard-earned dollars every year to pay for missile defense systems and the other paraphernalia of full-spectrum dominance. So the bogeyman about Israelis and Americans being vulnerable to attack—our familiar sacred cow of "national security"—is presented as a reason for such capability.

Assuming that full-spectrum dominance is not needed against state actors, however, would it not still be needed against al-Qaeda and other nonstate actors? Since they have no state against which to retaliate, non-state actors cannot be deterred by nuclear weapons. Does this not make full-spectrum dominance necessary to protect the people, however expensive it may be? Here again, the persuasiveness of such an argument requires a suspension of rational thought and discussion. If the real threat to American security is that of a suitcase bomb carried by a terrorist, why does the United States need tens of thousands of expensive weapons such as tanks, innumerable "conventional" bombs and missiles, jet fighter planes, submarines, and aircraft carriers? Why do we need over a million men and women in uniform stationed at hundreds of military bases throughout the world? And if we do not need any of this to defeat al-Qaeda, then neither do we need hundreds of thousands of civilian support staff and the single biggest bureaucracy on earth to administer the whole system.

This brings us to the hawks' ideological last stand. The United States needs global military capability, this final argument goes, in order to be able to disrupt and dislodge terrorist organizations in places like Afghanistan.[10] This claim, however, is no more rational than the others. Let us assume that the United States succeeds in securing Afghanistan with "boots on the ground" through a heroic sacrifice of blood and treasure.

---

10. In a December 2009 speech, President Obama cited the continued existence of al-Qaeda near the Afghanistan–Pakistan border to justify his policy of a troop surge in the Afghanistan war (Stolberg and Cooper 2009). While Obama himself may not be a hawk, as American politicians go, his role as custodian of the national security state and his vulnerability to criticism from hawks in Congress and the media may account for this choice of a hawkish policy.

It is by no means clear that this can be done, but let us assume for the sake of argument that it can. Will that have put al-Qaeda out of business? Of course not (Parenti 2002). Which country, then, will the United States invade next? Yemen? Kenya? Paraguay? And assuming that the United States could secure those countries, as well as Afghanistan, would *that* be the end of al-Qaeda? Simply to ask such questions exposes the absurdity of the boots-on-the-ground method of fighting terrorism.

In summary, full-spectrum dominance—the stated objective of U.S. national security policy—is not needed to protect American civilians from rogue states. A minimum nuclear deterrent, according to standard military doctrine, can accomplish that. Further, full-spectrum dominance, including "boots on the ground," cannot protect the U.S. population from nonstate actors. Tanks and fighter planes are not an effective remedy for a terrorist carrying a suitcase bomb. Further, there is no way to prevent such terrorists from being trained and equipped *somewhere* in the world. Reason dictates this conclusion: the vast bulk of America's trillion-dollar-per-year military behemoth has no function in protecting the U.S. population from attack. It can be legitimized only by symbolic appeals to "national security," a sacred cow that America's ruling elite invokes in much the same way that communist dictators invoked the "proleteriat" and kings invoked God or the gods to justify their control of vast wealth extracted from ordinary working people.

THE NATIONAL SECURITY STATE IS NOT DESIGNED TO SHAPE A DEMOCRATIC WORLD ORDER

Until now, my critique of U.S. national security policy has proceeded on the assumption that its sole purpose is to protect the population against direct physical threats. "Internationalists" readily concede parts or all of this analysis but go beyond it, arguing for a broader, more proactive, and long-term approach to security (Goldstein and Pevehouse 2011). Some, such as neoconservative architects of the Bush Doctrine, have advocated unilateral military intervention to shape a pro-U.S. world order (Jervis 2005). Others, "moderates" who typically come into power with Democratic administrations, want to combine continued U.S. military hegemony with multilateral diplomacy (Goldstein and Pevehouse 2011).

Further to the left are internationalists such as Richard Falk, Saul Mendlovitz, and the author of this book, who advocate demilitarization and promotion of global and regional security organizations (Burroughs et al. 2007; Deller, Makhijani, and Burroughs 2003; Falk, Kim, and Mendlovitz 1991; Global Action to Prevent War and Armed Conflict 2008; Mendlovitz 1999; Moore 2008). Like Ron Paul and other consistent libertarians, these left internationalists are highly critical of America's trillion-dollar annual expenditure on national security. But unlike libertarians, they address the challenge of how to fashion alternative international security arrangements, a task that only governments can take up.

Internationalists argue against "isolationism," the notion that the United States only needs to be concerned about its own security and should not be involved in international politics. Isolationism may have once seemed like a plausible alternative for the United States, protected as it was from Old World power centers by two oceans and endowed with the natural resources needed for its economic development. With the advent of steamships, airplanes, and intercontinental missiles, however, the security advantages of geographic isolation have receded.

Further, economic development has rendered countries increasingly interdependent. Advanced industrial economies currently depend on minerals and fossil fuels not available in sufficient quantity in any given country's territory, including the richly endowed United States. In addition, profit-maximizing firms seeking the cheapest raw materials and labor and the most promising markets for their finished products have expanded the country's global involvements.[11]

Indeed, such economic considerations form the backdrop of military policy documents such as *Joint Vision 2020*, which refer to the country's need to "project power" and defend "vital national interests." These documents assume that, in the absence of U.S. military hegemony, the country would be at the mercy of states more heavily armed than itself that would then be in a position to dictate whatever terms they want to an American population vulnerable to military attack and dependent on external resources.

But this is just another kind of bogeyman. As for the purely physical aspects of security, it is an axiom of military science that far fewer forces and less expensive armaments are needed to defend a territory than to conquer it (Møller 1996). Practicing neutrality for nearly two centuries, Switzerland has adopted purely defensive military policies, never

---

11. Left internationalists recognize that U.S. military policy is in reality motivated by economic considerations and the "strategic" military objectives that flow from them but hold that such policy is not in the public interest and is not consistent with international law (Deller et al. 2003).

acquiring the capacity to "project power" far beyond its borders. Yet it was never conquered during this time, even while far more populous and heavily armed European neighbors greatly outspent the Swiss on military capabilities (Dame 2001). This incidentally may be a model of how Israel could ensure its security without threatening its neighbors with nuclear weapons.[12]

Similarly, Japan, South Korea, and many European countries since World War II have maintained highly advanced industrial economies and gained access to whatever minerals and natural resources they needed without having the military means to defend their "vital national interests." But here apologists for U.S. military power will point out that these countries are not really self-sufficient since they rely on the United States for their security (Breen 2010; Mearsheimer 2010). A heavily armed democracy such as the United States is indispensable, they argue, to maintain a democratic world order against destabilizing threats such as fascism and communism. Possible candidates for future threats of this sort include "Islamofascism" or the emergence of a rival, undemocratic global power, say, China.

If the United States were to withdraw from its global role, the argument goes, the resulting power vacuum would actually encourage the emergence of new threats. To protect itself, the United States would then need to rebuild its military capabilities, at an additional cost to make up for the momentum lost during the interim. In a January 2011 interview with the *PBS NewsHour*, Defense Secretary Robert Gates made much the same argument to justify continued high levels of U.S. military spending (Gates 2011).

I have three responses to this argument. First, if the United States were to demilitarize, allies that feel insecure can and should take responsibility for protecting themselves. This would not require large standing armies or expensive long-range capabilities, as the example of Switzerland shows. If conservative politicians want to wean U.S. citizens from dependence on domestic government programs, should they also not be willing to wean allies from dependence on U.S. military power, maintained at taxpayer expense?

Second, if the United States shifted from a policy of world domination to one of global collaboration, it could make more effective use of the United Nations (Falk et al. 1991). In addition, the United States should

---

12. To be sure, Israel does not enjoy the geographical security advantage conferred by Switzerland's mountainous terrain. But comparable security can be achieved at relatively low cost using anti-tank weapons.

welcome defensive regional security organizations rather than resent other countries' reduced dependence on itself (Global Action to Prevent War and Armed Conflict 2008).

Third, and most important, increasing interdependence is greatly reducing the need for military power to maintain a democratic world order. Countries like Japan, South Korea, and the Netherlands have access to all the resources they need, not only because of U.S. military power but increasingly because they produce goods that other countries need. While Americans tend to think about interdependence only from the perspective of U.S. dependence on other countries, it is really a two-way street.[13]

Given that the United States enjoys more geographic security advantages than Switzerland did historically and more natural resource self-sufficiency than Japan and the Netherlands today, how can it require hundreds of billions of dollars in military expenditures every year to protect its political and economic sovereignty? Maybe these expenditures have little to do with *any* kind of security, even if broadly defined to include maintenance of a democratic world order.

On close examination, the "vital national interests" referred to in *Joint Vision 2020* and similar documents turn out to be in reality the interests of big U.S. corporations, whose profits depend on assured access on favorable terms to natural resources, labor, and markets in the developing world.[14] From the very origins of the modern corporation in the nineteenth century, the power of the state has been deployed on its behalf. In Europe, governments took the lead in staking out colonies, especially on an African continent rich in minerals, rubber, and agricultural products such as cocoa and palm oil, and in India, a lucrative market for European manufactures. It was this scramble, and the arms races that accompanied the commercial rivalries, that resulted in World War I (Stearns et al. 2011).

In the United States, the role of government was not to establish colonies but to engineer by more indirect means political arrangements

---

13. I argue in Chapter 5 that economic globalization has gone too far and that all countries should become more self sufficient in manufacturing and food production. By the time this occurs, however, a rapid spread of democracy in the world may make security concerns about access to resources obsolete. Alternatively, planning for a future scenario of pervasive resource wars could derail this democratic future by making resource wars a self-fulfilling prophesy. The global 99 percent should demand planning for the democratic and peaceful sharing of resources, the only hope for a humane future.

14. It should be noted that taking military action on behalf of economic interests is a form of war of aggression, which is a crime against peace under the Nuremberg Principles and a most serious violation of the UN Charter (United Nations 1945).

favorable to U.S. firms. This involved military intervention and other public policies that were just as deliberate as European colonialism. As early as 1852, marines were being dispatched to Latin America to prevent democracy from interfering with U.S. business interests (Zinn 2003). Reflecting on this history, U.S. Marine General Smedley Butler famously remarked that he had spent most of his career "being a high class muscle man for big business, for Wall Street, and for the bankers" (Butler 2003). While president of Princeton University, Woodrow Wilson stated in a lecture that "concessions obtained by financiers must be safeguarded by ministers of state, even if the sovereignty of unwilling nations be outraged in the process" (Zinn 2003, 362).

Politicians, of course, could not justify such an agenda openly in these terms. Ordinary Americans paying taxes or drafted for war were being asked to shoulder onerous costs, while the benefits accrued disproportionately to the rich. As president, Wilson urged U.S. entry into World War I to "make the world safe for democracy." Consistent with the ideological pattern discussed previously, this claim was absurd, except in the magical world of sacred cows. In reality, the United States entered the war on the side of an alliance that included czarist Russia, the most undemocratic regime on earth, and fought against imperial Germany, which at the time was being rapidly transformed into a democracy.

After World War I, to his credit, Woodrow Wilson did promote bold, multilateral efforts to institute a more democratic and peaceful world order. But his League of Nations initiative was doomed to failure for a number of reasons, including the continued synergy of military and industrial interests, the emerging conflict between fascism and communism, and American isolationism[15] (Mandel 1986; Stearns et al. 2011). So the great powers continued to leverage military power for commercial advantage, now with the United States having a place at the table. When Britain sought to gain complete control over Iraqi oil after the war, for example, the United States and France prevailed in carving out concessions for their own oil companies (Fusfeld 1988). Meanwhile, with the Versailles Treaty having undermined Germany's nascent democracy, another world war loomed on the horizon. Only in the aftermath of that carnage would the task of fashioning a demilitarized world be revisited.

---

15. Although President Wilson was a hero among the European masses for his promotion of a peaceful and democratic world order, at home Republican isolationists controlled the Senate and refused to ratify the League of Nations treaty that Wilson had negotiated (Stearns et al. 2011).

It is an interesting and important question why the main victors in World War II—Britain, France, the United States, China, and the Soviet Union—failed to "save succeeding generations from the scourge of war," in the words of the UN Charter. The answer reveals much about the world in which we live. There is no doubt that the Cold War paralyzed the UN Security Council and turned the "Third World" into a battleground between the Western democracies (the "First World") and the communist East (the "Second World"; Stearns et al. 2011). The conventional wisdom as to why this occurred is that Western policymakers feared a "red menace" of totalitarian dictatorships coming to power in country after country, increasingly isolating the First World until becoming powerful enough to conquer it and impose communism everywhere (Gaddis 2005).

While there is some truth to this picture, it does not adequately explain Western foreign policies in their original historical context. At the end of World War II, the Soviet Union was in shambles, while the more technologically advanced and industrially developed United States had suffered no such devastation to its homeland. The United States—Britain's successor as the most powerful country in the world—had a unique opportunity to negotiate security arrangements for a demilitarized world. Why did it engage in military confrontation with the Soviet Union instead?

If the real concern of the United States was expansion of communism in the Third World, the West could have come to an agreement with the Soviets and the Chinese that military aid to Third World countries would be for defensive capabilities only and that all military and economic aid would be contingent on the enactment of and compliance with democratic constitutions.[16] Such constitutions would include the legitimacy of communist parties, as already existed in Europe, for example.[17]

---

16. Here I engage in "counterfactual history," a thought experiment about how events might have unfolded differently. While many dismiss counterfactual history as idle speculation, in reality all reasoning about historical causes requires counterfactual assumptions (Bunzl 2004). For example, Gaddis's (2005) theory that U.S. policymakers confronted the Soviets militarily for security reasons assumes that they would not have done so if they could have achieved security by other, less costly means. I argue that such means were in fact available, and that the failure of U.S. policymakers to utilize them calls Gaddis's theory into question.

17. Gaddis (2005) would dispute the feasibility of such an arrangement given widespread KGB penetration of foreign communist parties. But the CIA also intervened in electoral politics beyond U.S. borders (Chomsky and Herman 1979), so the question remains why American policymakers did not take diplomatic initiatives to defuse this covert war. Gaddis would attribute their intransigence to Cold War ideology, which is correct as far as it goes, but he fails to address how that ideology functioned to legitimize the thrust of multinational corporations for global domination (Chomsky and Herman 1979). Gaddis himself uncritically buys into U.S. Cold War ideology, feeling along with the state capitalist elites that their selfish agendas also served a larger, noble purpose—defending the security of the "Free World."

Arrangements of this sort would have promoted democracy in the developing world and channeled the capitalist-communist conflict into peaceful political competition for hearts and minds.

That the U.S. power elite was not interested in any such arrangements is consistent with its foreign policy both before and after communism (Chomsky 2003). In the nineteenth century, for example, the United States supported "friendly" dictators in Latin America, so called because they were friendly to corporate interests (Zinn 2003). Since the dissolution of the Soviet Union in 1991, the United States has continued to provide military aid to heinous dictators in various parts of the world (Chomsky 2003, 2006; Johnson 2004), some of which have been toppled in recent years, most notably Pakistan's Pervez Musharraf and Egypt's Hosni Mubarak. Much of this aid, which is funded by U.S. taxpayers, flows to defense contractors, providing profits to investors and the means of terror and domination to dictators (Chomsky 2003, 2006; Johnson 2004).

Rather than make economic aid contingent on democratic arrangements, the United States and the International Monetary Fund (which the United States dominates) have insisted instead on "neoliberal" policies that benefit corporate elites and their shareholders (Chomsky 2003; Stiglitz 2003). For example, privatization promoted by the International Monetary Fund has frequently resulted in sales of state enterprises below market value, enabling rich purchasers to get richer at the expense of poor populations in the Third World and former communist countries (Stiglitz 2003). Aid is typically channeled into large infrastructure projects from which U.S. contractors like Bechtel and Halliburton profit rather than locally controlled projects that better meet the recipient country's real development needs (Stiglitz 2003, 2007). And the dictators propped up by U.S. military and economic aid are notorious for their corruption and subservience to Western corporate interests—a lucrative arrangement for America's rich that would be much harder to maintain in developing countries with democratic governments (Chomsky 2003, 2006; Johnson 2004).

THE NATIONAL SECURITY STATE REDISTRIBUTES WEALTH FROM THE MIDDLE CLASS TO BIG CORPORATIONS AND THEIR STOCKHOLDERS: CASE STUDY—THE OIL COMPANIES

Perhaps the clearest example of how corporate agendas have dominated U.S. foreign policy is the use of military power on behalf of the big oil companies and their stockholders. Herein lies a scandalous story of government malpractice at the expense of middle-class taxpayers (Fusfeld 1988). It is a product of America's reckless and dysfunctional national security state, which unfortunately produces similar policies across a wide range of industries and geographic regions (Chomsky 2003, 2006; Johnson 2004; Zinn 2003). The main setting of this particular story is the Persian Gulf region, which accounts for more than a quarter of the world's proven oil reserves.[18] In addition to its sheer volume, Persian Gulf oil is closer to the earth's surface than in most other parts of the world and is therefore cheaper to extract and more profitable (Fusfeld 1988).

The emergence of petroleum–powered ships, cars, and planes in the early twentieth century created an unprecedented demand for the fossil fuel, which had previously been valued primarily as a source of kerosene for lighting and heating. With the discovery of oil in Iran (1908), Iraq (1927), and the Arabian Peninsula (1930s), the Middle East suddenly became a source of extraordinary profits for Western oil companies (Fusfeld 1988).

After World War II, domination of the Middle East passed from the British Empire to the United States. Under both the British and the Americans, vast military power has been deployed in the region, including the U.S. Sixth Fleet stationed in the Mediterranean. The political agenda served by these forces is completely at odds with Western rhetoric about freedom, democracy, and human rights. Far from supporting democratic governments in the interests of free and fair commerce, British and American elites have allied themselves with corrupt monarchies and dictatorships, most notably the regimes of the Saudi royal family and of Iran's Shah Reza Pahlavi (Chomsky 2003). It is no coincidence that these policies—enacted at great taxpayer expense—have been typically crafted by defense and foreign policy officials who started out or ended up as executives, lawyers, or bankers working for the big oil companies (Fusfeld 1988).

The production of Persian Gulf oil has involved a collaboration of the region's governments, the major Western oil corporations, and the U.S. government (Fusfeld 1988). The earliest oil contracts allocated the lion's share of profits to the corporations. However, nationalist movements after World War II put increasing pressure on the governments and ruling families, especially in Iran and Iraq, to claim a larger and larger share

---

18. In descending order of the size of their reserves, the five most oil-rich Gulf countries are Saudi Arabia, Iran, the United Arab Emirates, Kuwait, and Iraq (U.S. Energy Information Administration 2011).

of the profits on behalf of their people. Such a reallocation would have cut into the oil companies' superprofits.[19] The U.S. government then created a legal scam for maintaining these superprofits at taxpayer expense. The royalties that corporations had to pay to the Persian Gulf governments would no longer be called royalties but rather "income tax." This could be used to justify deducting that amount of money from their U.S. income tax (Fusfeld 1988).

The big oil companies then "practically ceased to pay income taxes to the U.S. government, not only from their foreign operations, but from their domestic business as well" (Fusfeld 1988, p. 691). In other words, the U.S. taxpayer more than compensated the oil companies for the higher share of profits being demanded by Middle East governments. In 2009, Exxon Mobil actually had *negative* U.S. income tax, receiving a net bonus of $26 million from U.S. taxpayers, in addition to its $15.1 billion tax deduction for "income taxes" paid to foreign governments (Romm 2010). This whole arrangement is based on the legal pretense that corporations pay the governments because their operations happen to be in the latter's territory, not for the value of the oil itself. The scam takes income out of the pockets of middle-class taxpayers and redistributes it to oil company stock and bondholders, primarily the rich.

Meanwhile, the increased royalties did not satisfy Iranian nationalists, especially since the revenues were enriching the local ruling class to the neglect of the people. In 1951, the country's parliament nationalized the oil industry. In response, the Eisenhower administration approved a CIA covert operation two years later to remove the democratically elected prime minister, Mohammad Mossadeq.[20] For the next quarter century, the increasingly dictatorial Shah Reza Pahlavi ruled Iran, with support of the United States and a secret police notorious for its involvement in torture. The shah not only granted favorable concessions to big U.S. oil companies but also, like the Saudis, used a large portion of his country's share of the oil money to buy expensive weapons systems from U.S. defense contractors. The royal family and much of the country's

---

19. While oil is sold at prices set by a single global market, for geological reasons noted above production costs in the Persian Gulf region are lower than in most parts of the world, resulting in higher than normal profits (Fusfeld 1988).

20. Until this time, British, U.S., and other Western corporations had oil concessions in Saudi Arabia and Iraq, but the Anglo-Iranian Oil Company had a monopoly on Iranian production. After "Operation Ajax," Anglo-Iranian Oil was renamed "British Petroleum" and continued in Iran as part of a consortium of Western oil companies that now included five U.S. corporations (Abrahamian 1982). In 1958, nationalists also came to power in Iraq, prompting another Western-backed coup.

elite also invested their fortunes with Western financial institutions (Abrahamian 1982). These arrangements enriched the already rich investors in these oil, defense, and other Western firms at the expense of the Iranian and American people.

The United States reaped what these corporate-friendly policies had sown when a revolution toppled the shah's regime in 1979, giving rise to the Shi'ite theocracy that remains in power today. It cannot be emphasized too strongly that the existence of this regime—and the anti-American and anti-Israel kind of Islamism that it exports—was the natural consequence of bipartisan U.S. foreign policy from 1953 until the collapse of the shah's quarter-century reign of terror (Abrahamian 1982). But more damage remained to be done. The same Western elites that enriched themselves under the shah then orchestrated a new set of policies designed to maintain their power and profits. The result was a series of wars that claimed hundreds of thousands of lives in the region and cost U.S. taxpayers trillions of dollars.

In order to counteract the anti-American regime in Tehran, the United States now aligned itself with the even more brutal dictatorship of Saddam Hussein (Chomsky 2003). The duplicity and cynicism of America's corporate-friendly elites can be seen in their responses to Iraqi aggression. When the Iraqi dictator invaded Iran in 1982, there was little outcry from the United States, much less a counterinvasion. On the contrary, the Reagan administration was soon providing Iraq with military aid and crucial satellite intelligence on Iranian troop deployments (Chomsky 2003). This aid continued while Saddam Hussein was using chemical weapons against Iranians and even against Kurdish civilians, and this again elicited no diplomatic uproar from the United States (Hiltermann 2003).

By contrast, Iraq's 1990 invasion of Kuwait—which threatened U.S. oil company profits—was met by U.S. mobilization of an international coalition and military intervention, all cloaked in the righteousness of international law and the UN Charter (Chomsky 2003).[21] During the war, the United States destroyed much of the country's civilian infrastructure and supported harsh economic sanctions that lasted more than 10 years, causing hundreds of thousands of civilian deaths, mostly of children (UNICEF 1999). In addition to these horrendous human costs,

---

21. To be sure, the Iraqi invasion *was* a threat to the rule of law but most likely could have been reversed without a counterinvasion—or even prevented—had the George H. W. Bush administration wanted to avoid war (Hilsman 1992). By this time, however, Saddam Hussein's regime had become a threat to U.S. oil interests, and the destruction of his military in Operation Desert Storm helped neutralize that threat, at least for another decade.

the direct financial costs to U.S. taxpayers was estimated at $102 billion (Congressional Research Service 2010).

While President George H. W. Bush was content in 1991 to preserve Western access to Kuwaiti oil, 12 years later his son took oil geopolitics to a whole new level (Chomsky 2003, 2006). In *The Age of Turbulence*, Alan Greenspan (2008) wrote, "I am saddened that it is politically inconvenient to acknowledge what everyone knows: the Iraq war is largely about oil."[22] By November 2007, President Bush and Iraqi Prime Minister Al Maliki had signed a "Declaration of Principles" opening Iraq to foreign investment, "especially American investments" (Chomsky 2008). This agreement suggests that U.S. intervention in Iraq was part of a broader corporate agenda not limited to oil.

Seven months later, Exxon Mobil, Shell, Total, and British Petroleum—the same companies excluded from Iraq when the country nationalized its oil production in the 1960s—were negotiating no-bid contracts with Iraq's oil ministry (Kramer 2008). Billions of dollars in other contracts were awarded corporations with ties to the Bush administration, including Halliburton. Meanwhile, this one war alone claimed thousands of American and Iraqi lives. And its total direct and indirect financial costs to U.S. taxpayers are estimated to be $3 trillion (Bilmes and Stiglitz 2008), nearly $10,000 for every man, woman, and child in the United States.

Oil companies and their domination of U.S. Middle East policy are only the most outrageous case of a pervasive pattern. Throughout much of U.S. history, individual companies have pushed for military interventions, such as United Fruit in Central America and Anaconda Copper and ITT in Chile (Zinn 2003). More often, the state has acted on behalf of corporations collectively, including the 1854 trade agreement that Commodore Perry imposed on Japan (Cullen 2003), the "foreign investment law" enacted in 1967 by a new Indonesian dictatorship that the CIA helped to create (Chomsky and Herman 1979), and the 2007 "Declaration of Principles" opening Iraq to U.S. corporations (Chomsky 2008).

Indeed, a stated purpose of U.S. defense and foreign policy is protecting and advancing "national interests," a phrase that really means access by U.S.-based corporations on favorable terms to foreign natural

---

22. This explanation of the 2003–2011 Iraq War resolves what is otherwise an inexplicable mystery: the incompatibility with elementary military doctrine of the stated national security rationale for the war. According to Robert Jervis (2005), a leading expert on deterrence, a nuclear-armed Iraq would have posed little security threat to the United States or Israel because no Iraqi leader could even consider using nuclear weapons against another nuclear-armed state. But consistent with Greenspan's comment, Jervis was unwilling to acknowledge or explore the oil motivations behind Bush administration policy.

resources, low-cost labor, and markets (Chomsky 2003, 2006; Chomsky and Herman 1979). Robust democracies in the developing world or even nondemocratic governments that are independent (e.g., China) collaborate with Western corporations on terms more favorable to themselves, thereby cutting into corporate profits. Covert or overt uses of force (or the threat of use) are age-old tools of statecraft deployed by the United States, as previously by other great powers, to shape political conditions abroad that are conducive to profits at home (Kennedy 1989). Under current international law, it should be noted, such uses of force constitute what the Nuremberg Tribunal called "crimes against peace" and are most serious violations of the UN Charter (United Nations 1945).

THE NATIONAL SECURITY STATE LOOTS THE MIDDLE CLASS BY TAKING ITS TAXES AND PROVIDING NOTHING OF VALUE IN RETURN

Investors in U.S. corporations, who are the main beneficiaries of U.S. military power, are disproportionately the rich. This is evident in the concentrated ownership of stocks, bonds, and other financial wealth. In 2007, America's wealthiest 20 percent owned 91 percent of the country's financial wealth, while the bottom 80 percent—which includes most of the middle class—owned only 7 percent (Domhoff 2011). In addition to the wealth extracted from foreign populations as a consequence of U.S. military power, a large portion of military expenditure flows directly into corporations in the form of defense contracts, administered at public expense by the Pentagon's vast bureaucracy.

While the benefits of the national security state go overwhelmingly to the rich, the costs—both financial and human (e.g., people killed, maimed, or traumatized)—are disproportionately borne by the middle class. Recent data show that 60 percent of federal funds—the revenues that pay for the national security state—come from the middle class, defined as households with annual incomes between $20,000 and $200,000 (see Appendix 1.1). This translates into 600 billion tax dollars siphoned out of the middle class and into the national security state every year—an annual drain on average of $7,800 for some 77 million middle-class households.

As I have shown previously, only a small part of these revenues is legitimately needed for defense of the U.S. population from attack and for participation in international security missions. The rest—some hundreds of billions of dollars—is currently being used mainly to enrich those who are already rich at the expense of the middle class. To be sure, the national security state also provides over 2 million middle-class jobs.[23] But this number of jobs, in fact even more, could be created by alternative uses of these same resources (Pollin and Garrett-Peltier 2010). The real question, therefore, is what these alternative uses might be and how they might meet the needs of the middle class.

One unmet need that must be considered is effective prevention of terrorism. I have shown that military power cannot achieve this and is not designed to. An effective alternative is the eradication of extreme poverty in the world, which would cost about $50 billion per year,[24] a mere 5 percent of what the United States spends on its national security state. Funding that objective in the form of locally controlled development projects would create a groundswell of goodwill toward the United States, an important strategy for preventing terrorism. Nor is this only a matter of self-interest; it is even more fundamentally a matter of justice. Eradicating extreme global poverty is a moral imperative both in itself and as restitution to the world's peoples for the wealth extracted from them by U.S. corporations during decades of U.S. military hegemony.

Even after meeting all legitimate security needs, including terrorism prevention, hundreds of billions of dollars per year would remain for alternative uses. Of these, the most urgent are investments in a renewable energy infrastructure and more energy-efficient manufacturing, transportation, and other technologies. As discussed in Chapter 5, without a rapid phasing out of fossil fuel–based and energy-inefficient technologies in the United States and abroad, catastrophic and irreversible climate change from increasing carbon emissions in the near future is certain (Brown 2009). This will destroy most of world agriculture, leading to the starvation of billions of people and the destruction of civilization as we know it. Much of the human and physical capital currently being squandered on unnecessary national security programs must be diverted to producing the smart electrical grid, energy-efficient public transportation systems, and solar, wind, geothermal and other sustainable energy infrastructures needed to avert this imminent catastrophe (Rynn 2010).

Other possible uses of resources being spent on the national security state include equitable funding for public schools and health facilities that

23. In the latest years for which data are available, the U.S. Department of Defense alone employed .68 million civilians (U.S. Office of Personnel Management 2007) and 1.42 uniformed military personnel (U.S. Department of Defense 2009).
24. This is the estimated cost of the Millennium Development Goals, the international community's current plan to eradicate extreme poverty (United Nations 2011). Many question the way resources are being used under this plan but not the cost estimate.

serve the poor;[25] a first-rate system of public libraries with state-of-the-art computing, Internet, and multimedia resources; increased public funding for research and the arts; and rebuilding of the country's decaying bridges, waterworks, and other infrastructure. The tragic human costs of militarism were expressed most eloquently by President Dwight Eisenhower in 1953. His words could not be more relevant today:

> Every gun that is made, every warship launched, every rocket fired signifies, in the final sense, a theft from those who hunger and are not fed, those who are cold and are not clothed. This world in arms in not spending money alone. It is spending the sweat of its laborers, the genius of its scientists, the hopes of its children. The cost of one modern heavy bomber is this: a modern brick school in more than 30 cities. It is two electric power plants, each serving a town of 60,000 population. It is two fine, fully equipped hospitals. It is some 50 miles of concrete highway. We pay for a single fighter with a half million bushels of wheat. We pay for a single destroyer with new homes that could have housed more than 8,000 people. This, I repeat, is the best way of life to be found on the road the world has been taking. This is not a way of life at all, in any true sense. Under the cloud of threatening war, it is humanity hanging from a cross of iron. (Eisenhower 1953)

A national debate is needed on how to spend revenues currently being wasted on militarism and on the best means of providing such alternative goods and services. But one thing is beyond dispute: every dollar spent on unnecessary weapons systems, military bases, and Pentagon bureaucracy is a dollar not available for the kind of public goods and services indicated previously.[26] And it is mainly the middle class and poor—the

---

25. Jonathan Kozol (1991, 2005) has studied the large discrepancy in resources, including facilities and class sizes, between affluent suburban schools and those that serve the urban poor, who are primarily families of color. These inequities reflect the fact that nearly half the funding of U.S. public schools comes from local property taxes, giving most rich districts significantly higher per student funding than poor districts. As long as this system exists, there will continue to be an urgent need for federal supplemental funding to correct the discrepancy.

26. Some argue that the trade-off between military and nonmilitary spending is only partial because the former contributes to the civilian economy through technological spin-offs such as the Internet. This argument is misleading because it fails to take account of what economists call "opportunity costs." If the same money spent on military research and development were spent instead on government research and development involving equally challenging civilian applications, there is no reason to assume that it would produce fewer or less important spin-offs. In addition, it could produce something of economic value—say, nuclear fusion energy technology—instead of something of no economic value—say, a missile defense system. In fact, the Reagan administration faced precisely this trade-off and chose to devote scarce scientific and engineering talent to the latter instead of the former (Fitzgerald 2001; Freeman 2009).

99 percent—whom the national security state deprives of all these things.

DOWNSIZING THE NATIONAL SECURITY STATE

Apart from a bipartisan national security ideology and the corporate and plutocratic interests it serves, the single biggest obstacle to changing U.S. public priorities is the massive economic dislocation it would cause. Can the millions of people who owe their livelihoods directly or indirectly to the national security state be retrained and redeployed in the kinds of alternative activities indicated previously? Seymour Melman (1989), who coined the term "permanent war economy," believed that they could and developed "economic conversion" strategies for accomplishing this.

In addition, as discussed in Chapter 5, I advocate a policy of attrition based on the way any organization reproduces itself—by new hiring that replaces personnel who retire and new procurement that replaces structures and equipment that wear out or become obsolete. A freeze on new hiring and procurement would have the effect of rapidly downsizing the national security state in an orderly manner and with a minimum of economic dislocation. Some retraining of defense employees would be needed both to work in nondefense jobs and to be redeployed within the defense sector to accommodate reorganization due to downsizing. Exceptions to the hiring and procurement freeze would be allowed as part of the reorganization, but national security managers would have to pay for them by more rapid downsizing in other parts of the system. When the national security system reaches the final size and shape needed for legitimate defense, the hiring and procurement freeze would be lifted, and the much smaller defense system would maintain itself at that size.

Some libertarians might agree with this approach but would argue that resources freed up by downsizing national security should be released back into the private sector or used to repay the national debt.[27] This argument neglects two important issues. First, it makes the dubious assumption that revenues freed up by reducing government spending automatically create jobs in the private sector. This flies in the face of

---

27. While I favor reducing the national debt, this does not dictate a downsizing of government, much less decisions about which government programs to downsize. Those questions need to be answered on their merits, as I have set about doing in this book. After the optimal size and content of the public sector is determined on the merits, the separate question of how to responsibly and equitably fund that public sector can be taken up.

U.S. and international experience with recent business cycles, including recovery from the 2008–2009 recession. We now know that gross domestic product and stock prices can rebound while increases in employment remain much more sluggish (Aronowitz 2005; Mishel 2011; Wolfe 2011). This probably reflects in part long-term structural changes in the U.S. economy due to automation. There is no reason to believe that full employment can be achieved without a large and permanent public sector (Aronowitz 2005; Wolfe, 2011).

Even assuming that the private sector could produce enough employment to compensate for downsizing of the national security state, which is extremely unlikely, libertarians make a second dubious assumption—that the private sector would produce the kind of goods and services that the country most needs. But it is a truism of economics that markets, left to themselves, produce only private goods (Stiglitz and Walsh 2006). "Public goods," such as infrastructure, libraries, and schools, will not be adequately provided unless they are provided by government (Stiglitz and Walsh 2006). This may not concern the rich, but it should certainly concern the middle class. A large public sector, therefore, is indispensable for creating many of the jobs as well as the public goods and services needed for middle class prosperity. Such a public sector can be built in large part from resources freed up by downsizing the national security state.

In conclusion, the national security scam is one of the biggest threats to America's middle class. But it is not the only big threat. As noted at the beginning of this chapter, the United States was born in the same year that *The Wealth of Nations* heralded and promoted the rise of industrial capitalism. For 200 years, production for markets brought increasing prosperity, and democratic activists struggled to amelieorate the rising inequality, urban squalor, and abuses of power that accompanied this very progress. Industrial innovation and capital investment became the foundations of America's prosperity, enabling its corporations to prosper while still paying rising wages and benefits to increasingly unionized workers (Melman 1956).

By the nation's bicentenniel in 1976, however, the post–World War II social contract between capital and labor—the foundation of middle-class prosperity—was unraveling. Corporations began shutting down unionized factories in the Northeast, moving capital first to America's low-wage Sun Belt, then, under the protection of U.S. military power, to even lower-wage countries abroad. Even as corporate profits soared, median wages and benefits entered a period of stagnation that continues until this day, throwing the American dream itself into crisis. To these developments we now turn.

APPENDIX 1.1

Calculation of Tax Burden by Income Class

In FY 1999, the 76.8 million households with adjusted gross income in the range of $20,000 to $200,000 were taxed a combined $493 billion, which is 60.7% of the total tax liability for all taxable returns, some $812 billion (Tax Policy Center 2011). A family of four or more with an income of $20,000 would be below the U.S. poverty line (U.S. Department of Health & Human Services, 2011), but such families have no federal income tax liability and are therefore excluded from this analysis.

An approximate 60-40 ratio for the middle class—rich tax distribution applies to federal funds generally, not only personal income taxes. According to Office of Management and Budget data for FY 2010 (2011, Table S-4), three quarters of the $1.2 trillion of federal funds that were derived from taxes came from individual income taxes at the 60-40 ratio calculated previously. Of the other sources, $67 billion in excise taxes (which are regressive) fell mostly on the middle class and the poor, while $44 billion in customs duties and estate and gift taxes fell mostly on the rich—also a 60-40 ratio. The remaining source—$191 billion in corporation income taxes—were partly passed on to the middle class and poor in higher prices and partly passed on to the rich in lower profits. A tax burden ratio of 60-40 for all federal funds is therefore reasonably accurate for purposes of this book. This analysis excludes social insurance and retirement receipts, which are a separate revenue stream not used for defense and security programs.

CHAPTER 2

The Attack on Wages and Benefits

INTRODUCTION

American corporations have been shutting down manufacturing operations in the United States in search of cheaper labor for more than 30 years. Fewer than half of Americans now living remember what industrial relations were like before this era of capital flight. Unions negotiated and won better and better contracts, and management could agree to these contracts and still earn a normal profit because rising productivity increased the amount of income available for distribution between labor and capital. Rather than seek profit by reducing wages and benefits—which would occur in a technologically stagnant economy without labor unions—corporate management sought profit by investing in state-of-the-art production methods and equipment. This enabled them to pay the rising wages and benefits negotiated by unions, and the rising cost of labor in turn provided an incentive for management to mechanize production further, creating a virtuous cycle of industrialization (Melman 1956).

Figure 2.1 shows the level in real U.S. median compensation—combined wages and benefits corrected for inflation—from the post–World War II period to the present. In the 25 years between 1950 and 1974, real median compensation increased by 50 percent, a palpable improvement from year to year in the standard of living.[1] This was the heyday of the

---

1. Data for median compensation before 1951 are not available, but manufacturing wages were rising since at least 1890 (Wolff 2009). Since median compensation and manufacturing wages are correlated in the period after 1950, it is reasonable to assume that median compensation was also increasing in the earlier period.

Figure 2.1. Trends in Real U.S. Corporate Profits, Media Compensation, and Personal Saving, 1948–2009

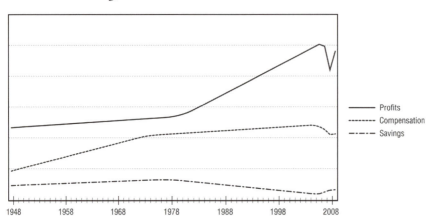

Note: (In this graph, there is no scale for the vertical axis because the three variables are measured in different units (percents, dollars, and billions of dollars). In order to conveniently display these trend lines on the same graph, I needed to transform the original units into index numbers and further adjust slopes and intercepts, as explained in Appendix 2.1. The resulting chart only shows temporal trends before and after deindustrialization, with slopes and intercepts that are necessarily arbitrary. Appendix 2.1, which supports the empirical claims made in this section, discusses the methodology used to construct the trend lines, cites the sources of the data, and shows individual graphs of the data in their original units.)

American middle class, when a majority of the country could aspire to unprecedented affluence, including home ownership and college educations for their children. To be sure, this American Dream remained beyond the reach of a large, predominantly black and Hispanic minority—what Michael Harrington (1962) called the "the other America." But for the non-Hispanic white population—which made up most of the country's workforce—industrial progress was steady, and its fruits were widely distributed, thanks in large part to labor unions.

By contrast, real median compensation increased only 6 percent in the nearly 40 years from 1974 to the present, an imperceptible annual change. This eclipse of the American Dream was caused primarily by corporate America's assault on organized labor and the deindustrialization of the U.S. economy that accompanied it (Bluestone and Harrison 1984). Beginning in the 1970s, corporate management began to move capital to low-wage regions, first within the United States, then abroad. This deindustrialized the highly unionized Northeastern region, later dubbed the "Rust Belt," and eventually the U.S. economy as a whole (Bluestone and Harrison 1984).

While capital flight was bad news for America's middle class, it was accompanied by soaring corporate profits—good news for the rich—as also shown in Figure 2.1. In the period from the end of World War II until 1980, real after-tax U.S. corporate profits had increased, on average, about $10 billion per year (in 2010 dollars). By contrast, in the period from 1980 to the present—the era of global capital flight—profits have increased by more than $30 billion per year. The rich, laying claim to the bulk of these profits, were now getting richer at an unprecedented pace, leaving the middle class behind.

As troubling as these developments were for ordinary Americans, two new ideologies prevented most people from understanding what was occurring. First, the notion of a "postindustrial" economy enabled corporate leaders to frame capital flight as part of a progressive and desirable development. The second ideology—neoliberalism—attributed the economic stagnation to unions and government.

IDEOLOGIES OF DEINDUSTRIALIZATION

Sociologist Daniel Bell's (1973) book *The Coming of Post-Industrial Society*, though not intended as corporate propaganda, gave America's business elite a convenient legitimation for destroying unions. Workers and labor leaders at the time were beginning to see American corporations shut down unionized factories and relocate production to low-wage regions. Bell's ideas enabled chief executive officers and capitalist-friendly politicians and pundits to present this assault on the very existence of trade unions as part of a benign historical evolution. He argued that America's manufacturing economy—the stronghold of trade unionism—was being eclipsed by an information economy of "knowledge workers" in such fields as telecommunications, computer science, marketing, finance, insurance, law, and mass media.

Bell viewed the coming of postindustrial society as the result of greatly increased productivity in manufacturing, which required fewer and fewer workers. Manufacturing employment would shrink, as agriculture had before it, and the manufacturing jobs would be replaced by information sector and other service jobs. While this analysis has some merit, it was a short step from the idea of a shrinking manufacturing sector to the incorrect notion that the United States no longer needed to manufacture most of the goods it consumed. If the latter was true, then shutting down American factories and moving production abroad could be presented as a good thing for all parties concerned. American workers would graduate from unionized factory jobs to more highly skilled jobs in the information sector, while agricultural workers in the developing world would also move up the economic ladder to manufacturing jobs. This new international division of labor between postindustrial and newly industrializing societies would, via trade, expand prosperity for all workers in all countries.

The second ideology—neoliberalism—complemented the first.[2] In order for the new division of labor to occur, a single global economy would have to be created in which manufactured goods, information services, and capital could flow freely across national boundaries. In an environment of unregulated global markets, neoliberals argued, profit-maximizing firms would bring about the most efficient allocation of resources, that is, an allocation that produces the goods and services people want with the least amount of waste. Achieving this would require the removal of barriers to free market capitalism—primarily unions and government. Without onerous union work rules and government regulations to stifle enterprise, a new age of global prosperity would dawn. And, without union wages and benefits, U.S. corporations would become more competitive.

This last point was especially appealing to U.S. corporate leaders in the 1970s, who found themselves defending America's post–World War II commercial supremacy from the very real threat of European and Asian competition (Micklethwait and Wooldridge 2005). The latter included Japan and the so-called Asian Tigers: South Korea, Hong Kong, Singapore, and Taiwan. China joined this group of rapidly industrializing countries in the 1980s, when communist leaders introduced

---

2. The founding father of American neoliberalism was Milton Friedman. Although he began publishing his ideas in the 1960s, Friedman did not become broadly influential until the 1970s and 1980s. It was only then that historical conditions were ripe for conservative politicians, such as California Governor Ronald Reagan and later President Reagan—bankrolled by corporate elites and the rich—to enact Friedman's laissez-faire agenda into law and public policy. The "Freshwater" economists at the University of Chicago and elsewhere have continued to develop Friedman's legacy into the present (Krugman 2009). Through its domination of the International Monetary Fund, the United States also imposed a package of neoliberal policies known as the "Washington Consensus" on developing countries, with disastrous consequences (Stiglitz 2003).

market reforms.[3] These Asian producers initially gained global market share largely on the basis of lower labor costs and became exporters of manufactured goods. Capitalist pundits incorrectly concluded from this that the United States was losing its comparative advantage in manufacturing, an idea that lent an air of rationality and inevitability to the outsourcing of U.S. manufacturing jobs. Again, the consolation promised to U.S. workers was a nonunionized but well-paid information sector that postindustrial ideology predicted would replace America's shrinking manufacturing sector.

After more than 30 years of corporate and public policies shaped by postindustrial and neoliberal ideas, there is precious little evidence that the policies have delivered—or ever can—the universal prosperity they promised (Goldstein 2009; Rynn 2010; Stiglitz 2003, 2007). To be sure, the proportion of America's gross domestic product accounted for by well-paid service jobs increased while the manufacturing sector's proportion decreased, as shown in Figure 2.2. But as for *numbers* of well-paid jobs, far fewer were created in the service sector than were lost in manufacturing (Rynn 2010). Many of the workers displaced by deindustrialization were either reemployed in lower-paid service jobs or ceased to work full-time (Goldstein 2009). These changes were reflected in America's poverty rate, which fell from 23 to 11 percent between 1959 and 1974, then went up in the period of deindustrialization and fluctuated around 13 percent until recent years, increasing to 15 percent in 2011 (Tavernise 2011; U.S. Census Bureau 2010).

Meanwhile, foreign direct investment on an unprecedented scale failed to broadly industrialize developing societies, which remained mostly producers of raw materials and agricultural goods (Chomsky 2003, 2006; Chomsky and Herman 1979; Cobb and Diaz 2009). In Latin America and parts of Asia and Africa, some economic growth occurred, but it was not widely shared within these societies, and there was little reduction of poverty. In much of sub-Saharan Africa, poverty rates actually increased (Stiglitz 2003).

---

3. Procapitalist pundits generally depict China's market reforms as the sole cause of its new economic growth. This picture neglects the continued and crucial role of government in the Chinese economy, the importance of which becomes clear when comparing China's market reforms with those in other communist countries. The former Soviet republics, which followed a model of rapid and radical privatization and deregulation promoted by capitalist economists and the International Monetary Fund, did not experience anything like China's performance. On the contrary, they experienced an economic collapse in the 1990s comparable to the Great Depression in the West, followed by much less impressive growth than occurred in China (Stiglitz 2003).

Figure 2.2.   Type of Industry as Percentage of U.S. GDP, 1974–2009

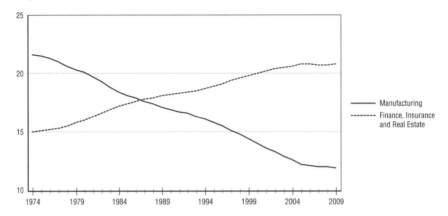

Source: Bureau of Economic Analysis, National Income and Product Accounts.

As in the case of national security, however, postindustrial and neoliberal policies enjoy the status of sacred cows, notwithstanding more than three decades of failure in the real world.[4] The reason for this status is simple—the policies would appear to be highly profitable for American corporations and their owners.[5] These rich beneficiaries, in turn, have enormous financial, political, and cultural resources to propagate and popularize the postindustrial and neoliberal ideologies that serve them so well. Ordinary people clearly need a tool kit of alternative concepts for understanding what is really happening to them in the era of capitalist globalization. The remainder of this chapter provides such a tool kit.

4. Even in the wake of stagnating wages and persistent, high unemployment, candidates for the 2012 Republican presidential nomination continued to promote the neoliberal notion that unions, excessive taxation and government regulations are the real causes of America's economic malaise, not capital flight and deindustrialization. Many mainstream pundits such as economist Christina Romer (2012) also continue to promote postindustrial ideology.

5. Marking the election of Ronald Reagan to the White House, 1980 was the beginning of a systematic implementation of neoliberal policies at the national level. Milton Friedman himself, in fact, was a Reagan adviser. A detailed causal analysis of the relationships between these policies and the increased growth of profits that accompanied them is beyond the scope of this book. There is no doubt, however, that the neoliberal era has been a highly profitable time for corporations and their shareholders and a time of economic stagnation for ordinary Americans, as shown in Figure 2.1 and Appendix 2.1.

THE ANATOMY OF DEINDUSTRIALIZATION

American postindustrial ideology is a perversion of an economic development theory that has much validity. According to this theory, economies go through stages of development from agriculture to industrial manufacturing to information and other services.[6] Just as the proportion of workers devoted to agriculture dramatically declined with the industrial revolution, the theory goes, so too the proportion engaged in manufacturing is now declining with the information revolution—the development of telecommunications, computing, and robotics. The industrial revolution began in Europe and America and then transformed or is transforming the rest of the world. The information revolution, according to this analysis, is now following a similar pattern of geographic diffusion.[7]

In the case of the United States, however, this developmental theory is an inadequate and misleading explanation for the decline of manufacturing employment. In the nineteenth and twentieth centuries, U.S. agricultural employment did not decline because food imports replaced domestic production. Rather, the country continued to produce food but did so with increasing efficiency such that only a small number of farmers were needed to sustain a large output.[8] But in the case of U.S. manufacturing, increased efficiency accounts for only part of the decline in employment. A substantial part of that decline results from the substitution of imports for domestic production (Rynn 2010). In other words, the United States never "deagriculturalized," as we might say, the way it is currently deindustrializing.

----

6. The typology of agricultural and industrial stages of development was developed by Marx and other nineteenth-century thinkers reflecting on the significance of the industrial revolution (Mandel 1982). Colin Clark's (1940) *Conditions of Economic Progress* added the service sector, creating a three-part typology of economic development that was further developed to incorporate the information revolution with Daniel Bell's *The Coming of Post-Industrial Society* (1973) and Alvin Toffler's *The Third Wave* (1984).

7. Note that the wealth created by increasing productivity in all sectors can be allocated in various ways by consumers and government—taking the form of shared prosperity, quality public goods, and a short work week, for example, or inequality and mindless consumerism.

8. To a large extent, this efficiency is related to unsustainable practices of agribusiness, such as monoculture farming and the highly chemical and machinery-intensive methods that accompany it (see Appendix 4.1 in Chapter 4). A return to organic, sustainable agriculture will necessarily require increased employment in that sector but not nearly to preindustrial levels (Rynn 2010). Sustainable technology can draw from both the industrial and the postindustrial revolutions. Indeed, the latter is really only a rapid acceleration of the application of knowledge to production inherent in technology itself (Rynn 2010). An example of postindustrial farming efficiencies is the replacement of pesticides with biological controls (e.g., introducing lady bugs to reduce the population of insects that destroy crops), based on advances in biological knowledge. Some of the increase in workforce that organic agriculture requires to tend crops can thus be offset by a reduced need for workers in the agricultural chemicals industry. Other efficiencies of a sustainable food system are discussed in Appendix 4.1 in Chapter 4.

The analogy between the shrinking of manufacturing employment and the earlier shrinking of agriculture would have been entirely valid for the United States if the country had continued on its mid-twentieth-century path of industrial progress. In that case, advanced robotic-assisted production would now be meeting nearly all the country's need for manufactured goods, as in fact is occurring today in Germany, Japan, and other highly industrialized countries. While such automation does reduce manufacturing as a proportion of total employment, it also supplies the other sectors of the economy with the abundance of inexpensive, high-quality machines and other goods that they need to expand, and thereby absorb the workers displaced in manufacturing, as envisioned by postindustrial development theory.[9] But this synergy is happening only to a limited extent in the United States, where domestic production of many categories of goods (including much capital equipment) is actually declining and being replaced by imports (Rynn 2010).

To be sure, manufacturing productivity in the United States continues to exhibit cumulative growth for those categories of goods that the United States still produces domestically (U.S. Bureau of Economic Analysis 2011). However, manufacturing as a proportion of total employment is shrinking faster in the United States than in Germany and Japan (Rynn 2010), even though the three countries are roughly comparable today in their rates of manufacturing productivity growth. This reflects the fact that the United States is a net importer of manufactured goods, while Germany and Japan are net exporters.[10] The fact that manufacturing workers in the latter countries are paid more than in the United States explodes the American postindustrial myth that high-wage countries cannot compete with low-wage countries in manufacturing (Rynn 2010).

Another fallacy of postindustrial ideology, related to the notion that the United States does not need to produce most of its manufactured goods domestically, is that these goods are peripheral to the emerging service and information economy. In fact, on close inspection, "services"

---

9. As explained below, the dichotomy between manufacturing and the non-manufacturing sectors can be misleading since all these other sectors—agriculture, services, transportation, and construction—as well as manufacturing itself, depend upon manufactured goods.

10. In addition to the United States being a net importer of manufactured goods, many products that it continues to make domestically are made with machine tools and advanced production systems that are themselves imported, and many other products are made in U.S.-based factories that are owned and managed by European or Asian corporations (Rynn 2010). Although not reflected in U.S. productivity statistics, these forms of dependency represent a decline in what Seymour Melman (1983, 2001) called "production competence." The same can be said for the complete loss of production know-how in areas of manufacturing where the United States has ceased producing altogether (Rynn 2010).

almost always require large amounts of machinery and other goods, and these goods need to be manufactured (Rynn 2010). This is apparent in health care, for example, which requires increasingly sophisticated imaging machines, surgical equipment, and medical supplies. Similarly, mass media and telecommunications require expensive recording, computing, and transmission equipment. Education requires laboratory and athletic equipment, computers, and instructional technologies. All these service fields require facilities that must be built from manufactured materials using construction equipment that is also manufactured.[11]

In summary, since the non-manufacturing sectors actually require large amounts of machinery and other manufactured goods, the dichotomy between manufacturing and the other sectors can be misleading. This is apparent in Leontief input-output analyses of the economy (Raa 2005). If the manufactured goods required for the other sectors are not produced domestically, they need to be imported, as the United States is indeed doing for many products. But the country's increasing balance of trade deficits indicate that the United States is not producing enough goods and services for export to continue paying for the manufactured goods that it imports (Rynn 2010). The loss of manufacturing employment in the United States associated with this net trade deficit is therefore an indication of economic decline, not postindustrial progress. Further, the dependence of the U.S. economy on high-value added manufactured imports, such as capital goods, has ripple effects throughout the economy. It increases the costs of automating—and thus of producing wealth more efficiently—in the non-manufacturing sectors, creating a drag on the entire U.S. economy.

Manufacturing is not just one sector among others in a developed economy (Rynn 2010). Machinery and other manufactured goods are essential to the productivity of *all* sectors—agriculture, services (including the information economy), transportation, construction, and, indeed, manufacturing itself. Given the pervasive importance of manufacturing, nearly all of it must be done domestically, since there is no way that other economic activity can generate all the exports that would be needed to pay for it.[12] The notion in recent decades in the United States that

---

11. Consistent with this analysis, in this book I apply the terms "production" and "industrialization" to all industries, not only to manufacturing. While the kinds of technology and machinery vary from one occupation to another, all are transformed by capital investment.

12. As discussed in Chapter 5, this is also true of developing countries, which therefore need tariffs on manufactured imports in order to industrialize optimally. The failure of the global free trade regime to eradicate global poverty is one of the most scathing indictments of neoliberalism (Stiglitz 2003, 2007; Reinert 2008; Diaz 2010; Cobb and Diaz 2009).

"manufacturing jobs are not coming back" reflects an ideology of deindustrialization that must be overthrown if the country is to maintain a high standard of living and do so using nonpolluting technology, renewable energy, and materials efficiency and recycling (Rynn 2010).

THE ANATOMY OF CAPITAL FLIGHT

Since American corporations paid rising wages and benefits in the post–World War II period, the question naturally arises why they adopted a union-busting, low-wage strategy beginning in the 1970s. One major development during the postwar period was the economic recovery of America's industrial rivals, which had been devastated by the war. By the 1960s, European- and Japanese-based corporations were cutting into global markets that their U.S. counterparts had previously dominated unchallenged (Micklethwait and Wooldridge 2005). Some relative decline of the U.S. economy was therefore inevitable. This, however, cannot explain why U.S. corporate leaders abandoned a win-win relationship with their workers and adopted the win-lose strategy of shutting down U.S.-based production in favor of low-wage production abroad. Indeed, one reason for German and Japanese success was precisely their high levels of management-labor collaboration (Deming 1984; Micklethwait and Wooldridge 2005).

To be sure, Japan and the Asian Tigers initially competed in part on the basis of relatively low-cost labor, a fact that looms large in the neoliberal legitimation of capital flight. But the United States could have compensated by raising its rate of productivity growth through increased research and development and capital investment in state of the art civilian production equipment and methods. Instead, the United States was diverting human and physical capital into its military sector on a massive scale, allowing Germany to surpass the United States in manufacturing productivity growth in 1956 and Japan to surpass the United States in 1972 (U.S. Bureau of Labor Statistics 2010). With their increasingly automated production systems and cutting-edge industrial robotics, these and other advanced industrial countries today collectively exceed the United States in manufacturing output. Although they now pay *higher* manufacturing wages than the United States, these countries still outcompete American manufacturers. This shows that high wages do not make corporations uncompetitive if managements also invest in the research and development, training and capital equipment needed to increase productivity (Rynn 2010).

There are good historical reasons why capital flight was invented by American capitalists and not Europeans or Asians. As early as the nineteenth century, strong labor unions and social democratic parties in Germany and other European countries created a variant of capitalism in which corporations were expected to serve—at least secondarily—the interests of their workers and other stakeholders, not only outside stockholders interested in profit. The Japanese developed a similar notion of corporate responsibility, reflecting their civilization's subordination of private interests to the national interest. In the United States, however, the corporation was viewed as an entity whose sole purpose was to make money for its owners.[13] And America's rich, with some notable exceptions, were ruthless and reckless about making money, being willing to throw their own middle-class neighbors out of work and deindustrialize the U.S. economy in pursuit of their short-term private gain. Even more remarkably, they were and are willing to kill the goose that lays the golden eggs, neglecting long-term investment in the very corporations they own, for the sake of higher quarterly profits.

Indeed, from this broader historical perspective, the era of strong labor unions in the United States from the 1930s through the 1960s was an anomaly. In the 18th and early 19th centuries, free workers in America did not form unions in part because their wages were high relative to the Old World, where labor was abundant and thus cheap compared with the other factors of production (Fusfeld 1988). As immigration increased the supply of labor in America, it became necessary to form unions in order to maintain the level of wages. Managers and shareholders accommodated the needs of organized labor when they had to—during the militant 1930s and 1940s—and when the country's commercial supremacy in the 1950s and 1960s enabled them to do so while still making increasing profits. But the era of rising wages in the United States came to an end after that, when European and Japanese competition began to cut into corporate profits.

Two factors dictated the low labor cost strategy that American corporations began to adopt in the 1970s. First, the bloated defense sector was tying up much of the physical capital and engineering skill that would have enabled the U.S. civilian economy to compete through increased

---

13. These differences between the European, Japanese, and American notions of the corporation are discussed by Micklethwait and Wooldridge (2005). Like the Americans, according to these authors, the British also viewed corporations as purely moneymaking entities. But Micklethwait and Wooldridge note that Americans were the first to reduce moneymaking to a science, create business schools based on it, and train managers in its doctrines and practices.

investment and accelerated productivity growth (Melman 1983). Second, the preoccupation of America's ruling elite with short-term gain meant an unwillingness to undertake the investment needed for greater productivity growth in the long run (Melman 1983; National Center on Education and the Economy 1990). Even managers who preferred to undertake such investment and continue the win-win social contract with their workers were forced to abandon those principles by Wall Street's corporate raiders, who threatened to unseat any chief executive officer who failed to deliver high quarterly profits (Micklethwait and Wooldridge 2005).

Along with their new low-wage industrial paradigm in the private sector, America's corporate elite—never shy about wielding power in Washington—became more aggressive on that front as well. In the 1970s, developing countries in Latin America and elsewhere were falling into debt caused by higher oil prices and depressed economic conditions. American policymakers, acting on behalf of business interests, took advantage of this situation to impose neoliberal policies on these countries as the condition for loans from the International Monetary Fund, which the United States dominated (Stiglitz 2003). Later dubbed "the Washington Consensus," this set of policies included privatizing government-owned enterprises (frequently sold to foreign capitalists at bargain prices) and opening their product and capital markets to the big transnational corporations and banks.

The Reagan administration continued this foreign policy, backed up by military and covert paramilitary operations against populist governments that resisted the neoliberal agenda (Chomsky 2003, 2006). In addition, Reagan adopted union-busting and deregulation policies at home, enabling corporations to increase their profits at the expense of workers' wages and benefits, workplace health and safety, and consumer and environmental protection (Zinn 2003). Finally, Reagan's military buildup meant a great increase in lucrative defense contracts at taxpayer expense (Zinn 2003). Combined with corporate America's low-wage strategy, these neoliberal and militarist foreign and domestic policies all contributed to soaring profits after 1980, even as deindustrialization proceeded and median income stagnated.

THE STRONG DOLLAR AND CAPITAL FLIGHT

An important factor contributing to capital flight, in addition to the low-wage strategy just discussed, was an international financial system that gave U.S. corporations an incentive to produce goods abroad.

As the biggest military and economic power by far to emerge from World War II, the United States was in a unique position to shape the postwar international financial system and insisted that it be dollar based. Pursuant to the 1945 Bretton Woods Conference, every currency in the system was convertible to dollars at fixed exchange rates, and the dollar was convertible to gold at a fixed price.[14] The dollar was the world's strongest currency at the time, and the fixed exchange rates locked in that supremacy for the next 25 years. The system could not last beyond that because the fixed exchange rates could not take into account structural changes in the world economy as other countries caught up to the United States economically.

Other things being equal, a strong dollar made foreign goods cheaper for American purchasers and American goods more expensive for foreigners, which was bad news for the country's exporters and balance of trade. But it also created new opportunities for moneymaking, and this may well be why the country's financial elite promoted dollar-based arrangements at Bretton Woods. That these profit opportunities were unsustainable and injurious to the public interest mattered little to the capitalists who dominated U.S. foreign policy.

The new system enabled U.S. mining and oil companies to pay their production costs in cheaper local currencies and then receive payment for their product back in the United States in dollars, with an extra margin of profit due to the favorable exchange rate. The same advantage from a strong dollar accrued to American firms buying raw materials from producers in developing countries. In the 1970s, the system was extended beyond the American economy when the country's foreign policy elite arranged with the Saudi royal family for oil on the international market to be dominated in dollars (Spiro 1999). This meant that, in order to buy oil, purchasers everywhere would need to exchange their local currencies for dollars and pay the Saudis and Western oil companies in the latter, making oil costlier for buyers and more profitable for the oil companies.

While oil and minerals had to be extracted wherever the deposits were, the same profitable logic of producing in foreign currencies and selling in dollars favored moving U.S.-based production abroad. In order for capital flight to be feasible, however, two logistical problems had to be solved cheaply. One was the cost of transporting a continuous, massive flow of goods around the globe, which was solved in the 1950s by

14. My account of the Bretton Woods system follows Cohen (2001).

advances in containerization, a kind of shipping technology. The second problem was timely communication between corporate headquarters in the United States and subsidiary offices abroad, which was only partially solved by having executives travel back and forth by jet. The ultimate solution was the instantaneous communication that became available in the 1960s and 1970s, when satellites and transoceanic cables opened thousands of telecommunications channels.

With inexpensive global shipping and communication, large-scale capital flight ensued, enabling American manufacturers to reap the benefits of not only cheap natural resources but also cheap labor to replace unionized labor back in the United States. And the artificially strong dollar made foreign labor even cheaper than it would have been otherwise.

The Bretton Woods system of fixed exchange rates and a dollar backed by gold was not stable in the long run. By making foreign imports cheap for Americans and U.S. exports expensive for foreigners, the strong dollar gave rise to persistent U.S. trade deficits. In a system of floating exchange rates, trade deficits are normally self-correcting. When a country buys more than it sells, it increases the supply of its currency in the foreign exchange market, causing the value of the currency to decrease. With its currency worth less and imports more expensive, the country then imports less (and vice versa for exports), thus correcting the trade imbalance.

A spontaneous correction of this sort could not occur in the case of the United States, however, because the fixed exchange rates under the Bretton Woods system prevented the dollar from decreasing in value against other currencies. The U.S. trade deficits therefore continued, increasing the supply of dollars in the world, a surplus fueled also by U.S. military spending abroad. This surplus of dollars caused their value to decrease against gold in the open market, making it profitable to redeem them at the U.S. Treasury, where they purchased more gold at the Bretton Woods price. With U.S. gold reserves dwindling, an official devaluation of the dollar became inevitable and occurred in 1971, when the Treasury stopped exchanging gold for dollars. The fixed exchange rates established under Bretton Woods were then replaced by a system of floating rates in which the values of currencies were determined on the open market.

While the value of the dollar in theory floated after 1971, in reality it continued to be artificially high and remains so today. The main reasons are that it continues to be the primary reserve currency for the world's central banks and the currency in which oil is denominated. This creates extra demand for the dollar that keeps its price higher than is justified in view of America's trade deficits and long-term government debt (Stiglitz 2007). While capital flight might have occurred in any case, the dollar-based international financial system has made it even more profitable. This has enabled corporate investors to get even richer at the expense of the middle class, who pay the price in the form of job loss due to the decline of U.S.-based production.[15]

FROM AMERICAN DREAM TO DEBT NIGHTMARE

From its colonial beginnings in the seventeenth century, America had been perceived by many in the Old World as a land of opportunity, where any person of humble origin could achieve prosperity through hard work and frugality. As discussed in the next chapter, however, this American dream came closest to realization not through the individual effort on which it was predicated but through collective bargaining in the twentieth century, which gave ordinary people a real measure of power in relation to corporations. With rising wages and substantial accumulated savings (lent to Uncle Sam during World War II), home ownership for the masses became a reality in the 1950s and 1960s, and more families were sending their children to college than ever before. By then, deeply rooted in the culture, the American Dream included the expectation that one's children would inherit better material circumstances than oneself.

Although median compensation essentially leveled off after 1974, this average long-term trend was hard to grasp at the time since actual compensation rose and fell with the business cycle (see Appendix 2.1B). Most insidiously, with their profits dependent on mass consumption, the same corporate elites who were chiseling wages and deindustrializing the U.S. economy now set about to prop up aggregate demand through an aggressive and deceptive marketing of easy credit (Ferguson 2010; Wolff 2010). Many middle-class Americans—blindsided by the expectation of ever rising incomes and property values and seduced by America's advertising-driven culture of consumerism—went along. It was therefore only when

---

15. It commonly said that the American consumer benefits from the strong dollar by getting imported goods that are cheaper than can be manufactured in the United States. But the associated loss of manufacturing employment in the United States means that the wealth needed to buy the cheaper goods is no longer being generated in the United States, making continued imports dependent on consumer credit and thus not sustainable. The root of the problem is that corporations—under pressure to produce high quarterly profits for their rich owners—are not making the long-term investments needed to raise the productivity of American workers so that the latter can compete with lower-paid workers overseas. Were such investment to occur, which would require the rich to accept lower profits (at least in the short term), Americans would have *both* more manufacturing jobs *and* inexpensive goods produced domestically in highly automated factories.

the resulting housing and consumption bubble burst in 2008 that wide-spread disillusionment with the American Dream set in.[16]

The rise of debt-financed consumption in the age of deindustrialization is reflected in a long-term decline in the rate of personal saving from 10 percent in 1980 to less than 3 percent in 2007, as shown in Figure 2.1 and Appendix 2.1C.[17] Along with persistent trade deficits, it indicated an economy that was consuming too much relative to what it was producing. In addition, this rise of debt-financed consumption spawned a massive increase in related white-collar employment. A housing bubble, for example, requires bank personnel to provide mortgages, real estate agents to buy and sell the houses, and other white-collar workers to process insurance policies. In the 1980s and 1990s, an accelerating growth of new and increasingly complex financial products and practices also expanded employment in the financial services sector.

In other circumstances, an expansion of housing, consumption and related services might indicate post-industrial progress. If high levels of civilian research and development, capital investment, and training in all sectors are making the economy highly productive and if middle class incomes are rising, such an expansion can be sustainable. This is in fact what occurred in the post-World War II housing boom.[18] Given the deindustrialization and stagnation of median income that began in the 1970s, however, the subsequent rise of financial and real estate services enabling a surge in consumption and new home construction indicated a serious misallocation of resources. As shown in Figure 2.2, between 1974 and 2009, manufacturing fell from 22 percent of U.S. gross domestic product to 12 percent, while finance, insurance, and real estate rose from 15 to 21 percent.

The change in structure of the U.S. economy depicted in Figure 2.2 and the consumption and housing bubbles that accompanied it constitute

---

16. Conservatives typically blame the housing bubble on government affordable housing policies, arguing that Freddie Mac and Fanny Mae promoted mortgages to people who could not afford them (Wallison 2011). Compared to the big private banks, however, a much smaller proportion of the loans made or guaranteed by Freddie, Fanny, and other government entities became seriously delinquent (Min 2011a, 2011b).

17. The rate of personal saving is an aggregate statistic that includes a high rate of saving by high-income households and negative saving—that is, debt—for many in the middle and lower classes. The decline from 10 to 3 percent represents mainly a large increase in debt.

18. This housing boom, however, was not a model of sustainable economic growth in the long run, which also requires an economy based on renewable energy, clean manufacturing, the recycling of materials, and sustainable agriculture (Rynn 2010). As discussed in Part II of this book, it requires as well a steady-state, post-capitalist economic system that is not based on ever-increasing private consumption.

a monumental failure of neoliberalism. According to that ideology, financial markets allocate capital efficiently to job-creating enterprises, and reducing taxes on individuals and corporations (and government regulations on the latter) frees up resources and entrepreneurial talent for the creation of wealth. But that is precisely what did *not* happen in most of the U.S. economy in the era of deregulation and low taxes that began in 1980. Awash in increased profits from capital flight and a strong dollar and pocketing much more of that money because of extraordinarily low tax rates (Adler 2010; Wolff 2010), the rich sought new financial investment opportunities. Far from channeling that money to productive and sustainable job-creating businesses, Wall Street instead promoted an unsustainable expansion of credit directed at consumers and would-be home owners.[19]

The financial mechanisms through which this occurred are complex, and I will not attempt to explain them here in any detail. In essence, to take the example of housing, investment banks created mortgage-backed securities (mortgages bundled into tradable securities) and derivatives (secondary financial products) intended to hedge the risks of these primary products. The capital used to buy the primary products made its way through the financial and banking system to home owners and through them eventually to construction firms and housing-related service providers, including the very financial institutions that operated this "securitization food chain."

Meanwhile, the money invested in derivatives—for example, the "credit default swaps" sold by A.I.G.—did not fund anything in the real world of homes and home mortgages. Rather, it entered a "risk market" that is parallel to the real economy. These derivatives were supposed to work like insurance (itself a kind of derivative), enabling those unable or unwilling to bear certain risks to pay others to assume them. By assigning prices to risk, derivatives, according to neoliberal theory, would ensure that capital invested in the primary market was allocated efficiently. And yet the actual outcome of unregulated capital and risk markets was the epitome of inefficiency and misallocation—a housing bubble in which scarce resources were expended on construction and the financing of home ownership, only to have the houses subsequently abandoned and left to rot. The bursting of the housing bubble left the banks with "toxic" mortgage-backed securities and distressed collateral while ruining the would-be home owners financially.

---

19. In the following analysis of the 2008 financial crisis, I follow Ferguson (2010) and Stiglitz (2010).

So why did Wall Street misallocate funds in this way? The answer is that firms will not raise capital and undertake new production if there is insufficient demand for their products, and the stagnation of middle-class incomes in the era of low-wage capitalism was constricting consumer demand (Wolff 2010).[20] And as long as corporations are exporting capital and deindustrializing the U.S. economy, insufficient real wealth will be produced domestically to sustain high wages and benefits. Under these circumstances, the only way to maintain economic expansion is by promoting consumer debt, making the expansion inherently unstable.

The financial elites surely knew or should have known that their short-term credit fix would create an economic catastrophe sometime in the future. But the costs of such a collapse—in joblessness, homelessness, and personal financial ruin—would be imposed mostly on the middle class, while the architects of the catastrophe fully expected to be bailed out by the taxpayer, as had occurred in the 1987 and 1997 financial crises. Nor were they mistaken, as we now know from the 2008–2009 bailouts.

THE ANATOMY OF AMERICAN STATE CAPITALISM

The utter failure of unregulated financial markets, at the cost of monumental waste and human suffering, should have put the nails in the coffin of neoliberalism. Lawrence Summers, who had the responsibility to regulate derivatives in the Clinton administration and refused to do so on the grounds of neoliberal ideology, should have been exposed as

---

20. It was this chronic sluggishness of aggregate demand that also explains why the Federal Reserve under Alan Greenspan (and more recently under Ben Bernanke) kept interest rates so low for so long. While conservatives blame this Fed policy—and thus "government"—for the housing bubble, central bankers are constrained by macroeconomic conditions and the twin goals of maintaining high employment and controlling inflation. Had the Fed followed a tight money policy under the conditions that Greenspan faced, the result would have been recession and deflation instead of a housing bubble. Thus, the Fed had no good options given the economy's weakening capacity to produce wealth and sustain the high wages and benefits needed for robust aggregate demand. The underlying causes of this weakness include such factors as capital flight and deindustrialization, the diversion of human resources and physical capital from civilian investment into an unproductive war economy, and the unwillingness of America's rich to forgo high short-term profits in order to invest in long-term productivity growth and to pay the taxes needed to properly maintain public infrastructure. Meanwhile, the misguided focus of conservatives on monetary policy deflects attention from the one thing Greenspan did do wrong and admits that he did wrong—neglect to adequately regulate the big banks (Greenspan 2008).

negligent, or at best incompetent.[21] Instead, he was put in charge of President Obama's economic team, a commentary on Wall Street's stranglehold on American democracy.

Why did the financial markets fail to perform as neoliberals predicted? In addition to the economic instability created by low-wage capitalism, as indicated previously, the answer to this question has two parts. First, unregulated markets in general allocate resources efficiently only under certain conditions (Stiglitz and Walsh 2007). One of these conditions is that buyers and sellers have equal information about the product on the market. Another is that all the costs of the product are included in its price and are not imposed on a third party that is external to the market transaction. To the extent these and some other conditions are not met, unregulated markets do not allocate resources efficiently, even in theory, and government regulation can often make them more efficient. Laws against deceptive marketing can limit predatory lending, for example, and banking regulation can help ensure that the risks of a bank's failure are not born by taxpayers. Consistent with this picture, the deregulation of financial markets and institutions that began in the 1980s was a major cause of the financial crises that followed in 1987, 1997, and 2008–2009, disconfirming neoliberal ideology's claims about the efficiency of unregulated markets.

All this points to a second and more fundamental issue—the concentration of wealth in America and the domination of government by the rich. This gets to the deep cause of recent financial crises and the housing and consumption bubbles that led up to them. In essence, American state capitalism is a kind of scam in which rich investors are permitted to assume risks on paper, profit greatly from doing so, and then run to the taxpayer for bailouts when the system periodically collapses. This is

---

21. Here is an obvious example of Summers' failure to do his job (Ferguson 2010). Only the owner of a house, car, or other asset is permitted to buy an insurance policy against that asset. No such rule governs the world of credit derivatives, in which an unlimited number of third party speculators can buy credit default swaps on the same asset. Further, while it is virtually inconceivable that all the houses in the country would burn down at the same time, requiring insurance companies to pay all their policyholders simultaneously, a general collapse of the financial system is not only much more likely but had actually occurred as recently as 1987 and 1997 (in international financial markets). Summers served as Treasury Secretary from 1999 through 2000, in the wake of the previous financial crisis, and yet opposed regulation of derivatives that might have prevented or at least mitigated financial catastrophe in a future crisis.

When that crisis came in 2008, A.I.G. was predictably unable to pay most of the credit default swaps it had issued. At that point, New York Federal Reserve Bank President Timothy Geithner, soon to be Barack Obama's Treasury Secretary, brokered a $60 billion bailout of the holders of these derivatives—mostly big banks—even as ordinary pensioners and homeowners were being wiped out by the financial crisis (Ferguson 2010).

exactly what occurred in 2008–2009, when the market for mortgage-backed securities and the derivatives associated with them collapsed. Financial institutions that had engineered and profited enormously from the housing bubble suddenly could not meet their obligations.

In order for capitalism to work the way neoliberals say it does, the investors who had assumed the risk of these outcomes and had made a killing from doing so should then have been required to bear the resulting losses. Instead, with breathtaking audacity, these investors insisted that the U.S. taxpayer reimburse them for their losses. Even more remarkably, they prevailed. The taxpayer bailout of A.I.G., for example, made its investors whole even as it did nothing whatsoever for the millions of Americans losing their homes and being financially ruined because of Wall Street's irresponsibility (Stiglitz 2010). No longer a truly capitalist society, America now lives under a *state* capitalist system in which profits are privatized while losses are socialized.

Such an outrageous resolution of the financial crisis, of course, could never have been enacted by politicians without some compelling cover story. Like a Greek chorus, thousands of American pundits, economists, and politicians from across the political spectrum proclaimed with one voice that only a government bailout could avert a complete collapse of the U.S.—if not the world—economy. What they did *not* say is that government could have saved the economy by nationalizing the financial giants, whether temporarily or permanently, and reorganizing them—as in any bankruptcy—so that the investors bore most of the losses (Stiglitz 2010).

This raises a most interesting and important question. Why is it entirely acceptable in America today for government to bail out private interests but unthinkable for it to take over failed financial institutions and reorganize them in accordance with the rules of capitalism itself? Because, the Greek chorus intones, we do not want government interfering with the free market. But the free market can work the way in which neoliberal pundits and politicians say it works only if investors are held accountable for the consequences of their financial decisions. And if government does not enforce this accountability, who will? Those who oppose that use government but support its use to transfer money from taxpayers to investors are engaging in class warfare against the middle class and on behalf of the rich.

On close examination, the state plays a number of roles that are essential to American capitalism, even as corporate elites and conservative politicians disingenuously bash government (Heilbroner 1985). In addition to periodic bailouts of the big financial institutions, the state uses taxpayer dollars to build expensive infrastructure on which private profits depend. Beginning in the 1950s, for example, construction of the interstate highway system—one of the world's largest infrastructure projects—constituted a transfer of income from middle-class taxpayers to investors in car, oil, and insurance companies—industries whose profits were tied to a private transportation system constructed at public expense. To be sure, in the 1950s the rich paid their fair share of such infrastructure projects, with the highest marginal tax rate at 90 percent (Adler 2010). But there was little public debate about whether private automobile or public rail-based transportation would better meet the needs of the middle class, the country as a whole, and the earth's ecology, notwithstanding the hundreds of billions of tax dollars at issue. Rather, the key policy decisions were made behind closed doors by corporate and government elites acting in their own interests.[22]

An even more lavish use of taxpayer dollars on behalf of corporate interests, as discussed in Chapter 1, is the deployment of U.S. military power in support of foreign regimes friendly to U.S. corporations, a prerequisite of capital flight. Fostering such regimes, which are inherently unpopular, has frequently required covert operations, military aid, invasions, wars, and permanent military bases in or near the host countries, all at great public expense. This process of making the world safe for American corporations took time and was the main objective of U.S. foreign and military policy from the end of World War II to the present (Chomsky 2003, 2006; Chomsky and Herman 1979). It was also expensive since "projecting power" throughout the world elicited countervailing responses from the communist countries.

While the human and financial costs of the national security state fall primarily on the middle class, the benefits accrue disproportionately to rich investors in U.S. corporations. In addition, the diversion of human resources and physical capital from civilian industry into the military sector contributed further to the decline of U.S.-based production. In short, the same middle class whose wages and benefits stagnated beginning in the 1970s because of capital flight and deindustrialization were subsidizing as

---

22. It could be argued in response to this analysis that the automobile is highly popular with the American middle class and that the interstate highway system responded to this preference, even if the policymaking process that created it was not explicitly informed by significant public input. However, the planning and construction of public highways began in the 1920s (Caro 1975), well before the vast majority of Americans even considered owning cars. Thereafter, preferences for cars, as with most consumer products, were heavily shaped by advertising, with car companies today spending well over a billion dollars a year convincing Americans to buy their product (Rachwal 2008).

taxpayers the military power that made capital flight and deindustrialization possible. Ordinary Americans would never consent to this looting, of course, except for a national security ideology that conceals from them the true purposes of U.S. military power, as discussed in Chapter 1, just as neo-liberal ideology conceals the true nature of capital flight and of Wall Street's financial scams.

BEYOND DEINDUSTRIALIZATION

The overvalued dollar discussed previously continues to be a source of increased profits for oil companies and for U.S. corporations who move production abroad. Ordinary Americans need to understand that their jobs in the long run depend on devaluation of the dollar and a rebuilding of the country's manufacturing sector (Krugman 2011a; Romer 2011). This can be facilitated by reform of the international financial system[23] and such policies as paying down America's national debt.[24] With a deval-ued dollar, the price of imports will increase, while consumers in many cases will not immediately have domestically produced substitutes. It will take time for American entrepreneurs to regain the production compe-tence needed to expand domestic manufacturing in many areas and thereby create new jobs and bring down the price of goods. Until then, employment in the private sector will remain depressed, and middle-class Americans, still dependent on imports that are now more expensive, will see their cost of living increase.

Here is the big political question raised by this analysis: who will com-pensate ordinary Americans who remain out of work or underemployed

---

23. The dollar will remain overvalued as long as it serves as the primary reserve currency for the world's central banks. It can and should be replaced in this role by Special Drawing Rights, a kind of currency issued by the International Monetary Fund for use by central banks, a proposal that has been further refined by Joseph Stiglitz (2007, 2010). While the Chinese government supports an expanded role for Special Drawing Rights, which is arguably in the global public interest, the U.S. financial establishment continues to resist the policy in order to maintain a strong dollar, a continuing source of short-term private gain for the rich paid for by job loss in America.

24. Paying off the entire U.S. debt will put more than $3 trillion into the hands of foreign invest-ors and governments, greatly increasing the surplus of dollars abroad. This need not create a pre-cipitous devaluation of the dollar if carried out over a long period of time and accompanied by a cessation of U.S. trade deficits and sharp curtailment of U.S. military spending abroad. But some devaluation is inevitable and desirable. Conservatives who demand a retirement of U.S. debt while simultaneously excoriating Federal Reserve Chairman Ben Bernanke for weakening the dollar demonstrate either an ignorance of international finance or a willingness to suspend the rules of logic in order to beat an ideological drum.

because of decades of capital flight? Who will compensate the middle class for their rising cost of living as the U.S. economy makes the transition from being a net importer of manufactured goods to being once again a producer with balanced trade accounts? Justice demands that those who profited from capital flight and unnecessary military programs now pay these costs. This means such policies as a large and permanent increase in taxes on rich individuals and households, a steep increase in taxes on oil companies, and monetary reform that enables the U.S. Treasury to recover revenues that properly belong to government but that are being appropriated as profits by private banks (American Monetary Institute 2011). All these revenues must be used to make restitution to the middle class.

There are a number of ways this can and should be done. Public works can be funded to build and repair the country's infrastructure, including schools and other public buildings, creating productive jobs for the middle class. Neglected school districts also need more teachers in order to reduce class sizes, a requirement for giving every child a quality education. In addition to these and other public investments, some revenues must be applied to paying down the national debt. By putting more dollars into circulation, this will reduce their value against other currencies, thereby creating conditions for a reindustrialization of America.[25] Most important, a green New Deal is needed to build the efficient and renewable energy and transportation infrastructures of the future and avert immanent climate change that threatens world agriculture and civilization itself.

Finally, the time is long overdue for far-reaching reform in the ownership and control of corporations (MacLeod 1997; Wolff 2010), as discussed in Chapter 6. Devaluation of the dollar will help discourage capital flight but not eliminate it. The latter can be achieved only when American workers gain sufficient ownership and control of their corporations to end the capitalist race to the bottom in search of cheap labor.

I will elaborate on this reform agenda in the second half of this book. But there is still more to say about ideologies that prevent America's middle class from embracing such reforms. Many pundits and politicians,

---

25. I am not arguing that America should repay its foreign debt rapidly, which would devalue the dollar precipitously, or do so by running persistent trade surpluses, which would likely be at the expense of trade deficits in developing countries. But while the United States need not become a net exporter, nor can it continue to be the world's importer of last resort and to stimulate foreign economies through its military spending abroad. When these unsustainable outflows of dollars are ended and after the world economy absorbs the new outflows from repayment of U.S. external debt, the value of the dollar will recover though not to the artificially overvalued level maintained during America's imperial heyday.

Republican and Democratic alike, argue that neoliberal policies are not the real reasons for the country's economic malaise. Rather, they say, public schools are not preparing the youth to compete in the global economy, taxes and government regulations are strangling free enterprise, and unions are sapping the individualist work ethic needed to restore American prosperity. To these issues I now turn.

APPENDIX 2.1: U.S. DATA ON CORPORATE PROFITS, MEDIAN COMPENSATION, AND PERSONAL SAVING

Figures 2.1A and 2.1B show graphs of U.S. after-tax corporate profits and median compensation in 2010 dollars and lines of best fit (trend lines) calculated using linear regression. Figure 2.1C shows a similar graph for rate of personal saving as a percentage disposable income. The data for Figures 2.1A and 2.1C were obtained from the U.S. National Income and Product Accounts (U.S. Bureau of Economic Analysis 2011) and for Figure 2.1B from the U.S. Social Security Administration (2011). The use of linear regression here is purely descriptive—to find lines of best fit in order to compare average rates of change in the periods before and after deindustrialization. I make no statistical inferences and thus have no need to assess whether the data are consistent with the assumptions of the linear regression model.

While deindustrialization of the U.S. economy is a continuous process that began at least as early as the 1970s, for purposes of comparing trends before and after deindustrialization, I needed an exact dividing point for each data set. I chose these dividing points based on characteristics of the data themselves as seen in nine-year moving averages; 1974 was a local maximum in median compensation and 1978 in personal savings, while 1980 was an inflection point in corporate profits. For Figure 2.1, the trend lines were transformed by using these dividing points as index years; slopes and intercepts were adjusted in order to display the three sets of trend lines conveniently on the same set of axes, and trend numbers for the last three years of the series were modified in order to depict changes in the data associated with the 2008–2009 financial crisis.

Figure 2.1A   U.S. After Tax Corporate Profits (billions of 2010 dollars)

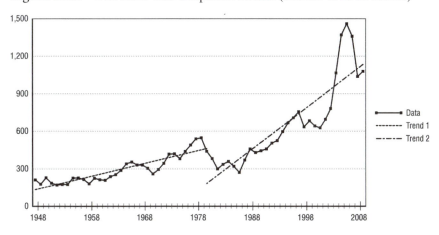

Figure 2.1B   U.S. Median Compensation (2010 dollars)

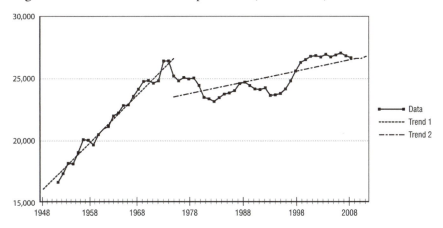

Figure 2.1C U.S. Rate of Personal Saving (percentage of disposable income)

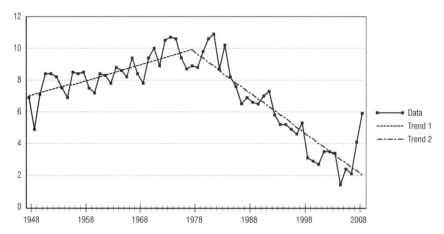

CHAPTER 3

School Reform and Other Diversions

INTRODUCTION

The national security, postindustrial, and neoliberal belief systems promised national greatness and ever-increasing prosperity. For more than three decades, however, there has been a growing chasm between these promises and the actual economic fortunes of tens of millions of Americans. Mass discontent increasingly threatens the plausibility of these ideologies and the state capitalist power structure they legitimize. Corporate elites deflect this discontent from themselves and maintain the sacred-cow status of their capitalism-friendly policies by attributing national decline to scapegoats—especially unions, "government" (defined to exclude the national security state and corporate welfare), and a public education system that is allegedly failing to prepare America's youth to compete in the global economy.

Further, through their ownership and control of vast media conglomerates, their domination of electoral politics and the state, and their influence over cultural institutions that depend on their philanthropy, America's ruling class propagates this self-serving ideology of sacred cows and scapegoats deep into the consciousness of ordinary people. This is not to say that all the rich and powerful are engaged in deliberate propaganda, though some certainly are. Rather, as in past ages, ruling elites generally believe in the ideologies they propagate, which serve to simultaneously legitimize their power in the eyes of others and enable them to feel good about themselves. The Spanish conquistadores, for example, thought of themselves not as oppressors but rather as enlightened leaders bringing lost souls to Christ. Similarly, British imperialists dwelt not on their appropriation of others' natural resources but instead on the "white man's burden" they were taking up.

So, too, most CEOs and other big power holders in America today do not think about the negative consequences of their policies for ordinary people. They no doubt believe their own ideology—that unions and government are impediments to the creation of wealth and that in clearing away these impediments they are promoting not only their own fortunes but also the prosperity of others. I begin this chapter with an important special case of such ideology—school reform neoliberalism—which holds that some communities are trapped in poverty not because capitalism is failing them but because incompetent teachers, protected by self-serving unions, are not providing the education that disadvantaged children need to succeed. That ideology is summed up in the 2010 film *Waiting for Superman*.[1] This same alleged failure of public education, according to the school reformers, is responsible for America's difficulties competing in the global economy.

Such beliefs about public education are widely held in the United States today. A front-page story in the *New York Times* titled "Teachers Wonder: Why the Heapings of Scorn?" (Gabriel 2011) elicited passionate letters to the editor from both critics and defenders. One reader wrote,

> It is a mystery why teachers fail to understand the public perception. They do not work a full day, they have significant time off during the day, they have extensive vacation time, they can be granted tenure and they have a retirement benefits package that is the envy of all except top corporate executives. Any additional activity, like being a coach, club leader or adviser, is generally compensated.

---

1. The director of this film and its star Geoffrey Canada, like many well-intentioned social entrepreneurs in the field of school reform, have somehow managed to overlook the fact that the foreign countries they think are outperforming the United States academically typically have unionized teachers. What these countries do not have are the vast extremes of wealth and poverty and inequitable school funding that are common in the United States. *Waiting for Superman* dismisses the role of money with the observation that spending per student has gone up in recent decades while academic performance has not. But such aggregate statistics say nothing about which school districts benefited most from the increase in spending, how additional money in poor school districts was actually spent, and the increasing challenges faced by poor districts during this same period (Adler 2010). The film implies that affluent school districts spend their money frivolously, ignoring the well-established role of smaller class sizes in academic performance (Class Size Matters 2011; Krueger and Whitmore 2001; Mishel and Rothstein 2002). For a well-informed critique of *Waiting for Superman*, see the DVD *The Inconvenient Truth Behind Waiting for Superman* (Grassroots Education Movement 2011). See also D'Agostino (2012b).

Now don't get me wrong. The uniformed unions also have over-reaching benefits that need renegotiation. But it is the teachers with whom the public has the greatest contact and who regularly whine about how poorly treated they are and demand raises from struggling taxpayers on whose shoulders their compensation falls.

It is high time they wake up and begin to understand that they do not exist in a vacuum and that their ivory towers need a dose of reality.

Another reader gave the perspective of most teachers:

I wish that everyone who thinks that teachers are "glorified baby sitters" who go home at 3 o'clock could spend a week doing the job. For decades I have nagged my husband to quit teaching because I can't stand his 70-hour workweeks. As a New York City high school teacher, he has on average 170 students each day. That translates into 170 tests and essays to mark on a regular basis, on top of having to create two or three lesson plans for each day.

It's a rare person who can do this job well. It's exhausting, and when you add the lack of appreciation of teachers, there's little motivation for a new generation to take on this vital task. In fact, I've been telling our kids since they were born not to become teachers. Now, watching their dad, they've come to the same conclusion.

One reader encapsulated volumes of school reform literature in three sentences:

Why the heapings of scorn on teachers and the unions? One word: performance. Until student performance improves, all deals are off.

The current wave of "school reform" arose with neoliberalism in the 1980s and employs its free market discourse (Compton and Weiner 2008). My perspective on this subject has been shaped by more than 20 years of work experience as a college and high school teacher. In the 1990s, I completed a long and expensive doctoral program in political science at Columbia University. Twenty years earlier, I would have been virtually assured of a career as a college professor. By the time I entered the job market, however, there was an oversupply of PhDs, and universities were replacing tenured positions with part-time "adjunct" jobs, some of which I held while I was still completing my doctorate.

I then taught in New York City public high schools for 11 years. My salary and benefits as a unionized teacher enabled me to make payments on my student loans and still remain in the middle class. Midway through my stint with the public school system, it was put under mayoral control. The city's billionaire mayor, Michael Bloomberg, chose as schools chancellor a former antitrust prosecutor and corporate lawyer, Joel Klein, whose lack of experience as an educator or schools administrator made him completely unqualified for the job.[2] But there was a method to Bloomberg's madness. The mayor saw the teacher's union as the primary obstacle to "reform," and Klein was well suited by temperament and professional skills to bust it.[3]

The implicit foundation of this antiunion agenda was a chain of reasoning that goes something like this: (1) New York's public schools are failing, (2) ineffective teachers are the single biggest reason for this failure, and (3) the teachers' union is protecting these ineffective teachers and is thus the single biggest obstacle to a quality education for all. Like the Bush administration's No Child Left Behind initiative, which had recently been enacted, Bloomberg's and Klein's school reform agenda was aggressively marketed as a bold plan to raise academic standards for all children. This would end what George W. Bush called the "soft bigotry of low expectations," which supposedly explained the "achievement gap" between affluent white and disadvantaged minority students. This same appeal to racial justice and equality would later characterize the Obama administration's Race to the Top, which made several billion dollars in federal grants and waivers from impossible federal mandates conditional on far-reaching, neoliberal school reform by the states.

The title of Bloomberg's and Klein's plan, "Children First," implied that public schools were failing because education professionals, including teachers' union and school district officials, were putting their own selfish agendas before the needs of the children they served. The ideology of disinterested school reformers rescuing children from the clutches of labor leaders, government bureaucrats, and other entrenched special interests legitimized the mayor's muscular agenda of remaking New

---

2. When Klein left in 2010–2011, Bloomberg appointed the equally unqualified Cathie Black, a publishing executive who lasted less than four months in the job. Klein went on to work for his good friend Rupert Murdoch, whose *New York Post* had supported his union-busting policies with a constant drumbeat of attacks on the United Federation of Teachers. In joining Murdoch's empire, Klein reportedly cashed in his public sector connections to pursue "entrepreneurial ventures that cater to the educational marketplace in which News Corporation could make seed investments" (Stelter and Arango 2010).

3. Bloomberg succeeded in undermining the union, at least for a time, but not in dismantling it. For a review of the mayor's school reform record, see D'Agostino (2009b).

York's public school system in the image of corporate America and the free market economy.

The current attack on teachers and teachers' unions—led by politicians, pundits, and wealthy businessmen across the political spectrum—is predicated on an assumption that is apparently uncontroversial: that American public education as an institution is, in fact, performing badly. School reformers have invested this assumption with a kind of moral authority such that anyone who has a more complex picture of what is actually going on in American schools is immediately suspect of being somehow dishonest or trying to get away with something, of protecting and excusing arrangements that are self-evidently bad.

Armed with this assumption and girded with its moral authority, school reformers press their indictment of public education without having to justify what is in fact a simplistic set of answers to questions that are far from simple and that merit an informed and respectful public dialogue. Further, in any such dialogue, teachers, above all, should have a valued place at the table, much as doctors do in discussions of health care, athletes on sports issues, and so on. And yet teachers in America today find themselves on the defensive, unable to question school reform orthodoxy without raising the suspicion of being self-interested apologists for a dysfunctional status quo. With their credibility impugned from the outset, teachers—the very people who can shed the most light on the real problems in public education—have been very largely shut out of the national discussion about the state and needs of the country's education system.

What, then, is the basis for the widespread and simplistic assumption that America's public schools are failing? In brief, the answer is an alleged decline in standardized test scores over time and the poor performance of America's youth on international comparisons. Yet most of those who actually study the educational testing data in depth and have the statistical expertise to understand it question both the overall picture of poor test scores and the notion that school or teacher quality is the primary causal factor in explaining test scores (Koretz 2008).[4]

Based on a comprehensive review of the available data in the mid-1990s, *The Manufactured Crisis* (Berliner and Biddle 1995) presented

---

4. In theory, "value-added" models can isolate teacher effectiveness and measure it separately from other factors that affect student test scores, such as class size and prior skill level of students. In practice, these models demonstrate poor statistical validity (McCaffrey et al. 2003) and distort the entire educational process by rewarding those who "teach to the test" (Baker et al. 2010; D'Agustino 2012c; Rothstein 2010, 2011). In addition, as discussed in Chapter 7, by pitting teacher against teacher, they undermine the very culture of collaboration needed to improve public education.

a scathing critique of the "failing public schools" picture, arguing that most of the decline in test scores could be attributed to an influx of low-performing students into the pool of those taking the tests. The authors also made the case that the international data were misleading because they could not adequately take into consideration differences in national curricula and other factors that complicate such comparisons. More recently, an analysis of New York City data called into question Michael Bloomberg's claim that the city's public schools were in decline before he took the helm as mayor (Brennan 2009).

The context of such research was the neoliberal attack on public education, which proved impervious to reasoned discussion. Experts who questioned the school reformers' interpretation of educational testing data were widely criticized for being complacent about the state of America's schools (Berliner and Biddle 1996; Stedman 1996a, 1996b). Such criticism showed the circular reasoning and ideological nature of school reform orthodoxy—"test data tell us that public schools are failing, and if anyone thinks the data tell us something else, that only shows they're in denial that public schools are failing."

In reality, the statistical evidence raises complex questions that merit open-minded and informed public discussion (Koretz 2008). However, such discussion would not serve the purpose of neoliberal reformers, who have little interest in understanding the real problems confronting schools but are hell-bent on remaking public education in the image of free market capitalism.

SCHOOL REFORM AND ECONOMIC STAGNATION

The climate of public hostility in which American teachers and teachers' unions find themselves today is rooted in nearly three decades of public policy. The current wave of school reform in America was launched in 1983, when a presidential commission of corporate, government, and education elites concluded that the country's education system was failing to produce a competitive workforce. "A Nation At Risk," the commission's famous report, warned that "the educational foundations of our society are presently being eroded by a rising tide of mediocrity that threatens our very future as a Nation and a people" (National Commission on Excellence in Education 1983).

The main evidence cited in support of this somber conclusion was an alleged drop in SAT scores between 1963 and 1980[5] and America's relatively poor performance on international tests. The commission's recommendations included "higher standards," better teachers, and "performance-based" teacher salaries. This same agenda has pervaded the education policies of all presidents, Republican and Democratic, from the 1980s through the Obama administration. It was and is echoed by corporate elites, politicians at every level of government, and local school boards. Compton and Weiner (2008) have shown that this movement in the United States is part of a broader neoliberal attack on teachers and teachers' unions occurring worldwide. They document the forms it is taking in different countries and the various ways teachers are fighting back.

Student test scores are central to the school reform movement in two ways. First, school reformers cite poor performance on international tests[6] as evidence of a crisis in American public education. Second, standardized tests—especially state reading and math tests—provide the data school reformers use in evaluating the success of both educational reform policies and individual teachers, administrators, and schools. In Chapter 7, I discuss why standardized test scores are not an adequate basis either for diagnosing what is wrong with public education or for creating better schools (see also D'Agostino 2012c). In this section, I limit myself to the question of whether public school performance, as measured by standardized tests, can be a relevant measure of how well prepared the country's youth are to be productive in workplaces when they leave school.

School reformers typically misconstrue the training deficits that confront American employers, most of whom are satisfied with most of their employees' traditional academic skills (National Center on Education and the Economy 1990). Employers who say they cannot find enough qualified workers are typically referring to something other than academic rigor. First, there are not enough job applicants with the specific

---

5. The "Sandia Report" later showed that the commission's finding of declining SAT scores was based on faulty statistical analysis. One of the report's authors told a journalist that it was suppressed by the Reagan administration's Department of Education, which had appointed the commission (Miller 1991). This is consistent with the obscurity of the report for nearly ten years; it was published only in 1993 in the May/June issue of the *Journal of Educational Research*.

6. Two widely cited international tests are the Trends in International Mathematics and Science Study and the Program for International Student Assessment (U.S. Department of Education 2011). Ironically, one of the main reasons for lackluster U.S. performance on these tests, aside from the high incidence of child poverty in the United States and inequitable funding of schools, is the country's preoccupation with "hard data" provided by multiple-choice tests. The most academically successful countries, by contrast, routinely employ holistic assessments, such as open-ended essay questions (Darling-Hammond 2010).

technical training needed in emerging industries. Successful European and Asian countries provide such training through free, government-run technical schools and retraining programs (National Center on Education and the Economy 1990), a solution shunned by American free market ideologues.

Second, there is a shortage of workers who can analyze needs and formulate and creatively solve problems, both independently and in collaboration with coworkers. These higher-order cognitive and social skills are cultivated by schools that feature learning teams and inquiry and project-based instruction. While such schools are the norm in highly industrialized foreign countries (Darling-Hammond 2010), they are ironically neglected (or even attacked) in the United States by school reformers preoccupied with multiple choice test data. To be sure, American school reformers do recognize that good jobs in the twenty-first century require higher-order skills, but they do not support the kind of schools that produce such outcomes because that type of school does not fit the reformers' notion of academic rigor (Meier 2009).

In summary, America is not faltering economically because of a shortage of rigorously educated workers. While it is true that the most successful European and Asian countries produce a larger proportion of college graduates than the United States (Darling-Hammond 2010), millions of the college graduates whom the United States does produce cannot find employment requiring their level of education (Matgouranis 2010). American corporations are outsourcing engineering and other skilled jobs to China and India not because there is a shortage of qualified Americans to do these jobs but because there are qualified foreigners who will do them for lower pay. Under these circumstances, graduating more engineers will not result in more wealth being produced in the United States; it will only lower the salaries of American engineers. While lower labor costs are in the short-term interest of corporations and their owners, it is not in the public interest to invest in human capital only to have it remain idle.

I am far from suggesting that the United States should provide less education for its people. My point is that corporate elites and rich investors who blame American education for the country's economic malaise are diverting attention, whether consciously or not, from their own responsibility for that malaise. Were these same elites and investors to build factories in the United States and provide industrial engineers with good salaries and benefits, more young people would want to go into engineering, and schools would turn out more engineers. Similarly, if America's ruling elites consented to pay the taxes needed to properly maintain roads, waterworks, and other public infrastructure from which they benefit, the resulting work opportunities in civil engineering would motivate more students to enter that field.[7] Instead, the low-wage strategy of American neoliberal managers and fiscal neglect of public infrastructure depress the job market for engineers in the United States, providing no incentive for students to enter the field or for universities to train them.

The limiting factor for America's production of wealth is not a shortage of highly educated people reflecting an alleged deficiency of public education. Rather, these factors include the exporting of capital by corporations seeking cheaper labor abroad, the squandering of human resources and physical capital on unproductive military programs, the unwillingness of rich investors to forgo high short-term profits in order to invest in increased productivity, and the unwillingness of rich taxpayers to invest adequately in the country's public infrastructure. The scapegoating of schools and teachers for America's economic decline is one way that the country's irresponsible ruling elites maintain their power, even as their policies batter the middle class and the poor.

To be sure, some proponents of school reform also have a critical perspective on U.S. corporate policies. The report *America's Choice: High Skills or Low Wages* criticized most U.S. businesses for neglecting long-term investment in training their personnel for high-productivity systems, partly because of pressures from Wall Street for short-term profits and partly because of attachment to an obsolete, assembly-line paradigm of work organization (National Center on Education and the Economy 1990). The report also argues that the United States is not adequately committed to training non–college-bound youth (and to retraining unemployed workers) for emerging industries, in contrast with Germany, Japan, Sweden, and Denmark. I agree with all these points.

A more recent report by the same organization, *Tough Choices or Tough Times*, deals more extensively with America's educational system, arguing that it is not preparing our youth for "high-value-added" jobs in such fields as research and development, design, marketing and sales, and global supply chain management (National Center on Education and the Economy 2007). The report contains many valid ideas, especially on

---

7. This assumes that political elites do not undercut American engineers when they do act to maintain infrastructure. In a kind of reductio ad absurdum of neoliberalism, however, New York City recently awarded a contract for repairing the Alexander Hamilton Bridge to a subsidiary of China State Construction Engineering Company (Semple 2011).

the need to replace local funding of schools with equitable state funding[8] and to reorient curricula from multiple-choice tests toward project-based assessments that value creativity. But the underlying assumption of this report, as with its predecessor, is that formal training and education are the limiting factors in America's economic performance. Both reports are remarkably silent about fundamental causes, especially the militarist and neoliberal policies that deprive the civilian economy of capital and well-paid jobs.

Robotic manufacturing is conspicuously absent from the list of high-value-added jobs in *Tough Choices or Tough Times*, a prime example of the postindustrial fallacy that the United States no longer has a comparative advantage in manufacturing and must now base its prosperity on services. In reality, as discussed in Chapter 2, services depend on equipment and other manufactured goods both directly (e.g., computers, office supplies, and telecommunications equipment) and indirectly (e.g., to construct and maintain facilities and generate needed electricity). All these machines and materials need to be manufactured, and the United States cannot correct its trade deficits unless most of this manufacturing is done domestically.[9]

In addition, human capital is not only developed through formal education or technical training but also arises continually from the interaction of workers with one another and with machines during the process of production in actual workplaces (Rynn 2010). The relocation of production abroad is therefore a fundamental reason for the deterioration of human capital (e.g., production skills and know-how) in the United States. Here, *Tough Choices or Tough Times* inverts cause and effect, arguing that a lack of skilled labor in the United States is driving capital abroad while in fact American corporations are not utilizing the skilled labor that the country already has and, by relocating production abroad, are causing production skills and know-how to atrophy.

---

8. As part of this proposal, the report advocates paying teacher salaries according to state civil service pay scales, with some modification based on merit. It is worth noting that Joel Klein, a member of the commission that produced the report, appended a statement dissenting from this proposal and affirming a more hard line school reform position (Klein 2007). While the report views teachers as highly skilled professionals and does not single out teachers' unions as a threat to quality, Klein was obsessed with breaking the teachers' union in New York City. One of his techniques was to create a budgeting system for schools that gave principals financial incentives to hire lower paid teachers irrespective of merit, consistent with the neoliberal attack on wages discussed in the previous chapter.

9. Further, the same corporate elites who outsourced American manufacturing jobs in search of cheaper labor are now outsourcing computer programming, telephone- and internet-based technical support, and other service jobs.

In summary, the deficiencies of American public education, real or imagined, cannot explain the long-term economic stagnation of the United States and its middle class. I turn now to the other claim of neoliberal reformers noted previously—that American public schools are failing to provide poor minority children with the educations they need to be successful. This is related to the so-called achievement gap, the persistence of poor academic outcomes for black and Hispanic youth relative to their white and Asian American peers.

SCHOOL REFORM AND THE ACHIEVEMENT GAP

As noted previously, school reformers present themselves as champions of equal educational opportunities and high expectations for all children regardless of race, class or ethnicity. While affluent families can afford private school tuition, disadvantaged black and Hispanic families depend on publicly funded schools. According to the reformers, traditional public schools are failing to close the educational achievement gap between disadvantaged and affluent children for two reasons (Hess 2006). First, public schools are government monopolies whose staffs have allegedly grown complacent because of a lack of competition. Second, contracts with teachers unions, which provide for tenure (job security) and which base salaries on seniority, allegedly protect incompetent teachers and fail to reward those who excel. This analysis is essentially an application of neoliberal ideology to public education.

The remedy, according to the school reformers, is to remake public education in the image of the competitive free market. This can be accomplished by abolishing tenure, instituting merit pay for teachers, and increasing school choice—that is, setting schools in competition with one another and empowering families to choose the best ones (Hess 2006). Increasing the number of publicly funded but privately managed charter schools (see Appendix 3.1) is a major strategy for expanding school choice. These reforms, according to their proponents, will reward excellent teachers and schools and weed out incompetence. With excellent publicly funded schools, the reformers say, poor minority families will finally have what they need to enter the middle class and prosper.

There is something seriously wrong with this picture. If government monopoly power and teachers' unions make public schools dysfunctional, then why are government-run, unionized public schools in affluent suburban districts doing so well? Why is there no movement in Beverly Hills, say, or Scarsdale to abolish tenure and institute merit pay? Clearly, the excellence of these schools flies in the face of reformers' theories about the pernicious effects of government power and unions. What, then, accounts for their high-quality programs and good academic outcomes? One factor is obvious—money, plain and simple. The large role of local property taxes in funding public schools in the United States produces a discrepancy in the resources per student available to most affluent suburban schools compared to those in poor rural and urban districts (Adler 2010; Kozol 1991, 2005). These differences in resources affect educational quality in a number of ways but especially class size, a well-established factor affecting academic performance (Class Size Matters 2011; Mishel and Rothstein 2002).[10]

The second major factor is socioeconomic (Koretz 2008). Children in affluent circumstances enjoy a number of key advantages denied to their counterparts struggling with poverty (Duncan and Murnane 2011). They go to school with their material needs met—including nutrition, health care, and freedom from violence—enabling them to focus on academic learning. Their early childhood experience was enriched by educational toys and a home culture in which reading and creative leisure activities such as hobbies played a prominent part. Their parents, typically college educated professionals, speak to them in standard English rich in academic vocabulary and impart the expectation of college and professional success as well as the associated work habits. They have quiet spaces to do homework and the time to do so since they do not have to earn money, provide child care to their siblings, or meet other unmet needs of the family at the expense of their own educational needs. They have attended good schools from the outset and are at or above grade level.

Schools populated with children having all these advantages cannot help but achieve better academic outcomes, on average, than schools serving the rural or urban poor. That would be so even if the former schools did not have smaller class sizes, highly qualified teachers, and all the other advantages that come from greater funding per student.

---

10. W. Norton Grubb (2009) disputes this, arguing that money has little impact on educational quality. While dismissing the importance of class size, Grubb focuses on the fact that teachers in underperforming schools on average spend more time on matters of administration and discipline and less on good pedagogy than teachers in high performing schools. But his assumption that pedagogical practice is independent of class size is unrealistic, indeed absurd to anyone who has actually taught in both kinds of school, as I have. A classroom of 20 high performing students may be very manageable, enabling the teacher to focus on pedagogy, while a classroom of 20 academically and socially-emotionally needy children may be completely unmanageable, making it virtually impossible for even the best teacher to employ the same teaching methods. While the class sizes are the same and the two teachers' practices vary greatly, a competent researcher will not conclude that the former plays no causal role while the latter does.

Compensatory federal and state spending for schools that serve the poor—which justice urgently requires—cannot entirely level the playing field for all children as long as extremes of wealth and poverty create highly unequal material and cultural circumstances for children before they even set foot in school (Duncan and Murnane 2011). The racial and ethnic achievement gap, a poison fruit of deeply entrenched class inequality, can be overcome only by egalitarian economic arrangements in the society as a whole.

Indeed, 10 out of 12 of the countries that outperform the United States on international tests have greater class equality than the United States, in most cases *much* greater.[11] To be sure, there is no easy way to assess the causal contribution to national test averages of this or any other single factor (Koretz 2008), nor is it even clear to what extent these averages are meaningful measures of academic achievement, as the debate between Stedman (1996a, 1996b) and Berliner and Biddle (1995, 1996) attests. But if these international differences mean anything—and school reformers are emphatic that they mean that American public schools are failing—then the data completely demolish the explanations that school reformers give for the alleged failure. Specifically, government monopoly power and teachers' unions cannot account for any academic underperformance that may exist since the countries with higher test averages have government schools much like those in America, most of them unionized. What those countries do not have are America's extremes of wealth and poverty and inequitable funding of public schools.

Given the crippling effects of poverty—which inner-city teachers wrestle with day after day with inadequate resources—the insistence of school reformers on high expectations for poor students is insufficient at best and a cynical diversion from the need for fiscal equity at worst. Public school teachers who work tirelessly to motivate disadvantaged youth do not need school reformers' lectures about high expectations. Nor is the problem that simple. In fact, the school reformers' definition and

---

11. I examined the 2009 scores on the Programme for International Student Assessment (PISA; Organization for Economic Cooperation and Development 2010) and recent Gini index data (World Bank 2011), which measures economic inequality within a country on a scale of 0 (complete equality) to 100 (complete inequality). Twelve countries scored significantly higher than the United States on all three scales of PISA (reading, science, and mathematics). Of these, 10 had lower Gini scores than the United States, which had a score of 41. Ranked from most egalitarian to least, these 10 countries with their Gini scores were Japan (25), Finland (27), the Netherlands (31), Korea (32), Belgium (33), Canada (33), Switzerland (34), Australia (35), Estonia (36), and New Zealand (36). Only two countries that outperformed the United States had greater social inequality: Singapore (42) and Hong Kong (43).

measurement of academic achievement in terms of standardized test scores has highly destructive consequences for disadvantaged minority students. Schools forced to close the achievement gap by that measure—which is the thrust of both the Bush and Obama administrations' policies, including No Child Left Behind and Race to the Top—are forced to substitute pedagogically worthless test preparation, which destroys the love of learning, for authentic education.

Consider, for example, a mathematics course designed to produce the highest possible scores on a standardized test. Such a course cannot devote a significant amount of time to ways of learning or topics that do not improve test scores, such as inquiry-based problems, student-chosen projects, and other activities that tap students' curiosity, cultivate creativity, and lay a foundation for lifelong learning (Lockhart 2009). While all schools face these trade-offs, those in affluent communities with students mostly at or above grade level have far more latitude in designing a curriculum that balances traditional skill building with projects and inquiry-based activities.

By contrast, a school serving disadvantaged students who are mostly below grade level—whether a charter or a traditional public school—must jettison a balanced curriculum that educates the whole person in favor of mind-numbing and spirit-killing test preparation. Such "excellence" is driving tens of thousands of America's best teachers out of the profession and millions of minority youth out of school (Noguera 2008). Most students who stay in such schools emerge permanently scarred with a lifelong hatred of academic learning. Any reader who thinks I am exaggerating needs to spend a single semester inflicting test preparation on disadvantaged children or at least listen—really listen—to the experience of teachers and children forced to endure such "education."

Authentic education and test preparation have diametrically different, profound, and lifelong effects on the self. A curriculum rich in projects and inquiry-based experiences continually sends children the message that their ideas matter. It cultivates independence of thought and initiative, essential traits of effective problem solvers, autonomous citizens, and authentic leaders. The test-oriented curriculum, by contrast, sends the message that only the test makers' ideas matter. It socializes youth into a culture of mindless conformity and obedience.

To be sure, this kind of authoritarian culture appeals to conventional employers, and for that reason many disadvantaged families struggling to enter the middle class acquiesce in test-oriented schooling or even seek it out. This is perhaps the main reason for the popularity of charter schools. Parents who want their children to succeed and who are struggling to raise them in neighborhoods afflicted by violence, jobless-ness, and substance abuse have few alternatives. Just as the hell of boot camp is a gateway to economic security in a military career, the regi-mented world of test preparation can open doors to regular employment in the private sector or the military itself. And the private sector route does not carry the risk of death or lifelong disability from battlefield injuries.

Young adults who emerge from the test-prep factory into college or private sector workplaces, however, and even those who enter the armed forces can expect little job security. To be sure, the winners at the test-prep game—those who have competed hard, learned to perform academic tasks under the direction of others, and been rewarded by high grades—are well trained to earn college-worthy SAT scores or hold jobs in authoritarian workplaces. Only a small minority, however, will excel at work in liberal arts colleges, which requires such creative and higher-order skills as formulating original topics, identifying relevant sources, and synthesizing diverse information into coherent term papers. Even those who do succeed will not have earned admission to the middle class, only the privilege of competing with millions of other underemployed college graduates for the increasingly scarce, well-paid jobs in corporate America (Matgouranis 2010). Finally, the ones who land these coveted jobs have only a precarious foothold in the middle class; they will never know if or when their job will be outsourced to an equally well educated, lower-paid foreigner.

In summary, the promise that education is a pathway to secure, middle-class prosperity in America today is fraudulent (Bowles and Gintis 2011; Collins 2011). Charter and other test-oriented schools may reduce the racial and ethnic achievement gap as measured by test scores, but they do so at the expense of the creativity and higher-order skills needed to excel in college or to hold well-paid private sector jobs, to the extent any-one can in capitalist America. The training in obedience and conformity provided by these schools prepare the vast majority of disadvantaged students who succeed in them for low-paid jobs or middle class but dangerous and often temporary jobs in the military.

If given a choice, poor parents might well prefer to send their children to schools where they will receive well-rounded educations that foster creativity, independent thought, and a love of learning, even if their test scores will be lower. But in reality, the parents have little choice. Neoliberal reformers like Mayor Michael Bloomberg have begun to shut down every public school in America that cannot or will not meet their demands for higher and higher test scores (Cramer 2011;

Ravitch 2011).[12] In a perversion of language worthy of George Orwell's novel *1984*, this is what neoliberals call "school choice."

Those who champion "high expectations" and are not themselves educators tend to simplistically equate "excellence" with high test scores. Some are well-intentioned social entrepreneurs who have chosen a particular educational option on behalf of the poor without even realizing they have made a choice. Others are cynical architects of a brave new world of capitalist-friendly education. In this world, low-paid, nonunionized teachers are forced to transform the country's youth into docile and disciplined workers for low-paid jobs in corporate America (Compton and Weiner 2008). But the intentions of school reformers matter little as long as they use power and money to dictate what goes on in classrooms.[13] In so doing, they are depriving the black and Hispanic poor of the very choice that they claim to promote, seizing control of neighborhood public schools from their stakeholders. This power grab by school reformers, who are disproportionately white and affluent, bears little resemblance to the civil rights movement in whose mantle they wrap themselves. On the contrary, it is of a piece with the long and painful history of domination that the civil rights movement fought implacably.

INDIVIDUAL FREEDOM: FANTASY AND REALITY

The bipartisan attack on public education in the United States is part of a larger narrative. Public schools are failing, the reformers say, because they are creatures of government and are beholden to labor unions, two institutions that are dysfunctional in their own right (Hess 2006). Attacks on government and organized labor have been, of course, a hallmark of

---

12. For example, the Bloomberg administration has closed or is in the process of closing dozens of "low-performing" public schools, most of which are located in poor minority neighborhoods, notwithstanding fierce opposition by the schools' stakeholders, including parents, students, teachers, and community leaders. The National Association for the Advancement of Colored People joined with the United Federation of Teachers in a lawsuit to prevent one round of closings, but the courts sided with the mayor (Cramer 2011). If the schools are truly as dysfunctional as the Bloomberg administration claims, it is hard to understand why so many parents would want their children to attend them and why so many teachers would want to work in them.

13. There are two ways to dictate what goes on in classrooms. One is to micromanage teachers from city hall through a vast bureaucracy, an approach initially tried by Mayor Bloomberg in New York City that failed dismally and was largely abandoned after several years (D'Agostino 2009b). The second approach, which Bloomberg tried next, is management by numbers (D'Agostino 2009b). When teachers can lose their jobs if they do not produce good-enough numbers, they need to orient their teaching to the test, even if that means killing their students' enthusiasm for learning and neglecting those for whom the test is too easy or too hard or who just learn better in ways that are not measured by the test.

right-wing politics since the 1980s. To be sure, Democratic politicians do not frame their school reform policies using explicitly antigovernment and antiunion discourse. But they support the same policies as conservative Republicans—such as merit pay for teachers and increasing the number of charter schools—policies that are predicated on an agenda of remaking public education in the image of free market capitalism (Compton and Weiner 2008).

The right-wing attack on government and unions is often framed in simplistic terms as a choice between individual freedom and the tyranny of collectivism. A Tea Party manifesto (Armey and Kibbe 2010) encapsulates this ideology in a quote from Ayn Rand's *The Fountainhead*:

> Our country, the noblest country in the history of men, was based on the principle of individualism, the principle of man's "inalienable rights." It was a country where a man was free to seek his own happiness, to gain and produce; not to give up and renounce; to prosper, not to starve; to achieve, not to plunder; to hold as his highest possession a sense of his personal value, and as his highest virtue his self-respect. (171)

Glenn Beck (2010) depicts unions as the antithesis of such individualism:

> While most of us rely on competition and a sense of personal achievement to bring out our best, public union employees are protected regardless of their talents or accomplishments. And that goes to the core of what is wrong with unions: they celebrate mediocrity. What is the point of exerting yourself when the reward doesn't change? What is the point of coming in early, staying late, or putting any extra effort into your job when your status and pay are defined by 500-page collective-bargaining agreements? (128)

There are three things wrong with this picture. First, it assumes a world in which workers have sufficient autonomy that individual merit and self-directed effort are the decisive factors in production. Second, it assumes that, insofar as individual merit and effort do matter, they are duly recognized and rewarded by bosses in the corporations and other organizations in which most people work. And third, it assumes that external reward is the primary reason that people excel rather than pride in one's work and the intrinsic satisfaction of doing good work.

As for the autonomy of workers and universal freedom, Ayn Rand's idealized America existed only to a limited extent in the past and is even less typical of workplaces today.[14] The middle- and upper-class English-men who founded the United States believed in Rand's "inalienable rights" for themselves but not for everyone. Black slaves, indentured servants, wage earners, and white women made up the bulk of the population and did most of the work. Of these, slaves had essentially no rights, while the others had some rights in theory but little chance of actually defending them in court. While white women for the most part had control over their work and could own and inherit property, their work was unpaid, and they had very few opportunities in the male-dominated money economy. Before the Civil War, it was common for states to restrict voting to propertied white males, in some cases even excluding religious minorities.

Except for family farmers and some others who were self-employed, nearly all workers in early America performed tasks under the direction of bosses. To be sure, indentured servants and wage earners—through hard work and frugality—had a shot at eventually owning their own land on the frontier. Indeed, it was this American Dream that drew millions of the working poor across two oceans from an Old World where social mobility was greatly limited by circumstances of birth. They worked for years under the direction of bosses, but those who could usually did move to the frontier and into the middle class,[15] such as it was, to be replaced by endless waves of new, poor immigrants.

But on the frontier, where the land was occupied by Native American tribes, the rule of success was hardly Ayn Rand's formula "to achieve, not to plunder." Rather, achievement *required* plunder, and private property carved out from the Indians' communal lands could be secured only with guns wielded both by the new landowners and by the U.S. Army. The mission of the latter was not the "noble" one of protecting the freedom of all, as Rand would have it, but the freedom of European Americans to prosper at the expense of Native Americans. Moreover, even this highly compromised path to individual success eventually came to an end when the nation's Manifest Destiny of coast-to-coast conquest was completed at the end of the nineteenth century. With the closing of the frontier, the continuing waves of immigration began to depress wages in the New World.

---

14. My discussion of this point in the following paragraphs is indebted to Zinn (2003), as is my discussion of the impact of labor unions and government in the following section.

15. Even for independent farmers, it should be noted, success or failure depended largely on factors beyond the individual's control, such as the weather, economic conditions, the vicissitudes of accident and disease, and the loyalty of friends in time of need.

In summary, conservatives need to ignore a vast gulf between their fantasies of individual freedom and America's actual history. And the rise of industrial capitalism in the nineteenth and twentieth centuries reduced worker autonomy further. After the Civil War, business magnates such as J. Pierpont Morgan, Andrew Carnegie, and John D. Rockefeller absorbed thousands of small, independent businesses into monopolies of unprecedented size. This meant that even bosses who had enjoyed some measure of autonomy earlier in the country's history were now being subordinated to a small number of extremely powerful people. In the twentieth century, such concentrated power was vested in the hands of professional managers—precursors of today's CEOs—who imposed bureaucratic order on the unwieldy commercial empires they inherited.

The millions of white-, blue-, and pink-collar employees of today's corporations can hardly be described as autonomous workers. Some have power over others, but except for the CEO, every boss reports to a higher boss. This is the reality of American capitalism today, which is very far removed from the individualism that conservatives imagine. The quality of people's decisions and efforts in these collectivized corporations do matter to some extent, but individuals are largely interchangeable and dispensable. Even where individual merit and self-directed effort are recognized and rewarded, they are not the decisive factors in production, as conservatives incorrectly assume.[16]

The second assumption of individualist ideology—that modern capitalism in fact recognizes and rewards merit and hard work—is just as problematic as the first. It is true that competitive markets, other things being equal, favor firms that produce the best products at the lowest prices. But this purely economic picture neglects the fact that firms are also social organizations in which power plays a decisive role. A capitalist boss wants his or her employees to be smart and competent but does not want them running the enterprise or corporate department. Such a shift in power would reduce the boss's role to that of coordinator, thus delegitimizing his or her appropriation of the profits (in the case of small business owners) or higher salary (in the case of professional managers).

Yet the workers collectively have more specific knowledge about the enterprise—including its suppliers, workplace, products, and customers—than any one person can, even the smartest and most competent boss.

---

16. It could be argued that this picture of corporate life omits the dynamic small-business sector that accounts for half the employment and most of the innovation in America's private sector (U.S. Small Business Administration 2011). But, as in the case of economic life in early America, most small businessmen today are bosses who typically control the organization of work.

To retain control of the department or enterprise, a boss must therefore keep the workers divided and reserve for himself the right to dictate how production will be organized. There is an obvious conflict between these imperatives of power and the need to fully mobilize the intelligence and competence of workers, and the ownership structure of capitalist firms requires that power take precedence over merit.

This is a major reason why bosses, even those who are not authoritarian by temperament, often feel threatened by workers who are especially smart and competent and do what is necessary to "keep them in their place." Those who communicate openly about problems and injustices in the workplace are particularly threatening. Bosses generally favor workers who are obedient and compliant over those who are independent minded and self-directed, even if the latter are more capable and hard-working. The requirements of power thus ensure that merit and hard work, while valued in themselves, are not consistently rewarded in capitalist enterprises.

The third of the previously mentioned conservative assumptions is that individuals will not work hard and achieve excellent results unless motivated to do so by external rewards, especially money. But there are far too many counterexamples for this to be a valid generalization about human nature. Such examples include teachers, clergy, and others in the helping professions who are motivated by the satisfaction of making a positive difference in the lives of others. Artists, scientists, and others engaged in creative pursuits are motivated by the intrinsic satisfaction of the work itself, as are tens of millions of ordinary workers who do their jobs well without external supervision because they enjoy their work and/or take pride in it.[17]

Even those in the corporate world competing to be CEOs are motivated by intrinsic rewards, such as the power that goes with the job and the satisfaction and excitement of applying their gifts to a challenging task. There is no shortage of highly talented and qualified people wanting to be top managers nor would there be a shortage even if they were paid only a fraction of what they are typically paid today. In the past, in fact, CEOs were paid much less than they are today, and the country's

---

17. Many economists assume that it is common for workers to "shirk" their job responsibilities when given the opportunity to do so and that it is only the threat of unemployment that keeps them in line. As Adler (2010) points out, however, these economists invoke shirking as a theoretical construct to explain labor market phenomena and have never studied it empirically in its own right. Far from being a general expression of human nature, shirking, to whatever extent it does occur, would appear to be a paradoxical by-product of organizational cultures in which managements try to control workers (Deming 1984, 2000).

economic performance was better. The notion that corporations must offer CEOs lavish compensation packages in order to attract the best talent is not consistent with what is known about human motivation and serves only to legitimize unconscionable greed and corporate corruption.

Note that all this intrinsically motivated achievement occurs in spite of a capitalist system that, because it serves the imperatives of power and concentration of wealth, does not consistently reward merit and hard work. There is every reason to believe that transforming capitalist firms into worker-owned and -controlled enterprises, as discussed in Chapter 6, would unleash an extraordinary amount of talent and effort that is currently being wasted. The superior productivity and commercial success of the Mondragon Cooperative Corporation, the world's largest organization of worker-owned and -controlled enterprises, supports this view (MacLeod 1997).

GOVERNMENT, UNIONS, AND THE AMERICAN DREAM

The America Dream was the idea that the United States is a land of opportunity in which every person can achieve prosperity through hard work and frugality and expect that their children would have a higher standard of living than their own. To be sure, this vision was marred by racism, sexism, and other artificial barriers to advancement, which even conservatives acknowledge and do not condone. But these barriers have been largely dismantled by the civil rights and women's movements, progress that was dramatically symbolized in 2008 by the rise of Hillary Clinton, Sarah Palin, and other female candidates for national office and by the election of Barack Obama. While Americans today disagree about the nature and extent of the social change that has occurred, there is an emerging consensus that prejudice has no place in the economic and political realms.

Ironically, however, the country's first black president presided over widespread disillusionment with the American Dream. The immediate cause was a multiyear economic crisis that included several million home foreclosures and double-digit unemployment in many parts of the country (Stiglitz 2010). In retrospect, these depression-like conditions were just the culmination of a long-term economic crisis that had begun in the 1970s (Wolff 2010).

Conservatives had a simple explanation for this demise of the American Dream, which wove together the individualist ideology discussed above with a single-minded fixation on the problem of debt. Americans were living beyond their means, they argued, and had abandoned personal responsibility for the nanny state's false promises of security and prosperity. According to this narrative, home owners themselves had created the housing crisis by taking on bigger mortgages than they could repay (Santelli 2009), and an unprecedented, debt-financed expansion of the federal government was siphoning capital from the productive, job-creating private sector (Beck 2010). Just as the causes of the crisis were simple, according to conservatives, so were the solutions—a return to America's core values of frugality and individualism. The dismantling of big government and greedy public employee unions would accomplish both: austerity would be the price paid for irresponsible spending, and the renunciation of collectivism would go hand in hand with a renewal of individual freedom and responsibility (Beck 2010).

According to Glenn Beck, America's crisis of values and institutions can be traced as far back as Woodrow Wilson but especially to Franklin D. Roosevelt, architect of big government as we know it. Beck rewrote the history of twentieth-century America as the story of increasingly out-of-control government debt and the addiction of ordinary people to collectivism, represented by big government, unions, and "progressive" public schools. In Beck's version of history, government and unions sought to fix what wasn't broken[18] and in the process undermined the real sources of the country's prosperity—frugality, individualism, and a commitment to free market capitalism (Beck 2010). But this picture again idealizes the past, conveniently ignoring the downside of capitalism for ordinary people and the role of government and unions in ameliorating its destructive effects.

In reality, the vast majority of hardworking and frugal white Americans were not achieving prosperity in the nineteenth and early twentieth centuries (Clark 1951; Zinn 2003). Family farmers—squeezed between low prices for their crops and the high costs of credit, equipment, and other factors of production—fought losing battles against debt, exacerbated by gold standard–induced deflation. With the closing of the frontier around 1890, workers dependent on urban employment faced wave after wave of new immigrants willing to work for lower wages than themselves.

---

18. Although conceding that unions originally served a legitimate purpose in protecting working people from exploitation, Beck (2009) does not see such exploitation as an endemic feature of capitalism. He goes on to attack the very foundations of trade unionism on the assumption that any individual who works hard and saves his or her money can enjoy prosperity in capitalist America today.

Disease, disability, and death were routine consequences of unsanitary cities, poorly built and maintained buildings, unsafe and unhealthy workplaces, and filthy meatpacking establishments.

While hard work and frugality did remain essential ingredients of success, they are not what turned the tide for ordinary Americans. Rather, it was activist government and unionization that created America's middle class as we know it. Government intervention took many forms. Building and health codes, food safety laws, and other regulations—enforced by armies of government inspectors—effected a revolution in health and safety. Cities levied taxes on their citizens in order to build waterworks and other public infrastructure and to provide sanitation, public health, fire protection, and other municipal services. Public schools, funded by tax revenues, gave native-born and immigrant children alike access to the literacy and numeracy needed for citizenship and economic success.

Unregulated capitalism was crushing the vast majority of hardworking family farmers, and it was the federal government that lifted them out of poverty. With millions of farmers competing to sell their crops in commodities markets and ever-expanding yields due to advancing agricultural science and technology, crop prices were spiraling downward. At the same time, farmers had to pay monopoly or quasi-monopoly prices for capital, fertilizer, equipment, energy, rail transport, and other factors of production. Without antitrust laws and prosecution, agricultural subsidies,[19] rural electrification projects, and other Progressive Era and New Deal government programs, family farmers had few prospects for middle-class prosperity.

It was labor unions and federal legislation protecting them that lifted millions of Americans working on railroads and construction sites and in mines, textile mills, factories,[20] and other workplaces into the middle class. Wave after wave of immigrants, beginning especially in the nineteenth century—Germans, Irish, Chinese, Poles, Italians, Greeks, Russians, and others—uprooted themselves from ancestral homelands to come to the land of opportunity. This was a bonanza for capitalist

---

19. While farm subsidies were originally enacted to make family farms economically viable, today they enrich mainly big agribusiness at taxpayer expense and distort global food markets to the disadvantage of poor farmers in the developing world (see Appendix 5.1 in Chapter 5).
20. Henry Ford, who voluntarily paid his factory workers higher-than-market wages in the World War I era, had other than altruistic reasons for doing so. He ran his assembly lines at an inhuman pace, making car manufacturing a punishing way to make a living. In order to expand his operations in a tight labor market and minimize the chances of a strike that would shut down his expensive factories, Ford needed to pay higher wages than other employers (Adler 2010). It was only through collective bargaining that autoworkers later gained some significant control over their compensation and working conditions.

employers: desperately poor people from dozens of countries—divided by language, religion, and ethnic custom—competing with one another for work opportunities. A small fraction of these newcomers lifted themselves into America's middle class by starting small businesses. Many more tried and failed, and the vast majority remained stuck in what today would be called "dead-end" jobs.

Labor organizers formed these motley ethnic groups into unions against great odds. Employers played off one group off against another and retaliated against union activists and sympathizers, resorting to police, the courts, and private violence to prevent organizing and break strikes. Most unions were marred by racism, which proved an Achilles' heel of organized labor as African Americans passed over by white organizers were enlisted by employers to break strikes. Despite all these challenges, an increasing percentage of America's workforce became unionized, raising the income of ordinary people and improving safety and other workplace conditions. Unions won the five-day workweek for all Americans and helped abolish child labor. And finally, the 1935 Wagner Act gave working people legal protections to form unions and strike and required employers to engage in collective bargaining with the worker's representatives.

The role of government in maintaining full employment is another area where historical progress occurred through the "collectivism" so maligned by Glenn Beck. According to neoclassical theory—the dominant viewpoint of mainstream economists before the 1930s—unregulated markets are self-correcting, with the laws of supply and demand quickly eliminating wasteful shortages and surpluses through changes in price. According to this view, multiyear periods of involuntary unemployment (a surplus of labor) is impossible because the surplus will cause a decrease in wages, and at lower wages, employers will hire everyone who wants to work (Adler 2010). This theory was never consistent with the evidence of history. From its very origins in the eighteenth century, modern industrial capitalism has witnessed multiyear recessions and depressions in which high unemployment persisted in spite of reduced wages. In the United States, such economic downturns lasting three or more years began in 1797, 1807, 1815, 1839, 1873, 1882, 1918, and 1929, events for which neoclassical economists had no satisfactory explanation (Gordon 1986).

In his 1936 classic *The General Theory of Employment, Interest, and Money*, British economist John Maynard Keynes (2010) provided the first scientific explanation of the business cycle. Previous thinkers, such as neoclassical economist Jean Baptiste Say, had been aware of the circular flow of money in a market economy, in which the wages paid to workers are used to buy the goods and services that the workers produce and thereby the workers' own wages in a later time period. Keynes explained why this circular flow does not automatically maintain full employment. In order for that to occur, the money that households save (e.g., deposits in savings accounts) would have to be invested in new production (e.g., construction of factories). According to the neoclassical economists, this must in fact occur because the financial markets will quickly correct any mismatch between savings and investment through changes in interest rates, that is, the price of borrowing money. For example, if businesses do not invest as much as households save, a temporary surplus of funds will produce a decline in interest rates, and at the lower interest rates, businesses will invest more until the amount being invested matches the amount being saved.

Keynes noted, however, that interest rates have a limited impact on a firm's decision to invest. If businesses become pessimistic about the economic outlook, they will not undertake new investment even if interest rates are very low. This was evident in the United States in the years following the 2008 housing bubble collapse, when business investment in U.S.-based production declined or was sluggish in spite of extremely low interest rates. In such cases, money that is being saved is removed from the circular flow, and the unemployment created by reduced investment will not be corrected by the financial markets. In fact, unemployment becomes a vicious circle; when the unemployed spend less, other businesses lose customers and lay off some of *their* workers, who then spend less and so on. Left to itself, the free market economy can therefore enter periods of persistent, high unemployment. Such conditions existed in the 1930s, when Keynes was writing, and they exist in the United States today. Keynes concluded that only government intervention, through deficit spending, can break the vicious circle and restore full employment.

Although neoclassical theory enjoyed a revival in the United States beginning in the 1970s,[21] Keynesian theory has been the dominant

---

21. The neoclassical revival began with Milton Friedman's work in the 1960s and went mainstream in the 1970s, when stagflation shook the confidence of policymakers in the Keynesian paradigm. Friedman (1962; Friedman and Schwartz 1963) was both a laissez-faire ideologue and an innovative and competent economist. He showed how Federal Reserve policies contributed to the Great Depression (Friedman and Schwartz 1963) and laid a foundation for sound monetary policy, such as the successful anti-inflation measures of Fed Chairman Paul Volcker. However, there was no real contradiction between Friedman's "monetarism" and Keynesian economics, as his famous comment "we are all Keynesians now" indicated. Friedman's neoclassical successors, such as Edward Prescott and Eugene Fama, combined his right-wing ideology with sophisticated mathematical modeling disconnected from the real world. For example, their theories entailed the absurd conclusions that housing bubbles cannot occur and that all unemployment must be voluntary (Krugman 2009).

influence on fiscal and monetary policy. It also explains the stabilizing effects of two policies that predated Keynes's *General Theory*: the progressive income tax and the federal-state system of unemployment benefits. When the economy enters a recession, unemployment benefits and reduced tax rates (due to people with reduced incomes entering lower tax brackets) pump money into the economy to maintain the flow of spending. This combination of increased government payments and reduced taxes, other things being equal, results in a government deficit.[22] When employment and the private sector are booming, by contrast, the reduction in benefits and increase in taxes automatically remove these stimuli and, other things being equal, produce a government surplus. The Federal Reserve also counteracts the business cycle by expanding the money supply during recessions and contracting it during boom periods. During particularly serious periods of unemployment, as in the 1930s and in the years after the housing bubble collapse in 2008, fiscal stimulus policies in addition to these monetary and automatic fiscal stabilizers may be necessary to restore full employment.

Notwithstanding neoclassical criticisms, Keynesian policies have been consistently successful: there has not been a single recession lasting three years or longer since the Great Depression (National Bureau of Economic Research 2011), compared with eight such recessions between 1797 and 1929 (Gordon 1986). Republican demands that the federal government and the Federal Reserve abandon successful Keynesian policies in the midst of severe, recession-level unemployment after 2008—legitimized by neoclassical economic theories—were at best a foolish attempt to turn the clock back more than seventy years. At worst, they were a nihilistic exercise in economic sabotage intended to unseat a black Democratic president.[23]

---

22. Neoclassical economists argue that government borrowing to finance deficits, by reducing the supply of funds in the capital markets, "crowds out" the private sector investment needed for economic recovery. If private firms were willing to invest, however, there would be no recession in the first place. It is only when government deficit spending begins to pull the economy out of recession that private firms will invest and, with a favorable outlook for sales, will do so even if interest rates are higher.

23. This is not to say that the Keynesian conceptual framework by itself provides an adequate economic analysis or basis for public policy. I would argue, in fact, that the maintenance of aggregate demand through Keynesian fiscal and monetary policies is a necessary but not sufficient condition for full employment. Other necessary conditions include adequate investment in human capital, manufacturing, and infrastructure (Dumas 1986; Rynn 2010); an egalitarian distribution of wealth and income that allocates purchasing power to those with unmet needs (Adler 2010; Wolff 2010); and public policies that correct externalities and other market distortions, that make adequate provision for public goods, and that align international trade and finance with the global common good (Brecher et al. 2009; Stiglitz 2007, 2010).

One of the most enduring, important lessons of Keynesian economics is that high wages, far from depressing employment as predicted by neo-classical theory, actually help maintain full employment and general prosperity by keeping consumer demand high (Adler 2010). In this regard, the 1935 Wagner Act remains one of the most important legacies of the New Deal. By facilitating the formation of unions and collective bargaining, this legislation helped set in motion more than thirty years of rising wages and benefits, the basis for an era of unprecedented prosperity for ordinary working people. It is no exaggeration to say that unions, with the support of government, created the American middle class as we know it.

Ironically, the American Dream—which was supposed to be accomplished by individual effort and frugality alone—was finally realized for tens of millions of households only with the help of "collectivist" institutions demonized by the right. And capital flight and deindustrialization—results of the unregulated capitalism glorified by the right—are today bringing this era of prosperity to an end. Along with the military industrial complex, these neoliberal policies enable the rich to get richer at the expense of America's middle class.

But there is more to capitalist ideology than these ideas about collectivism and individualism. Even if "big government" in the past did bring all the benefits enumerated here, some conservatives would argue, how can Americans continue on that path if the country simply cannot afford it? Capitalism may be flawed in all the ways indicated above, and some expansion of government may have been necessary to correct these flaws. But what if the correctives have gone to such an extreme that a major downsizing of government is now needed? And what if the "socialist" alternative to America's admittedly imperfect economic system is a dysfunctional and unjust cure that is worse than the disease? To these critical issues I now turn.

APPENDIX 3.1: WHAT ARE CHARTER SCHOOLS?

Having autonomy from local school districts and exemption from many regulations, most charter schools are funded by the states and accountable to the states for educational outcomes as measured by test scores. In some cases, such as New York City, local school districts themselves issue charters and grant the same kind of autonomy and accountability as states. Whether chartered by the states or by large urban districts, these schools are typically not unionized (though some are) and have a longer school day and year. Their teachers are typically less experienced and more likely to lack state certification (Rui and Boe 2012)

While charter schools in theory are not permitted to discriminate against academically needy children, their culture is typically test oriented, and they provide fewer supports for English language learners and other students with special needs. Largely because of this reputation, fewer families of academically needy children apply to charter schools, and those who do are more likely than others to be "counseled out" (encouraged or pressured to leave) by administrators anxious to maintain high school–wide test scores. As a result, charter school enrollments are de facto academically selective (Knopp 2008; Grassroots Education Movement 2010).

Many charter schools receive supplemental funding from private sources. Where local school districts create charter schools, in some cases they give them preferential treatment at the expense of the traditional public schools they administer. New York City, for example, frequently takes scarce building space away from its traditional public schools and allocates it to new charter schools, creating great resentment among parents and staff of the former (Grassroots Education Movement 2010, 2011).

The claim of reformers that charter schools outperform traditional public schools is dubious (Center for Research on Education Outcomes 2009; Renzulli and Roscigno 2011). Even in those instances where charter schools compare favorably with the latter by the criterion of test scores, it is unclear how to interpret that difference. Given that most charter schools have a smaller proportion of academically needy children and in some cases more resources because of private donations and preferential treatment by school districts, some improvement in test scores would be expected independently of school quality. More fundamentally, charter schools are known for teaching to standardized tests, an approach to education that neglects critical thinking skills, development of creativity, and the kind of exciting educational experiences that create lifelong learners. Higher test scores, by themselves, are therefore not an indication of overall school quality.

CHAPTER 4
The Attack on Government

INTRODUCTION

There are two aspects of conservative ideology that go beyond my previous discussion of individualism versus collectivism. The first is the notion that government, whatever good it may achieve, is for the most part parasitic on the private sector economy and imposes arbitrary rules on it that interfere with the production of wealth. Further, politicians seeking their own power and unconstrained by the exigencies of earning profits in the competitive marketplace will expand this parasitic institution without limit if permitted to do so (Beck 2010). Second, and related to the above, conservatives argue that government expropriates wealth that successful individuals have earned through hard work, talent, and frugality and redistributes it to others who have no legitimate claim to it (Nozick 1974; Santelli 2009).[1]

Given this view that government undermines both prosperity and justice, the problem is not merely to fund it in a responsible way but to

---

1. In fact, government, from its Neolithic origins to the present, has indeed been paid for through the extraction of wealth from those who produce it (Mandel 1982). Conservatives, however, ignore the fact that the accumulation of wealth in the private sector is based on a similar expropriation, as will be discussed later in this chapter. Thus, to the extent that government taxes the rich and uses that wealth to provide public goods for the entire population, it is returning to the common people some of the wealth that was taken from them by the rich (Adler 2010). Further, when it corrects market distortions and provides infrastructure and other public investments, government plays a positive role in the creation of wealth. Ironically, the most parasitic part of government is the national security state idealized by conservatives, which is paid for primarily by middle-class taxpayers but provides them virtually nothing of value in return, as discussed in Chapter 1.

downsize it as much as possible. Hence, the virtually unanimous demand of Republican politicians that Washington and the states put their fiscal houses in order entirely through spending cuts or, equivalently, that the growth of government debt is an evil commensurate with the growth of government itself (Beck 2010). Further, if the growth of government is an evil, then the growth of government debt—which is inherently exponential—takes on apocalyptic dimensions. For Republicans, this problem trumps every other facing the country and poses the single greatest threat to future generations.

In reality, however, government debt is only a symptom of more fundamental problems. The fixation of conservatives on the symptom diverts attention from the underlying challenges, which are what really endanger future generations. These real threats do not arise from government; in fact, the latter is an indispensable tool for averting them. But just when a well-funded and effective federal government is most needed to secure a humane and sustainable future, conservatives are most energetically destroying that tool.

GOVERNMENT DEBT: ANOTHER DIVERSION

In one sense, of course, debt cannot be a fundamental problem since the annual budget deficits that create it represent the difference between two quantities—revenues and expenditures. On the revenue side, most Republicans want to shield the rich from tax increases, branding any such proposals as "class warfare." I will have more to say on tax equity in the following sections. On the expenditure side, they have no scruples about cutting government jobs and programs that affect the middle class and poor while wanting to keep off the table corporate welfare such as ethanol, oil, and agricultural subsidies and unnecessary military programs. Framing the fundamental issue as one of debt is a way of deflecting public attention from these underlying problems of social justice and fiscal priorities.

The so-called debt issue masks other underlying problems as well. Of the $9.5 trillion in federal debt owed to the public,[2] nearly half is held by foreign entities, including the Chinese government. This costs

---

2. The remainder of the U.S. government's total debt of $14 trillion, which is $4.5 trillion, or about one-third, is held by the Federal Reserve, the Social Security Trust Fund, or other federal entities. These accounts and their associated interest payments are conveniences of public finance that exist on paper only, not true debt in the sense of claims on the U.S. government by external parties. The constant reference of mainstream pundits to the country's "$14 trillion dollar debt" is therefore misleading.

American taxpayers tens of billions of dollars in annual interest payments and for that reason should be eliminated over time. But doing so will not settle America's accounts with the rest of the world as long as hundreds of billions of dollars continue to flow out of the country every year because of trade deficits and massive military spending abroad.

If foreign recipients of this vast surplus of dollars do not have the option of buying U.S. Treasury securities—and repaying the debt will put even more dollars in their hands—they will buy other dollar-denominated assets, like U.S. corporate securities or real estate. That state of affairs would be no more sustainable than an accumulation of government debt, since the U.S. economy would eventually run out of assets for foreigners to buy. To have a sustainable relationship with the world economy, the United States needs to rebuild its manufacturing, replace oil imports with domestically produced renewable energy, and dramatically scale back its expensive military operations and bases abroad, which it cannot afford.

The upshot of this analysis is that debt is not a fundamental problem but rather a manifestation of other problems, especially the unwillingness of rich Americans to pay their fair share of taxes; corporate welfare and pork-barrel weapons programs; persistent trade deficits caused by deindustrialization and addiction to foreign oil; and unsustainable military spending abroad. By focusing on debt, conservative politicians and corporate elites are diverting attention from all these problems.

In fact, the same deficit hawks who promote the notion that debt is the biggest threat to their children and grandchildren tend to systematically neglect threats to future generations even more urgent than those just listed. By far the most ominous of these is climate change, which is destroying conditions for agriculture throughout the world and thus the foundations of civilization itself. Other urgent threats include pollution and deforestation—the other main causes of ecological collapse besides greenhouse gases—as well nuclear weapons proliferation, the global AIDS pandemic, and the persistence of poverty at home and abroad. While there are straightforward solutions to U.S. public debt, these global problems unfold in complex political and physical systems that are inherently more difficult to manage and where the stakes are incomparably higher.

For example, pollution and deforestation are irreversibly destroying entire ecosystems, while irreversible changes in world climate due to carbon-driven global warming can decimate agriculture and kill a majority of the world's population through starvation in a matter of decades (Brown 2009; Wright 2004). While mounting debt can be reversed, the same cannot be said about demolition of a city by a nuclear weapon, which could also set off a spiral of further violence worse than the Afghanistan and Iraq wars. The hundreds of thousands of people dying every year from AIDS cannot be brought back to life, and the pandemic is expanding. Hundreds of millions of people worldwide live in extreme poverty, many being killed and maimed by malnutrition, lack of access to clean drinking water, and preventable diseases. Sub-Saharan Africa is the most impoverished region and simultaneously the one most severely affected by the global AIDS pandemic. Such extreme, preventable human suffering should be an urgent moral problem for all leaders, but especially for Republican politicians who make a public display of their Christianity.

Government is not causing any of the urgent problems just indicated, and in fact it is a necessary part of the solutions. One of the simplest ways to end global warming is a carbon tax (Stiglitz 2007), a solution fiercely resisted by big oil and coal companies (Gelbspan 2004). The global dimensions of this and other urgent problems require bold American leadership on behalf of real solutions—international environmental and nuclear disarmament regimes, new rules of world trade that can help developing economies, and increased foreign aid to eradicate extreme poverty and preventable disease. All these initiatives are legitimate and urgently needed interventions of government, and some of them can be paid for by new taxes, such as value added and carbon taxes.

Finally, it is necessary to explode right-wing nonsense about taxing the rich, whom conservatives laud as "job creators." Here the Republican ideologues flunk Macroeconomics 101. As every college freshman taking this course knows, marginal propensity to consume decreases with income, so taxing the rich has minimal impact on consumer demand. During periods of negative or weak economic growth, such as the years following the 2008–2009 financial crisis, the macroeconomic problem is inadequate consumer demand. Firms invest in new production only when they expect consumers to buy their products and do not raise capital when the economic outlook is uncertain. During such periods, the rich therefore put their income in other investments that do not produce jobs in the domestic economy.

By contrast, if the federal and state governments tax that income and invest it in human resources and physical capital (e.g., education, health care, and green infrastructure projects), they will directly create and maintain jobs in the present—contributing to consumer demand—and through the public capital created increase the country's capacity to create wealth in the future (Rynn 2010). By taxing the rich and spending on the needs of the middle class and the country as a whole, government can help expand the economy in a sustainable way and is the only institution that can do so when the private sector fails. In fact, such failure is a long-term feature of low-wage capitalism and requires, among other things, a large, permanent public sector. By creating productive jobs and needed goods and services on a continuing basis, government can reclaim income from the rich, in whose hands it produces little or no wealth, and invest it in ways that create general prosperity.

OPPORTUNITIES AND OUTCOMES: WHAT IS JUSTICE?

As persuasive as the above analysis may be from the viewpoint of the common good, it is not sufficient. The whole notion of the common good rings hollow for many Americans when government policies are perceived as running roughshod over individuals and deeply held principles of justice. Such was the case, for example, when CNBC Business News Editor Rick Santelli (2009) blasted the Obama administration's plan to help refinance the mortgages of home owners facing foreclosure. In this February 2009 broadcast, Santelli accused the administration of essentially stealing from hardworking and responsible citizens to bail out profligate home owners who took out mortgages that they knew or should have known they could not afford (Santelli 2009).[3] Notwithstanding that Santelli wielded all the moral authority of the nation's derivatives traders, his broadside resonated with millions, going viral on the Internet and galvanizing the nascent Tea Party movement. It is essential that a progressive mass movement engage such widely shared and passionately held ideas, which tap fundamental beliefs about justice that go beyond the specifics of the housing crisis.

Arguably the strongest and most intellectually serious attack on government redistribution of wealth was Robert Nozick's (1974) classic *Anarchy, State and Utopia*. The author views redistribution of wealth through government as a moral evil because, he argues, it treats the individual as a means to an arbitrary social end, violating the sacrosanct principle that persons are ends in themselves. Redistribution of wealth is arbitrary, according to Nozick, because it ignores the question whether the individuals being taxed are *entitled* to what they have. Someone who steals another's wealth is clearly not entitled to it, but someone who earned it is in a different category.

---

3. In reality, the unregulated mortgage market had spawned over a hundred kinds of complex, adjustable rate mortgages about which Federal Reserve Chair Alan Greenspan reportedly said, "If you had a doctorate in mathematics, you wouldn't be able to tell which ones are good for you and which ones aren't (Ferguson 2010)."

A distribution of wealth is just, Nozick argues, if and only if it has come about through a fair process in which every individual has an equal opportunity to pursue prosperity. Government has a responsibility to insure equal opportunity but, once it has done so, must not interfere with the distribution of wealth that emerges. In Nozick's theoretical world, taxing the rich to provide income and services for the middle class or the poor is equivalent to stealing from the rich or forcing them to work for the benefit of others. The legitimate role of government is not to create equality of *outcome* for individuals or groups but only to ensure equality of *opportunity*. The latter exists when every citizen (1) possesses what they freely acquire on their own (without taking it from another), (2) possesses what they acquire through free exchange, and (3) receives the protection of their property by government. While scholars continue to debate the implications of these ideas (Varoufakis 1998), for purposes of this book we may consider Nozick's distinction between equality of outcome and equality of opportunity as the foundation of American conservatism today.

Whatever the strengths and weaknesses of Nozick's theory in the realm of ideas, the biggest problem with it, in my view, is the way it is routinely used to legitimize existing property arrangements. Although never explicitly stating it, conservatives who invoke the "outcome versus opportunity" distinction make an enormous assumption: that Nozick's three conditions for equality of opportunity mentioned previously—free individual acquisition, free exchange, and property rights—operate in the real world the way they do in Nozick's theoretical world. But there is little basis for this assumption in the American experience, past or present.

First, the production of wealth is rarely achieved by isolated individuals; it generally arises out of a process that is inherently social.[4] In a capitalist system, the owners of a business and its workers have a conflict or potential conflict over how much of the product should belong to each (Adler 2010). In the case of unionized firms, this conflict is decided through collective bargaining, but in most other cases it is decided by existing property law—that is, by the state—in favor of the owners.

Second, exchange in so-called free markets is generally free only in the weak sense that buyers and sellers have equal rights under the law, a fact that omits the realities of power. Big corporations, for example, are vastly more powerful than the individual consumers or employees who must deal with them. While in theory consumers are free to not pay high prices

---

4. Nozick ignores this fact of life by illustrating his theory with highly nontypical examples of acquisition—such as finding something of value that does not already belong to someone else or inventing something—that can be carried out by isolated individuals.

for rent or food,[5] in reality they need to live somewhere and eat. While a nonunionized worker is in theory free to reject a low wage offered by their employer, if his or her only alternative is joblessness, that is a choice he or she can hardly afford.

Third, while a capitalist government does protect property of the rich and spares no effort to return it when stolen, this same government does nothing to return wealth that capitalist businesses and their owners have appropriated from those who coproduced it (Adler 2010). Indeed, by Nozick's criteria, the only wealth that rich persons can claim as their own is what they produced entirely through their own labor and then exchanged for other wealth. This generally accounts for at most a small part of a rich person's property; the rest was produced through a social process and appropriated by the rich through the coercive power of the capitalist state, which gives the stockholders and proprietors of productive enterprises sole ownership of what is produced. If anyone doubts this description of capitalist property arrangements, try working in a factory and taking home one of the products you made with your own hands. If you get caught, the police will say you stole it, make you give it back, and may even put you in jail.

To be sure, workers in advanced industrial economies do not generally produce any good entirely on their own, and complex rules are needed to determine who gets what. But there is no reason to assume that these rules, which are made by those who have the power to do so, are just. In fact, in the most egregious case of violent appropriation of wealth in American history—slavery—there was no effort to make reparations, which could have been done by redistributing land. Nor are any such reparations attempted today to return wealth that the rich have appropriated from ordinary working people. These examples illustrate the bias of existing property arrangements, past and present, in favor of the rich. While reparations in the strict sense are not feasible in most cases, a strongly progressive income tax is a practical way that economic justice can be implemented.

ECONOMIC RENTS AND TAXATION

In justifying economic inequality, Robert Nozick neglected a crucial distinction between the roles of work and luck in the acquisition of

---

5. The agribusiness firms that produce food possess what economists call market power; that is, they are so big that they can charge higher prices than would prevail in a perfect market (Stiglitz and Walsh 2007). Rental housing is owned by landlords who collect what economists call economic rents (discussed next), which allow similarly inflated prices.

wealth. For example, he argues that a star athlete is entitled to be rich because so many people are willing to pay to watch him or her perform (Nozick 1974). While no one would dispute that an athlete should be paid for their work, including the time and effort committed to training, the notion that someone is entitled to be rich because nature happened to endow him or her with unusual gifts is dubious. Indeed, most public justifications of inequality appeal to work, not luck. Those who attack the estate tax, for example, do not argue that a person born with a silver spoon in their mouth has a right to keep what they inherit but that a person who has accumulated wealth through hard work and frugality should not be penalized by a "death tax" (McCaffery 2010).

The roles of work and luck in acquiring wealth are actually easier to disentangle than most people realize. When people are paid more to do a job than is actually needed to induce them to do it, the extra income they receive is generally what economists call an "economic rent" (Stiglitz and Walsh 2006). I would argue that this quantifies the part of a person's pay that is due to luck, for example, the fact that he or she happens to be endowed with certain scarce gifts such as athletic ability, mathematical aptitude, or artistic talent. To say that something is scarce means that its supply is fixed or nearly fixed and that the price paid for it will depend on demand. In American culture, there is a greater demand to watch basketball games than Shakespearean plays, for example, so professional athletes are paid more than Shakespearean actors even though the talents at issue may be equally scarce.

The social justification of laissez-faire capitalism is that unregulated markets, through the laws of supply and demand, produce the goods and services that people want at the lowest possible cost. Economic rents, however, are a pervasive violation of such market rationality. If a star athlete would be willing to do what he does for $100,000 per year instead of $3 million,[6] then his fans are paying $2.9 million more for his services than justified by free market principles. In fact, they are paying even more because the ticket price also includes economic rent to the sports team owners. The upshot of this analysis is that government can impose a steep income

---

6. The pay that a person is willing to accept to do a job is generally determined by what economists call her opportunity cost, that is, the pay she could otherwise earn doing something else. I am far from arguing, however, that an inner-city youth with athletic gifts but few other opportunities should be paid, say, what she could make at a minimum wage job. Rather, I am proposing that a person who is poor should be permitted to collect economic rents for her gifts, but subject to increasingly high tax brackets as in the case with any prosperous American, limiting her ability to become rich by virtue of her good luck. Indeed, there is no other way to pay for the sustainable and productive public jobs at living wages needed to lift all Americans out of poverty.

tax rate on professional athletes, team owners, CEOs,[7] and other high-income earners without in any way interfering with the operation of markets or diminishing the supply of services they provide.[8]

A similar analysis applies to other sectors of the economy, such as real estate and the mining and mineral extraction industries. Land in cities is inherently scarce, and high demand raises rents and property values to higher levels than would occur in a perfect market. The latter assumes that high prices serve as an incentive to increase supply, but since the supply of land in cities cannot be expanded to meet demand, those who own it are collecting more income than is justified by free market principles. The same can be said for the inflated price that oil and coal companies receive for the scarce resources they own. Government can and should tax these economic rents, which would make resources available for public works and services without sacrificing the principle of market rationality. Indeed, the nineteenth-century philosopher Henry George (2006) argued that all the revenue government needs could be raised through taxation on such rents, a proposal that has not received nearly the attention it deserves.

In summary, the argument that high taxes reduce incentives for the rich to work hard is complete and utter nonsense. Many people who are rich do work hard, but that is not why they are rich, nor would taxing the economic rents they collect reduce their level of effort. Most Americans work hard but do not become rich, so working hard cannot be the reason people accumulate wealth. The latter occurs either through high salaries and other compensation for work performed and/or through unearned income from gifts and investments.[9] Some are paid more than

----

7. In the case of CEOs, only part of their high pay stems from scarcity of their skills; most of it, by far, stems from the sheer corruption of corporate governance, in which CEOs in cahoots with corporate boards pay themselves outrageous salaries completely out of proportion to their skill level. If economic rents should be recovered for society through taxation, the principle applies even more obviously to ill-gotten gains due to legalized corruption.

8. It is generally not feasible for government to directly reimburse the purchasers (e.g., the sports fans) for the economic rent they have paid. If government taxes the recipient of the rent, however, and uses the revenue to provide public goods for all, the purchasers receive back something of value in return for the rent they paid.

9. The one exception to this statement is the case of small entrepreneurs who risk personal savings and are truly entitled to any resulting profits. The tax code and bankruptcy laws should be adjusted to protect such entrepreneurs —both individuals and cooperatives—enabling them to keep all profit they earn entirely by risking personal savings. This is both a matter of individual justice and a matter of maintaining social incentives that should attach to entrepreneurial activity. If successful in investing their own savings, however, most entrepreneurs expand using bank loans and other funds from outside investors, thus risking other people's money. These outside investors generally hold portfolios that are diversified across enterprises, industries, and asset classes and thus incur far less risk than entrepreneurs risking their own savings (Banks 2007).

others because their skills are in high demand and labor markets cannot increase the supply of people with such skills. In other words, they are paid more because they are lucky enough to be endowed by nature with gifts that are scarce and highly valued and for which they collect economic rents, not because they work harder than others.

To be sure, talents and gifts are potentialities that generally require education or training and hard work to develop into marketable skills for which society is willing to pay. But these legitimate costs are not included in economic rents; the latter arise only inasmuch as the underlying gifts are in short supply and cannot be increased through education.[10] Nor can the higher compensation due to education as such be a source of wealth accumulation; in a competitive labor market, such a windfall would draw more people into the profession, thus lowering compensation to the level at which it just covers the cost of education. When this does not occur, it is generally because there is a limited supply of people with the requisite underlying gifts. The extraordinary compensation packages of star athletes and other celebrities are mostly economic rents that far exceed what is needed to bring their services into the market and as such are legitimate objects of a progressive income tax.

Apart from the economic rents that account for the high pay of some individuals, wealth accumulation occurs almost entirely through the inheritance of wealth and through financial investments. Since heirs have done nothing to earn what they inherit, a high estate tax is entirely reasonable. Investors do risk their capital and on that basis are entitled to keep more of the income generated by investments. The U.S. tax code in fact takes this into account, taxing capital gains at a lower rate than ordinary income. This is entirely appropriate in the case of middle-class investors, who can accumulate only modest amounts of capital through investments. For the rich, however, the capital gains rate is one of the many loopholes that need to be reformed in order to create an equitable system of taxation.

In addition, a steeply progressive income tax should be reinstituted, up to the 90 percent on marginal income of the rich, which prevailed under

---

10. In America, education is generally paid for by the students, either in advance or through student loans. Such costs of education must therefore be recovered by the individual in the form of higher compensation. These costs are not included in economic rent because without the higher compensation, no one would agree to pay for the education needed to enter the profession. Note also that a society needs to compensate people for the costs of their education only if it forces them to pay for it in the first place. This problem does not arise in more egalitarian societies that provide free higher education to any person with demonstrated gifts and prior academic achievement.

the fiscally responsible Republican administration of President Dwight Eisenhower (Adler 2010). Paul Krugman (2011b) notes that the top 0.1 percent of taxpayers—mostly people with annual incomes over $2 million—account collectively for hundreds of billions of dollars in annual income, making a steep marginal tax on this segment of the population a potentially important source of public revenue.

This concludes my analysis of the policies, institutions, and ideologies on which rule by the rich depends. It is intended as a conceptual tool kit for those in the middle class—and those struggling to enter or remain in it—who want to understand and challenge the state capitalist system that is undermining their prosperity and eroding the country's democratic heritage. Part II, to which I now turn, is devoted to the questions of how to reconstruct American government, labor, and education on just and sustainable foundations in the global context of the twenty-first century.

PART II

A NEW PROGRESSIVE AGENDA

CHAPTER 5

Government for the People

INTRODUCTION

According to planetary science, physical conditions necessary for life—which may be a rarity in our universe—are likely to exist on earth for another billion years, after which increased radiation from the sun will wipe out our biosphere (Caldeira and Kasting 1992). From a human perspective, a billion years is an eternity. But environmental crises created by humans, if not reversed in the current decade, will likely destroy billions of human lives through starvation, dehydration, disease, and political violence within the life span of babies being born today or, at the latest, of their children.[1]

As adults, this generation—or, rather, the part of it that survives this hell of ecological collapse—will live on a barren planet stripped of hundreds of thousands of species that took the last half a billion years to evolve. Nature will not make an exception for America, as the extreme weather events currently decimating agriculture worldwide attest. Entire regions that are growing grains today will be unsuitable for farming, and the remaining humans will live in a continual state of war over the arable land and potable water that remain (Brown 2009; Klare 2002; Wright 2004). Those miserable people—our children and grandchildren—will be struggling for physical survival, not worrying about repaying government debt.

---

1. Such are the consequences of large scale destruction of agriculture that will be caused by catastrophic climate change, which is imminent and can only be averted, if at all, by emergency action (Brown 2009; Harvey 2011; Klare 2002; Richardson et al. 2009; Wright 2004).

This or some similar nightmare is humanity's certain fate in the twenty-first century unless citizens in the coming years act to reverse the polluting and other human activities that are destroying local ecosystems and the carbon fuel use that is driving global warming. The fate of our planet is quickly spinning out of human control, and the need for action is urgent (Brown 2009; Nordhaus 2012; Wright 2005). Against this sobering backdrop, no question is more important that this: what is the proper role of government in averting global ecological catastrophe? Related to this is another question: if governments fail to act, will market rationality save the day?

According to conventional wisdom, these are difficult and complex questions that are fraught with disagreement among the experts. They are not. Although experts can and do differ over strategies and technical matters, there is widespread agreement on fundamentals. For example, some economists support a carbon tax and others a cap-and-trade system, but there is virtually no disagreement among scientists that CO_2 emissions must be greatly reduced in the near future to avert catastrophic global warming (Brown 2009; Nordhaus 2012). Nor is there disagreement among economists that some kind of government action is required (Nordhaus 2012).[2] The problem is that many of these same experts leave their scientific training at the door and abuse their academic authority when they go to work as propagandists for oil companies and other big corporations or as public intellectuals promoting laissez-faire ideology. In any case, America cannot afford to postpone debate and action on viable solutions to known crises that threaten civilization itself (Nordhaus 2012).

All economists, even neoliberals, know that markets are not rational under certain conditions. One such condition is when the parties to a market transaction do not bear its full costs, which economists call the problem of "externalities." Every time a motorist fills up at the pump, for example, an externality occurs. Exxon-Mobil and its shareholders make money, and the motorist gets the fuel needed to drive to work. But neither party pays the most important cost of the transaction—the contribution to global warming that occurs when the product is used.

This cost can be quantified. It is the amount of tax that would have to be imposed on such transactions in order to reduce overall carbon fuel consumption enough—and soon enough—to reverse global warming.

---

2. All economists recognize the existence of "market failure" under some circumstances and the corrective role of government in many such cases (Stiglitz and Walsh 2007). Unabated global warming is an extreme case of market failure and a classic example of the "free-rider" problem for which government and multilateral treaties can provide a solution (Klein 2001; Olson 1971).

The calculations are complex and require technical assumptions, but the underlying principle is simple and uncontroversial. An excessive[3] amount of gasoline will be produced and consumed in an unregulated market system because those buying and selling the product are not paying the costs of global warming, which are externalized and imposed on others in the future. The free market does not produce rational outcomes in this case or any other where significant externalities occur. But government can make the market rational by instituting carbon taxes or some equally effective policy for reducing emissions.[4] Government can impose the future costs of global warming on those who buy and sell gasoline today, and then they will buy and sell less of it. The free market cannot save us from global warming, but government can.

To be sure, global warming by its nature is a problem that cannot be solved by the United States alone. Tropical rain forests, for example, remove large quantities of carbon dioxide from the atmosphere and should be part of the solution to global warming. Yet these forests are being destroyed for their lumber because the free market does not value their ecological benefits, another kind of externality. In fact, in cutting down these forests, loggers are destroying not only trees but also entire ecosystems containing hundreds of thousands of irreplaceable species, including many plants with unique medicinal properties. The need to protect tropical rain forests is irrefutable, but capitalism, left to itself, is destroying them. Justice, respect for nature, and concern for future generations demand that some of the revenue collected from carbon taxes in advanced industrial economies be used to subsidize maintenance of these forests, thus compensating poor countries for the foreign exchange revenue they would otherwise have received for their lumber.

As the most powerful country in the world as well as the largest emitter of carbon dioxide and other greenhouse gases in history, the United

---

3. By excessive, I mean relative to the efficient amount that would be produced and consumed in a perfect market. All economists today recognize the need to modify the perfect market model under certain conditions, such as externalities, oligopoly, and information asymmetries (Stiglitz and Walsh 2007).

4. For example, higher gasoline taxes would give motorists incentives to greatly reduce their use of gasoline through conservation, hybrid vehicles, or public transportation. To compensate motorists for the costs of changing their energy consumption patterns (without undoing the incentive), a payroll tax reduction of the same amount can be given to all working people, funded by this gasoline tax and other carbon taxes. The higher gasoline taxes and reduced payroll taxes can be phased in by perhaps one dollar per gallon every year for 10 years. A carbon tax on coal can create an incentive for utilities to produce electricity from renewable sources, providing green energy for hybrid cars. Finally, expanded public transportation built as part of the green New Deal can enable a large reduction in automobile use overall.

States has a special responsibility to lead the world in stopping global warming.[5] That can never occur, however, as long as the American political system is dominated by huge corporations like Exxon-Mobil, Chevron, and coal giant Peabody Energy Corporation (Gelbspan 2004). Nor is the problem limited to individual politicians and corporations. It arises out of the rules of American state capitalism that permit corporate elites to move in and out of top government positions and to dominate politicians through lobbyists, campaign contributions, and super PACs. While some exceptional politicians and corporations do act in socially responsible ways in spite of all this, the system itself rewards self-destructive greed and narrow, short-term interests.

Anyone who wants their children to have a humane future needs a crystal-clear understanding of what is really going on here. The root of the problem is *not* that government is dysfunctional by nature and politicians inherently corrupt and self-serving. Rather, the problem is a state capitalist system that systematically undermines the integrity of even the most dedicated public servant. The American people need government to solve problems that will otherwise destroy us, but it has to be a government for the people, not a state capitalist government for corporations and the rich. Only a revolutionary mass movement can create a government for the people, and such a movement is now an urgent necessity for the future of civilization.

For the reasons indicated, carbon taxes (or an equivalent CO_2 emissions reduction system), a strong and well-funded Environmental Protection Agency, and other policies that can protect the earth's ecology are essential goals of any public interest movement worthy of the name. Government regulations to correct other externalities, such as those involving the health and safety of workplaces, are also justified and necessary to impose rationality on markets. This is also the case with food safety standards and other consumer protections that prevent participants in market transactions from imposing costs on third parties, such as private and government health insurance providers.

PLANNING FOR HUMAN SECURITY

The implications of global environmental crises for humanity's future remind me of a comment by Albert Einstein. While uttered over 60 years

---

5. For a critical review of U.S. policy on the United Nations Framework Convention on Climate Change and the Kyoto Protocol, see Deller et al. (2003).

ago about another unprecedented threat, his words could hardly be more relevant to the problem of climate change today. "The unleashed power of the atom," Einstein said, "has changed everything save our modes of thinking and we thus drift towards unparalleled catastrophe." The "modes of thinking" that made nuclear weapons seem inevitable were rooted in a system of security based on heavily armed states. Entire industries and occupations depended on that system, all of which had been legitimized for centuries by militarist ideologies.

Similarly, America's economic system has been based for over a century on inexpensive fossil fuels—first coal for steam engines and electrical generating plants and then petroleum to power internal combustion and jet engines. Because fossil fuels were plentiful relative to demand and thus cheap, there was no incentive to economize on their use, and the country's transportation and other physical systems used lavish amounts of them. In the twentieth century, America's cities and its entire pattern of land use were redesigned to accommodate the automobile, and extravagant amounts of energy were used building roads, single-family suburban dwellings, and the energy-wasteful cars themselves. Coal-fired power plants provided cheap electricity used with little concern for efficiency to light, heat, and cool buildings; to manufacture a vast, endless flow of goods; and to operate innumerable appliances.

Indeed, while America's preeminent position in the world has rested on its military power, including nuclear weapons, its entire domestic civilization has been based on cheap fossil fuels. To discover, therefore, that burning these fuels is precipitating changes in climate that imperil agriculture and indeed life as we know it is an inconvenient truth that few have been prepared to take seriously. Until recently, the average person in capitalist America rarely thought about such things as nuclear proliferation or global warming, devoting most of their time and energy traveling to and from work, surviving their dysfunctional workplaces, and maintaining relationships with family and friends. Few politicians would risk their careers by challenging such pillars of American power and prosperity as the weapons contractors and oil companies. Even peace and environmental activists—and the foundations that funded them—found themselves ignoring the big threats to humanity in order to focus on this or that legislative priority and wield what little influence they could inside the Washington Beltway (Cabasso 2007b; Gelbspan 2004).

All this is changing. Reminiscent of the 1960s and 1970s counter-cultural revolution, the Occupy Wall Street movement that began in September 2011 triggered similar protests in dozens of other American cities. The middle class is fighting back at a system of state capitalism that is destroying their livelihoods, their security, and the ecological foundations of future peace and prosperity. Pentagon officials and corporate CEOs —masters of the universe during the so called "American century"—are no longer the only ones defining "reality." The obsolete modes of thinking that had locked America into a trajectory of war and ecological collapse are losing their grip. Einstein would be pleased. Whether it will prove to be too little, too late remains to be seen. But political conditions are emerging for a transformation of state capitalism that can secure a just and humane future, if anything can.

What is the nature of this transformation? The Occupy movement is now in the process of defining its goals. I would like to suggest that its protagonists are, most fundamentally, searching for what has been called "human security" (Cabasso 2007b). By contrast with "national security"—which served the interests of nation-states and power elites—human security is the condition in which ordinary people can meet their basic and higher needs.[6] It is similar to what President Franklin D. Roosevelt called the "Four Freedoms": (1) freedom of speech and expression, (2) freedom of religion, (3) freedom from want, and (4) freedom from fear (Cabasso 2007b). Human security—defined in these or similar terms— is the true aim of government, not the freedom of rich and powerful people to accumulate more wealth and power at the expense of others.

The concept of human security differs in three ways from the old state capitalist modes of thinking (Cabasso 2007b). First, it is truly universal, rejecting the double standards that have plagued America throughout its history. Poverty, for example, disproportionately affects certain groups, such as blacks and Hispanics, a state of affairs indicating that the needs of some people are currently considered more important than those of others. Human security is a condition that applies equally to all.

Second, human security is global, not something that can be achieved only by Americans while poverty, violence, and disease afflict hundreds of millions of people in other parts of the world. This global sensibility is already familiar to Americans, who respond empathically to news

---

6. By "basic needs," I mean freedom from violence; an unpolluted environment; access to clean water and healthy food; access to other necessities, including clothing, housing, and health care; and employment at a living wage in a nonabusive, safe, and healthy workplace. By "higher needs," I mean political and religious freedom, political participation, time for and access to cultural activities, loving community, and self-realization. Maslow (1987) provides a similar typology. As explained later in this chapter in my discussion of subsidiarity and responsibility, I am not arguing that government can or should directly supply all these needs. What I am arguing is that the true purpose of government is to enable all people to satisfy these needs, not to enable the few to dominate others and accumulate wealth without limit.

coverage of wars, natural disasters, and other conditions that cause appalling suffering abroad. Such coverage, however, rarely explains the role of the American power elite in much of this suffering. The U.S. government, for example, has a long history of providing military aid to dictatorships, and the oil and coal companies are the driving force behind the climate change that makes extreme floods, droughts, and hurricanes increasingly common worldwide. Along with an awareness of global problems, citizens need to understand their causes, including the role of state capitalist institutions and policies.

Third, and following from its universal and global character, human security is indivisible. This means that the security of some groups cannot be advanced by negating the security of others, as when austerity measures spare the wealthy while balancing government budgets on the backs of those who can least afford it. Similarly, the pursuit of military supremacy violates the principle of indivisibility because it advances the security of one country at the expense of others. These characteristics of human security—its universality, global dimensions, and indivisibility—require new modes of thinking that break from violence-based, state-centered national security as well as from capitalist accumulation of wealth through exploitation of ordinary people's labor.

In the remainder of this chapter, I will identify the core policy strategies through which a government for the people can make the good life a reality for every American while simultaneously enhancing human security throughout the world. Here, I want to note the essential role of government planning in formulating and implementing such policies (Klein 2011). It is a widely held myth in the United States, cultivated by conservatives ever since the New Deal, that government planning is the hallmark of socialist and communist societies and is alien to America's free market traditions.

In reality, government planning is as American as apple pie. It is what built the county's roads, bridges and tunnels, culminating in the interstate highway system in the second half of the twentieth century. It is what mobilized the country's human and physical capital to defeat Nazi Germany and imperial Japan. Government planning is responsible for such diverse inventions as the atomic bomb and the Internet. It is what landed humans on the moon and brought them safely back to earth and what built and administered the largest military and commercial empire in history. I have never met a conservative who repudiates any of these achievements, yet conservatives unanimously denounce with great fury the government planning that made them possible. This contradiction makes a mockery of American conservatism and the Republican Party.

Peace and sustainable prosperity cannot be secured without government planning. The latter needs to be done in concert with individuals and enterprises acting in markets, to be sure, but markets alone could never have achieved the previously mentioned technical and organizational feats, nor can it achieve similar feats in the future such as building a green infrastructure, reversing climate change, and eradicating global poverty. The question is not whether the U.S. government should or will engage in planning on a massive scale but rather to what ends that planning will be directed and whose needs it will serve. Planning for human security on behalf of all the people is now the only rational option, and time is running out to choose that option and implement it.

THE ENERGY CHALLENGE: SPEEDING UP THE TRANSITION

Big challenges such as nuclear proliferation and climate change, when they are addressed in the halls of power, are addressed in entirely the wrong way. Many policymakers concede that nuclear disarmament and reducing levels of CO_2 emission are desirable goals but dismiss them as not possible or feasible in a short time frame, say, 5 or 10 years. Instead, they adopt a planning framework that takes the underlying problem as a given and then ask what more limited steps can be taken to mitigate it. This indicates that leaders are paying lip service to a goal but not really taking it seriously. The contrast with other goals that *were* taken seriously is instructive.

In October 1939, for example, Franklin D. Roosevelt received a letter from Albert Einstein informing him that it might be possible to build a nuclear fission bomb of unprecedented destructiveness and that Nazi Germany was stockpiling uranium and proceeding with fission research. The president immediately formed an advisory committee and through a series of further actions set in motion the Manhattan Project, culminating in the detonation of the first atomic bomb in the New Mexico desert less than six years later.

Like other great achievements, this one in retrospect has come to seem inevitable. In 1939, however, it was by no means clear that an atomic bomb could actually be built, as Einstein himself admitted. It would have been easy for Roosevelt to dismiss as mere speculation the inconvenient truth that such devices might actually be built and remain focused on military problems of more immediate relevance. But the president judged the possibility of Hitler developing an atomic bomb before United States to be an unacceptable risk, and he allocated and mobilized the resources needed to minimize that risk.

Nor was the mission of the Manhattan Project to determine whether an atomic bomb was possible. Rather, proceeding on the assumption that it was, the project's mission was to build one and to do so in the shortest possible time. This required an extraordinary amount of government planning and the administration of science and technology on an unprecedented scale to accomplish something that might, in the end, have been impossible. But the stakes were deemed too high for delay or indecision, and policymakers rose to the occasion, taking all necessary actions to accomplish the goal and deferring for the future the question of whether it was possible to do so.

The existential threat to American security posed by Hitler in 1939 and the resolve, creativity, and competence with which the country met that challenge constitute a precedent for the threat of ecological collapse today and the kind of government planning and action needed to avert it. In the present case, climate scientists know that reducing CO_2 emissions will reverse global warming, and the challenge is to accomplish this before a catastrophic and irreversible change in the earth's climate occurs. Specifically, given the dependence of existing technologies and the world economy on fossil fuels, how can renewable energy technologies be developed and deployed fast enough to reverse global warming? Most energy economists agree that renewables will become cheaper than fossil fuels in perhaps another decade, at which point market forces will effect a transition from the latter to the former. Climate scientists warn that such a timetable is much too slow (Brown 2009; Harvey 2011; Richardson et al. 2009), but it is not obvious whether or how the transition to renewables can be speeded up in time to avert ecological collapse.

Reflecting the inertia of the fossil fuel economy, the conventional wisdom in Washington and corporate America is that a significantly faster transition to renewables is simply not possible or feasible and that global CO_2 emissions will continue to rise during the interim. In such a planning framework, it is entirely reasonable for America to expand the production of its own fossil fuels, especially coal and natural gas, which it possesses in abundance. The United States should also promote research and development on renewables, according to this state capitalist view, but should defer large-scale implementation until cost-efficient technologies have been developed.

In order to adopt this planning framework, however, policymakers must ignore or deny the certainty of ecological collapse if current trends are not altered in the very near future. While the exact length of time available for making this transition is not known, Roosevelt faced similar uncertainty about development of the atomic bomb and did not invoke such uncertainty as an excuse for inaction. In reality, the only relevant question today is not whether reducing CO_2 emissions in the short term is possible or feasible but rather how to do it. If the feat proves impossible, humanity will at least go down fighting, and the outcome will be no worse than would occur with business as usual. But if there is indeed a way out—and the only rational course is to proceed on that assumption—solutions must be pursued with the utmost speed. Since the state capitalist system seems incapable of responding to the climate crisis and other urgent challenges in this appropriate way, rational and responsible people need to replace it with a government for the people that can serve the needs of human security. And this revolution must occur in the shortest possible time.

As explained next, a set of three interrelated policy strategies provides the best hope of decreasing global CO_2 emissions in time to stabilize earth's climate. Taken together, these three strategies map out a green New Deal, a path to the sustainable society of the future. First, a steep carbon tax is needed to make renewable energy technologies less costly than those based on fossil fuels and to create incentives for the efficient use of energy and materials. Second, a massive program of public investment in renewable energy infrastructure is needed to absorb and redirect the human and physical capital idled by the rapid phasing out of the fossil fuel economy and other wasteful economic activity, including the bloated national security state. Third, the scale and types of public investment must be tailored so as to utilize all idle human and physical capital in the economy, and government must provide all necessary job retraining needed to accomplish this.

TOTAL EFFICIENCY: ENERGY AND MATERIALS

The amount of CO_2 reduction needed for human security and the requirements for achieving it have been rigorously determined. A report by the International Alliance of Research Universities (Richardson et al. 2009) estimates that holding average atmospheric temperature at a ceiling of 2 degrees Celsius above preindustrial levels is needed to avert dangerous climate change. This, in turn, would require an immediate 60 to 80 percent reduction in global CO_2 emissions. Recognizing the implausibility of such an achievement, the report concludes, "To limit the extent of overshoot, emissions should peak in the near future." Fatih Birol, chief economist at the International Energy Agency, has calculated that global fossil fuel infrastructure being constructed at its current pace will lock the world into irreversible climate change by 2015 (Harvey 2011).

These warnings are not alarmist propaganda but the sober conclusions of eminent scientists backed by a large body of peer-reviewed research. Rationality demands an immediate, all-out mobilization of the U.S. government to slash CO_2 emissions while working collaboratively with top leaders from China and other large CO_2-emitting countries. Whatever the outcome of such collaboration, the United States should be racing into the future to reduce emissions—not waiting for other countries to act but doing its own part and influencing them through its example and diplomacy. Nor is this only a matter of global responsibility since the first country to retool for a sustainable future will gain a competitive advantage in the world economy, a point not lost on Chinese leaders. Let Republicans frame the problem as a national security and commercial race against China, if they wish, and Democrats as a race against global warming. The result is the same—the need for a total mobilization of human and physical resources comparable to the U.S. war effort against Hitler.

The measurable requirements for achieving the needed carbon emission reduction are also clear. In 1993, Japanese energy economist Yoichi Kaya identified the relevant parameters and their relationship in a single equation (Kaya and Yokobori 1993). Now known as the Kaya identity, it states that global CO_2 emission from human sources is obtained by multiplying four factors: population size, gross domestic product (GDP) per capita, energy use per unit of GDP, and carbon emissions per unit of energy consumed. The first of these, population, is an important variable for the intermediate and long term but is not amenable to reduction by public policy in the relevant time frame. Reduction of carbon emissions therefore hinges on the remaining three factors, which are easily translated into policy objectives.

Two of the factors—GDP and energy use per unit of GDP—can be reduced substantially with little adverse impact on the quality of life of ordinary people through a green New Deal. Major policy elements of such a strategy include rapid downsizing of the defense sector, as discussed later in this chapter; modification of all building construction plans to conform to LEEDS standards for energy efficiency; suspending the manufacture of appliances that do not meet stringent efficiency standards, nonessential manufacturing that uses energy-intensive or energy-wasteful processes, the manufacture of unnecessary, energy-wasteful luxury and consumer products, such as private jets and sport-utility vehicles; and substitution of whole foods for highly processed and packaged foods (which will actually produce health benefits, reducing health care costs). In a kind of reverse multiplier effect, stopping all this inefficient economic activity will produce further reductions, such as canceling the construction of new mining, manufacturing, and office facilities that would have been needed to support all the economic activities listed above.

All nonessential household consumption must be postponed, much as occurred in the United States during World War II. But as the above list indicates, a vast amount of the country's GDP consists of economic activity that does not contribute to the standard of living of ordinary people. Indeed, one of the most pernicious examples of obsolete, state capitalist modes of thinking is the confusion of GDP with quality of life (Cobb, Halstead, and Rowe 1995). The former includes spending on war, energy use that pollutes the environment, and medical treatment for preventable illnesses and injuries—economic activities that are negatively correlated with quality of life. By contrast, the latter includes such noneconomic "goods" as clean air, freedom from workplace stress, and more time for cultural activities and political participation. New measures of quality of life, such as the Genuine Progress Indicator (Gast 2010), must be adopted in place of GDP, which should be retained only for statistical purposes as an aggregate measure of energy-consuming activity.

The final factor in the Kaya equation—carbon emissions per unit of energy consumed—indicates the need for an immediate cessation of oil, coal, and natural gas exploration as well as cancellation of planned construction of extraction and processing facilities for these fossil fuels and a rapid phasing out of the production and use of these fuels to very low levels.

The economic reductions indicated above can be achieved largely through market mechanisms by instituting carbon taxes that set the average price of energy from fossil fuels higher than from existing renewable technologies. Oil, coal, and natural gas should be taxed at rates reflecting the emissions they generate when burned (Stiglitz 2007). Subsidies for fossil fuels and agribusiness should be diverted to the design and rapid deployment of a renewable energy infrastructure and for such activities as reforestation, preservation of tropical rain forests, and less capital- and energy-intensive organic agriculture (see Appendix 5.1). Additional funding for these initiatives can come from the carbon taxes, a progressive consumption tax,[7] and increased income taxes on the rich.

----

7. Like a value added tax, a progressive consumption tax would have very high rates on luxury items, high to moderate rates on non-essential consumer goods, and no tax on food and other necessities. This kind of tax would create incentives for households to forgo unnecessary consumption while having minimal impact on the poor.

PUBLIC INVESTMENT, SUBSIDIARITY, AND RESPONSIBILITY: PATH TO A GREEN NEW DEAL

The steep carbon tax (or equivalent carbon reduction policy) proposed here is an absolute, objective requirement for averting catastrophic ecological and social upheavals that are already beginning to engulf the world. For that reason, the policy should be an urgent and nonnegotiable demand for democratic mass movements in the United States and elsewhere. But all public policies have economic consequences, and an effective mass movement must understand what these are and how they can be managed. Indeed, a single policy strategy, such as a carbon tax, must be pursued as part of a coherently designed set of synergistic strategies that move in the same direction of a humane and sustainable future.

The most obvious consequence of steep and rapidly implemented carbon taxes is the massive unemployment and idling of physical capital that would occur—in the absence of countervailing policies—during the period of transition from an energy wasteful economy based on fossil fuels to an efficient one based on renewable energy. The needed countervailing policy strategy is a well-planned program of public investment—at the federal, state, and local levels—in the green infrastructure of tomorrow. "Well planned" means coherently designed to meet the economic needs of human security, not a hodgepodge of pork-barrel projects and earmarks designed to serve the short-term political priorities of legislators or the profits of contractors. Public investment is the second of three synergistic policy strategies proposed here. It should be determined through a process of democratic planning and coordinated among the levels of government through the principle of subsidiarity, that is, in the most decentralized way possible consistent with national and international goals and objectives.[8]

For example, anything that can be done efficiently by individuals, cooperatives, and firms should be done at that level, delegating the rest to government. Of the remaining policy needs, municipal governments should undertake everything that can be done at the local level, delegating the rest upward and so on up through the states, regional planning bodies, the federal government, and the United Nations and other global planning forums. Subsidiarity ensures that the federal government

---

8. The concept of subsidiarity that I am proposing here is an approach to coordinating grassroots, local initiatives with national government planning, both of which are necessary to averting catastrophic climate change, as discussed by Naomi Klein (2011).

undertake only such planning and implementation as cannot be or is not being handled by lower levels. As for the United Nations, its powers are limited not only by subsidiarity but also by its dependence on nation-states for financing and authorization of major policies.

The principle of subsidiarity may be understood as the general presumption that decentralized actors do not need authorization from a higher level to act. This must be combined, I would argue, with the principle of responsibility, according to which every actor at every level has an *obligation* to take effective and appropriate action on behalf of human security. This entails social responsibility by individuals and firms as well as the responsibility by various levels of government to correct externalities and other market failures to the extent that they can be corrected. If entrepreneurs do not want government imposing onerous regulations, then let them practice social responsibility, making such regulations unnecessary.

The days are over when it is acceptable for corporations to externalize their costs onto their workers and to saddle future generations with the ecological consequences of short-term profit seeking. Whenever the private sector is unable or unwilling to act in ways consistent with the public interest, responsibility passes to the next-highest level beginning with municipal governments. It continues up through the governmental hierarchy so that the problems that eventually land on the president's desk and the congressional docket are only those that cannot be (or at least have not been) solved at lower levels. An aroused public must hold individuals, firms, and every level of government accountable for discharging the responsibilities appropriate to the various levels.

In *Manufacturing Green Prosperity: The Power to Rebuild the American Middle Class*, Jon Rynn (2010) depicts in greater detail what the program of public investment I am advocating—a kind of green New Deal—might look like. Needed projects include rail and other public transportation systems, urban construction designed for sustainability and energy efficiency, and a green energy infrastructure that includes solar, wind, and geothermal technologies. Rynn notes that public investments of this kind and scale would set in motion a rebirth of American manufacturing, revitalizing the private sector and putting the country back on the road to prosperity for the middle class, though this needs to be redefined in a postconsumerist framework (Cobb et al. 1995; Klein 2011).

In addition to this infrastructure and manufacturing agenda, human security requires public investment in what some call biological capital. First, the United States needs an energy-efficient and health-promoting food system based on organic plant and animal agriculture, minimal food processing, and minimal intermediaries between food producers and consumers (see Appendix 5.1). Government subsidies paid to agribusiness should be eliminated immediately and the revenues used to pay the transition and start-up costs for this sustainable food system, which will be operated mostly by small farmers and farming cooperatives (see Appendix 5.1). Rynn (2010) suggests that the outermost ring of land around a given urban area be devoted to such food production, with clean, energy-efficient manufacturing in the middle ring and residential and commercial spaces in the core. Finally, the planting of trees and other projects to restore and conserve vital ecosystems (Brown 2009) are important components of the program of public investment proposed here.

TOTAL UTILIZATION: HUMAN RESOURCES AND PHYSICAL CAPITAL

The third policy strategy, operating in concert with new taxes and massive public investment, is the total utilization of human and physical capital. This strategy cuts the Gordian knot of macroeconomic controversies about full employment with the simple proposition that governments at every level must be the employers of last resort. Any citizen who wants to work or needs the income is entitled to a productive job, which must be provided by government if it is not available in the private sector. The notion that governments at every level must cut back services and public employment in order to balance their budgets is a perverse way of reckoning costs and constitutes an intolerable attack on human security. Such austerity is the logical if vicious consequence of state capitalism and thus a *reductio ad absurdum* of its fundamental assumptions.

The public investment projects outlined above can be expanded to any desired level in order to meet the employment needs of the country. A government for the people will undertake public works on whatever scale is necessary to fully utilize the country's human and physical capital. Projects must be created that utilize skills and physical resources that are currently or will be idled by the phasing out of obsolete institutions and technologies.[9] Along with such planning, a great deal of training and

9. Many of the planning tools for accomplishing this already exist or can be created by adapting existing tools. The field of "input-output analysis" contains a vast body of theory and successful policy applications involving similar problems (Raa 2005).

retraining will be needed. Much of this can be achieved by assigning those needing jobs to various projects as apprentices based on transferable skills they already have.

As with the New Deal, experimentation will be needed, and some solutions will emerge through trial and error. America has succeeded at this before. New Deal projects, such as the Tennessee Valley Authority, construction of the Triborough Bridge, and the Civilian Conservation Corps put tens of millions of people to work and created public infrastructure and biological capital of enduring value. As a matter of public policy, all manufacturing and other contracts created by public investment must be used to employ U.S. citizens, except where Americans with the requisite skills are not available.

Where would the funding for all this come from? Some of it would come from carbon and progressive consumption taxes as well as higher income taxes on the rich. Some of it will come from existing tax revenues currently being squandered on the national security state, which is also the source of much physical capital and human resources that will be required. Finally, some of it will come from government borrowing, at least in the short term. This can primarily take the form of small-denomination government bonds purchased by middle-class citizens, who, as in World War II, will be reducing unnecessary consumption to meet a pressing national emergency and thus having funds to invest. Since the Green New Deal's public investments will greatly increase the country's capacity to create wealth in the future, even a large increase in new government debt incurred for that purpose would be sustainable, unlike much of the existing debt that was incurred for unproductive military and other pork-barrel programs.[10]

---

10. The American Monetary Institute (2011) correctly notes that government can simply print money to pay for investment in productive infrastructure inasmuch as such investment increases the real economy and thereby requires an increase in the money supply to prevent deflation. This method of funding will not be available during the early years of a Green New Deal, however, during which GDP will be reduced as part of an overall plan for averting catastrophic climate change. Note that such a reduction in GDP, which would normally result in reduced employment, can be accompanied by *increased* employment as long as capital- and energy-intensive and high-value-added activities like weapons manufacturing are replaced with labor-intensive and low-value-added activities such as planting trees and installing solar energy panels. To avoid inflation, people employed in these low-value-added activities cannot initially be paid at the same level as existing government employees, which was also the case in Roosevelt's New Deal. As the energy-efficient and renewable economy is phased in, however, the country's capacity to produce increasing wealth with minimal carbon emissions will enable an increase in public wages and funding of further public investment through an increase in the money supply.

There is absolutely no excuse for even a single person in America to be looking for productive, paid work and being unable to find it. That includes teenagers looking for summer jobs, the elderly, and the disabled. It is the responsibility of government to combine human and physical capital and organize production to meet real human needs whenever and to whatever extent the private sector fails to do so. That state capitalism fails miserably to accomplish this is a scathing indictment and sufficient reason to replace it with a government for the people.

The rapid phasing in of steep carbon taxes and the rapid downsizing of America's national security state, discussed next, will create an unprecedented amount of economic dislocation. Massive public investment will mitigate these effects and facilitate a rapid and efficient adaptation of human and physical capital to the new, sustainable economy. The retraining programs required to accomplish this are themselves part of the needed investment and must be provided by government to whatever extent the private sector fails to provide them.

Related to this, time and resources must be allocated to job counseling and placement in order to make maximum use of the country's human resources. If a person has academic skills, for example, she will probably be better off apprenticed to a public school than to a tree planting operation, but an even better use of her unique mix of gifts and interests may exist. Such solutions benefit both the individual and society. Job counselors who can help find them are a higher-order human resource that government should mobilize to whatever extent the private sector fails to do so.

One area of pubic investment that can absorb large amounts of human and physical capital to good effect is primary and secondary education. Renovating, building, and equipping adequate facilities in school districts that serve the poor will both employ millions in poor neighborhoods[11] and help reclaim the human potential of disadvantaged children.

---

11. Accomplishing this will require novel solutions to novel problems. On the one hand, priority in hiring must be given to unemployed residents in poor neighborhoods. On the other hand, few of these residents are members of construction unions and most will require training. One solution is to greatly expand union apprenticeship programs. This can be done in the context of Mondragon-type producer cooperatives (Nembhard and Haynes 2002), formed through democratic collaboration between unions and community organizations, a model that can also be applied to housing. An important principle in all such initiatives is the need to build "social capital"—which involves relationships and community—not only tangible "bricks and mortar" products (Karan 2002).

Similarly, a large expansion of the teaching workforce is needed to reduce class sizes in underfunded school districts to the same levels that exist in affluent suburban districts. The unmet needs in the country's public schools are discussed in greater detail in Chapter 7.

Finally, making the transition to a low-carbon economy in time to avert ecological catastrophe will require a massive mobilization of science and technology. Some American scientists and inventors are already doing cutting-edge renewable energy work. Government should be providing every possible support for such work, including ample funding. It should simultaneously assemble its own renewable energy team, building on and learning from the experience of the Manhattan Project, NASA, and other successful government research-and-development programs. Consistent with the principle of subsidiarity, the federal government's program should focus on needed research that private industry, universities, and lower levels of government cannot do well (or at all) or are simply not doing for whatever reason.

It is not my concern in this book, nor should it be the concern of the masses of people joining the progressive movement, how all this can be accomplished at the detailed policy or technical levels. Roosevelt was not and did not have to be a research administrator or nuclear engineer to set the country's scientific and technical personnel to work building an atomic bomb. It was his role only to frame the overall policy goal of building a bomb before the Third Reich did. Today, the policy goal of overriding importance and urgency is reducing CO_2 emissions in time to reverse catastrophic climate change, and the masses of people must demand it since elites appear unwilling or unable set priorities appropriately.

If there are policy strategies more effective and viable to this end than those sketched here, let others put them forth immediately and let Congress debate them and enact the best ones in the very near future. If Congress or the Supreme Court obstruct or delay such action, let the American people assert their unique, sovereign power to institute new constitutional arrangements—as the founding fathers did in 1787—in the present case by putting the alternatives to a direct vote of the people in a national referendum (see Chapter 8).

SELF-DEFENSE AND COLLECTIVE SECURITY

The transition from a "national security" paradigm promoting the power of the state and its elites to one based on human security and the needs of ordinary people will free up a vast amount of human resources and physical capital currently being squandered on unnecessary military programs. There are only two circumstances in which the use of force is legal and legitimate under the UN Charter and current international law (United Nations 1945). The first—"self-defense"—is narrowly defined under Article 51 of the UN Charter as a state's right to repel an armed attack on its territory, for example, the Syrian and Egyptian attack on Israel in 1973. The second—"collective security"—is when a state participates in a UN-authorized military action to repel such an attack, protect citizens from genocide, or address some similarly serious threat to international peace and security. In 2011, for example, the UN Security Council authorized air strikes against the forces of Muammar Gaddafi when their slaughter of the civilian population of Benghazi appeared imminent.

American elites commonly discuss whether a given military action serves U.S. "interests." It was in those terms, for example, that many Republicans opposed U.S. participation in the operation against Gaddafi's forces. In fact, however, any threat or use of force in pursuit of "national interests"—which in practice generally means *corporate* interests—is an act of aggression and is defined under the Nuremberg Principles as a "crime against peace" (United Nations International Law Commission 1950). Whenever an American politician or pundit utters the phrase "national interest" in the context of possible military action, a progressive mass movement should pounce on them and identify their discourse as criminal.

The same elites who justify war by invoking national interests typically—and not surprisingly—dismiss international law as utopian and the United Nations as irrelevant. But most ordinary Americans believe that the true purposes of U.S. military power are, in fact, to protect the country from attack and uphold peace and human rights abroad. They need to understand that these commonsense beliefs about what are legitimate uses of force are actually aligned with international law, and that elites who vilify the latter are seeking to justify self-serving abuses of military power. Further, a progressive mass movement must be alert to deceptive appeals to humanitarian imperatives and self-defense to legitimize aggression. This occurred, for example, when the George W. Bush administration invoked Saddam Hussein's heinous human rights violations and alleged possession of weapons of mass destruction to justify an invasion that was really in the service of corporate interests (Chomsky 2003, 2008).

Clarity about the only legitimate uses of force must be the starting point for any analysis of the troops and weapons a country truly needs. Such clarity rules out the vast bulk of what the United States currently spends on national security. As in the case of energy policy, a mass movement does not need to concern itself with debates about technical policy matters but does need to understand in broad terms the military capabilities the United States really needs to promote human security at home and abroad.

As discussed in Chapter 1, U.S. military and other national security expenditures support a policy of "full-spectrum dominance" or "projecting power" around the globe, policy objectives for which there is no basis in international law. These capabilities include over 700 military bases on foreign soil, some 1.8 million troops, and tens of thousands of vehicles and weapon systems, including fighter jets, missiles, aircraft carriers, battleships, tanks, and several thousand nuclear warheads deployed on bombers, submarines, land-based missiles, and other delivery systems. In addition, hundreds of thousands of civilian personnel administer the whole system from the Pentagon and local offices. The national security state includes additional workers and physical infrastructure in other entities besides the Department of Defense, such as the CIA, the State Department's military aid programs, the Department of Energy's nuclear weapons complex, and the defense divisions of civilian corporations, which operate under contracts administered by the Pentagon.

Very little of these human resources and physical capital are designed to either repel attacks on U.S. territory or participate in UN-authorized collective security actions, the only uses of force that are legal and legitimate. These extraneous capabilities include most of the country's nuclear arsenal and its air-, sea-, and land-based delivery systems. Nuclear weapons, however, raise special security problems that we must now confront. The same is true of missile defense systems, that is, missiles and other technology—much of it in the research-and-development phase—designed to intercept incoming missiles.

Many religious leaders and legal scholars have long questioned the legitimacy of nuclear deterrence on grounds that virtually any use of such indiscriminate weapons would involve the mass slaughter of civilians and radioactive contamination that cannot be contained to the battlefield (Chullikatt 2011; Moxley, Burroughs, and

Granoff 2011).[12] In a 1995 advisory opinion, the International Court of Justice definitively affirmed this position, ruling that the threat or use of nuclear weapons is generally prohibited under international law and that the complete abolition of nuclear weapons is an urgent legal and political imperative (Burroughs 1998). While President Obama did express support for abolition—the only president other than Ronald Reagan to do so—his administration has done little or nothing to plan for it. On the contrary, nuclear deterrence remains an integral part of U.S. military policy (Moxley 2011).

A government for the people should move rapidly to expedite a nuclear weapons convention, that is, an international treaty for abolishing nuclear weapons (United Nations 2007; Weiss, 2011). It is a conservative myth that such a treaty would unrealistically require the United States to trust other countries to carry out their disarmament obligations. Rather, a nuclear weapons convention would include a system of inspections to ensure that all nuclear weapons are being duly dismantled and that no radioactive material is being stockpiled for future military use (United Nations 2007). Such a system can never be foolproof, of course, but its inherent dangers are far less than those of current arrangements. By eliminating existing weapon stockpiles and putting radioactive materials under strict international surveillance, for example, a nuclear weapons

---

12. Apologists for U.S. nuclear policy concede the illegitimacy of mass destruction but argue that the whole point of deterrence—the threat to use nuclear weapons—is precisely to *prevent* their actual use (Ikle et al. 1988; Kissinger 1969). They typically argue that the nuclear-armed United States and Soviet Union refrained from major war for more than forty years, evidence that nuclear deterrence works. These arguments do not hold up to rational scrutiny.

First, it is a well-established principle of international relations that a threat can be effective only if it is credible, which requires a resolve to actually follow through on the threat (Schelling 1981). Consistent with this principle and rarely discussed publicly, the United States and other nuclear-armed states are constantly engaged in operational planning for nuclear war, and America's nuclear weapons are currently on hair-trigger alert and ready to be used in minutes on orders from the president. In law, the threat or preparation to commit a crime is itself a kind of criminal act, known as an "inchoate crime," and criminal acts are not rendered legal by any theories that the actors use to justify their acts to themselves and others (Lifton and Falk 1982; Lifton and Markusen 1990).

Second, the apparent success of the U.S.-Soviet "balance of terror" was almost certainly the result of luck, not the supposed rationality of being willing to perform the unthinkable in order to prevent it (D'Agostino 1993). There were numerous incidents during the Cold War, also rarely discussed publicly, when nuclear war would most likely have occurred because of an accident or miscalculation and was prevented only by some lucky event. During the Cuban Missile Crisis, for example, a Soviet commander mistakenly believed that his submarine was under attack and wanted to launch a nuclear counterattack that could easily have triggered World War III and the annihilation of both superpowers. He was persuaded not to do so only because an insistent subordinate managed to calm him down (Lloyd 2002).

convention would greatly reduce the chances of a terrorist group acquiring a nuclear weapon. During the time it will take for a nuclear weapons convention to be negotiated and implemented, a government for the people can unilaterally downsize the country's nuclear arsenal to a minimum deterrent of perhaps a few dozen weapons, unwind its deterrence posture by taking weapons off alert, and begin planning for security without nuclear weapons.

As for missile defenses, first promoted by Ronald Reagan as an alternative to nuclear deterrence, the whole notion is reminiscent of France's Maginot Line, a system of fortifications that was easily circumvented by German forces in 1940 (Kaufmann et al. 2011). How would a missile defense system, for example, prevent a nuclear weapon from being delivered by ship and detonated in a port city of the target country? Or how would it prevent a "rogue state" from delivering a nuclear weapon on a commercial airliner? In addition, missile defense systems are vulnerable to being overwhelmed by decoys and other countermeasures (Moore 2008). Research and development on missile defense systems is a complete waste of taxpayers' money and should be canceled immediately.

Given America's geographic isolation and borders with countries that pose no military threat and given the ineffectiveness of missile defense systems to protect the country's territory, the United States has little need for "self-defense" forces under Article 51 of the UN Charter. It does need measures to prevent terrorism, of course, but military forces are of little use for that purpose. The only remaining question is what forces it should retain to participate in UN collective security actions. This is a question that can and should be debated by experts, but however it is answered, collective security will legitimately require only a fraction of the military forces that the United States currently maintains. This is good news indeed, because the United States cannot continue to send over a hundred billion dollars abroad every year to maintain a far-flung empire and needs every bit of physical capital and human resources it can muster at home to make a rapid transition to a sustainable economy.

To be sure, demilitarization by the United States will involve many changes in the current system of international security. Global Action to Prevent War and Armed Conflict (2008) has assembled a set of policy ideas for a phased reduction of national armed forces worldwide and the simultaneous buildup of regional and global security arrangements. While American state capitalism is the single biggest obstacle to such a plan, a government for the people could be its single biggest champion. The United States can and should immediately shift its foreign policy planning framework from one predicated on an international system based on heavily armed states to one characterized by demilitarization along the lines envisioned by Global Action. Given the absence of conventional military threats to the country's homeland due to its geographic isolation, such a shift can be made unilaterally without in any way compromising the country's national security. This same geographically based security advantage, combined with its economic preeminence, also puts the United States in a unique position to proactively promote a new, demilitarized system of international security.

There are three policy strategies for accomplishing the needed downsizing of America's national security state: attrition, redeployment of personnel, and economic conversion of plant and facilities. Like any other organization, the national security state is a dynamic system that is continually hiring new recruits and civilian employees and purchasing new facilities and equipment as other personnel retire and equipment wears out or becomes obsolete. A policy of attrition consists of a hiring freeze and a moratorium on procurement of new military equipment and facilities. The policy can be waived in special cases but only on the condition that national security managers pay for the new hiring and procurement with equivalent cuts in other parts of the system.

Redeployment and economic conversion, the other downsizing strategies, are really only special cases of the previously mentioned strategy for total utilization of human resources and physical capital. Personnel no longer needed in the national security state should be retrained and redeployed in the civilian economy. Many troops and civilian employees learned transferable skills in the military and can work as machinery operators, mechanics, drivers, physical education teachers, or police officers. Many troops with knowledge of foreign languages and countries can be put to work on poverty reduction programs in those places, including the building of waterworks and other infrastructure. Many white-collar workers leaving the Pentagon or private sector defense contractors can continue in their previous occupations as accountants, secretaries, computer technicians, and researchers. Weapons engineers can be retrained as math and science teachers or as builders of the green energy and transportation infrastructures of the future.

Economic conversion involves finding alternative uses for military bases, weapons manufacturing facilities owned by defense contractors, and other physical structures not needed for human security. If this enormous transition were left to the free market, a massive amount of physical capital would be discarded or redeployed in a wasteful manner. But if the U.S. government can operate the Department of Defense—one of the largest planned economies on earth—why can it not redeploy and convert all these resources in support of ecological sustainability and civilian prosperity? As discussed above, such a transition should be undertaken in accordance with the principle of subsidiarity. Workers who manufacture weapons, for example, are far better positioned to find alternative uses of their plant and equipment than government officials in Washington (Melman 1989).

ENDING GLOBAL POVERTY AND POLITICAL VIOLENCE

The indivisibility of human security and its global dimensions are nowhere more apparent than in the issue of poverty, which affects rich countries in at least three ways—the transmission of infectious diseases, downward pressure on wages, and terrorism. First, human contact through travel—vastly accelerated by commercial aviation—spreads throughout the world epidemics that originate in unsanitary conditions in developing countries (Wolfe 2011). This was the case with AIDS, for example, which most likely originated in the Congo River valley (Pepin 2011). Similar spillover effects occur within countries, as when infectious diseases in the South Bronx and other poor neighborhoods triggered by municipal service cuts were spread by commuters to affluent suburbs and then nationwide (Wallace and Wallace 2001).

Second, global poverty exerts downward pressure on wages in rich countries through immigration, whether legal or illegal, which increases the supply of labor. In addition, the availability of cheaper labor abroad creates an incentive for capital flight, which deindustrializes advanced economies and reduces the demand for domestic labor. While capital flight began in the United States in the 1970s, the practice eventually made its way to Germany and Japan, whose capitalists have more recently joined the global race to the bottom.

Third, extreme inequality between countries and the resentment it produces create political conditions in poor countries conducive to terrorist movements. This inequality results primarily from a system of international trade that enables the rich countries to become richer by exporting manufactured goods to the poor countries and impedes the latter's efforts to develop their own manufacturing industries (Cobb and Diaz 2009; Diaz 2010; Reinert 2008; Stiglitz 2003, 2007). At the same time, capitalist advertising and consumer culture—transmitted through global media—heighten the awareness in poor countries of their poverty even as they undermine religious traditions and local cultures

(Sachs 2002). It is surely no accident that the 9/11 hijackers—who were religious fundamentalists—struck the World Trade Center, a potent symbol in developing countries of capitalist economic and cultural domination.

For all these reasons, anyone interested in advancing human security needs an understanding of what causes global poverty and how it can be eradicated.[13] According to neoliberal theory, a global economy with no national barriers to the movement of capital or goods was supposed to industrialize the developing countries. The International Monetary Fund, backed by the power of the United States, imposed such "liberalization" on much of the developing world beginning in the 1970s, and Western banks and economists promoted it to the former Soviet republics in the 1990s. These policies produced disappointing results at best in Latin America and Asia, actually increased poverty in sub-Saharan Africa, and created a decadelong economic catastrophe in the former Soviet republics before the latter recovered to the merely disappointing level (Stiglitz 2003).

Meanwhile, a number of Asian countries—most notably South Korea, Japan, China, and India—followed a diametrically different path and achieved dramatically better results (Reinert 2008; Stiglitz 2003). In this approach, which might be called the Asian development model, governments maintained formal and informal trade barriers to protect their own industries from American and European corporations. While neoliberal theory predicted that sheltering firms from the rigors of competition would reward incompetence, their corporations in fact thrived to the point of being able to produce high-quality goods at lower cost than their Western competitors. (China started on this path later than Japan and South Korea and is still working on the quality of its consumer goods.) As discussed in Chapter 2, their lower costs were initially based on cheaper labor, but the Asian development model also featured indigenous finance and capital accumulation, enabling Asian firms to catch up to and even exceed Western producers in capital investment in mechanization and automation.

In fact, contrary to neoliberal theory, Western countries that are rich today industrialized not through free trade but precisely through such government limitation of free trade (Reinert 2008; Stiglitz 2003). In the eighteenth century, for example, India was the world's leading producer of quality textiles. In order to develop its own textile industry, Britain first

---

13. In the analysis of global poverty that follows, I build on Cobb and Diaz (2009), Diaz (2010), Reinert (2008), and Stiglitz (2003, 2007).

had to ban the import of Indian products (Toussaint 2009). That policy gave British producers protected access to the British market, enabling them to stay in business long enough to learn to match the price and quality of Indian products. To be sure, it was industrial technology that eventually enabled British industry to compensate for India's lower labor costs. But that industrialization took time and could never have occurred without the import ban enacted by Parliament.

Once Britain surpassed India in textile manufacturing, the former no longer needed trade barriers to compete. It was only then that Britain preached free trade to the rest of the world, turning the tables on India and getting rich by exporting more than it imported. Similarly, the United States could not compete with British manufacturing except by imposing steep tariffs on British imports. By the twentieth century, American producers were surpassing their European rivals, and after World War II, the United States became the world's leading promoter of free trade.

At the present time, the developing countries of Latin America, Africa, and parts of Asia need tariffs on foreign imports in order industrialize and capital controls to protect their emerging financial sectors from the big multinational banks (Reinert 2008; Stiglitz 2003, 2007). But the United States, Europe, and Japan use the World Trade Organization and other instruments of political and economic power to oppose such measures. Further, even while preaching free trade, they hypocritically maintain trade barriers against agricultural exports from the developing countries, the latter's main source of foreign exchange revenue. Specifically, the advanced countries generously subsidize agribusiness, harming not only poor farmers in developing countries but also ordinary people in the advanced countries.[14]

A government for the people, recognizing the indivisibility and global dimensions of human security, will take the eradication of world poverty as one of its goals. This can be accomplished by donating as foreign aid about 5 percent of the money that the United States currently spends on its national security state. In order to be effective, such aid programs must be controlled by the recipients, who understand local needs far better than outsiders (Stiglitz 2007). In addition, and most important, the United States should eliminate subsidies to U.S. agribusiness and

---

14. As discussed in Appendix 5.1, agribusiness increases its profits by externalizing costs in a number of ways, including neglect of its workers' and customers' health needs, and by using unsustainable farming practices that boost present crop yields while imposing ecological costs on future generations.

promote an international trade regime that abolishes agricultural subsidies worldwide and permits developing countries to erect tariffs and capital controls, the only proven path to industrialization.[15]

As for ending political violence, it is not enough to eradicate global poverty, which interacts with noneconomic factors, such as the rage and desire for revenge rooted in individual and group trauma and humiliation (Beisel 2009; deMause 1982; Morrock 2010; Strozier et al. 2010). Al-Qaeda, for example, was formed largely in response to such events as the 1979 Soviet invasion of Afghanistan, the ongoing Israeli occupation of Palestine, and Saudi reliance on U.S. forces for protection from Iraq in 1990 (Dudek et al. 2006). When Saddam Hussein invaded Kuwait in that year, Osama Bin Laden approached Saudi leaders with an offer to lead an international jihad against the Iraqi dictator but was rebuffed (Dudek et al. 2006). Bin Laden and his followers denounced the presence of American troops in Muhammad's native land as an intolerable desecration of Islam, a message that resonated with many Muslims throughout the world and swelled the ranks of Al-Qaeda's supporters and recruits. Bin Laden then launched a plan to destroy the World Trade Center, making his first attempt less than three years later.

To be sure, al-Qaeda is essentially a fundamentalist cult (Strozier et al. 2010), which it would have been regardless of military actions by the Soviets, the United States, and Israel. But it was these actions that transformed what might have been at most a local criminal enterprise into an international terrorist movement. Consistent with this analysis, the second target of the 9/11 hijackers was the Pentagon, which represents nothing if not the arrogance of U.S. military power. All this underscores the need for a new kind of foreign policy based on nonviolent methods for resolving political conflicts. Military power is both ineffective in dealing with such conflicts and provocative of further violence (Johnson 2004). Consistent with this demilitarization of foreign policy, terrorist

---

15. Like many developing countries, the United States also needs to increase its exports in order to balance its trade accounts. In order for developing countries to industrialize using an export-driven model, highly industrialized European and Asian countries, which are currently net exporters, need to become net importers. This would occur naturally, other things being equal, in the kind of global trade regime discussed above, where agricultural subsidies are dismantled and developing countries erect tariffs on imported manufactures. The effect of these policies will be an eventual depreciation of the euro and the yen against the currencies of developing countries, which should be welcomed as an indication of increasing global equality. The United States, which has been the world's net importer of last resort for more than a quarter of a century, and China, which has been a net exporter during the same period, each need to achieve balanced overall trade accounts. This will require a depreciation of the dollar and an appreciation of the renminbi.

acts by nonstate actors must be framed as crimes and handled as such in national and international courts, not as acts of war against political groups that merit group responses.

These principles of demilitarization and the eradication of global poverty provide the framework for a foreign policy that can actually achieve human security, which—as discussed above—is necessarily universal, global, and indivisible. To be sure, none of this is possible under America's system of state capitalism, in which oil companies, defense contractors, and other corporate interests dominate foreign and defense policy on behalf of the rich. But the Occupy movement and its counterparts in other countries—such as the Arab Spring, UK Uncut, and the Spanish Indignants' movements—suggest that the era of state capitalism may be coming to an end (Global Teach-In 2012). Political forces are now in play that make an American government for the people conceivable and, with that, the kind of foreign policy outlined here.

BEYOND GOVERNMENT: HEALING INDIVIDUALS AND COMMUNITIES

The establishment of human security requires action by governments, and an American government for the people can exercise important world leadership toward that end. But there are limits to what any government can achieve inasmuch as human relationships are deformed by the traumas and narcissism of individuals and entrenched social pathologies, such as racism, sexism, and other forms of prejudice and group hatred (deMause 1982; Morrock 2010). Such problems cannot be completely resolved without the healing of individuals and communities, which requires the involvement of nongovernmental organizations, psychotherapists, anthropologists, religious groups, women's networks, and other forms of what political scientists call "civil society" (Civico 2010, 2012; Conaway and Sen 2005; Lederach 1995, 2005; Orme-Johnson et al 1988; Pintacuda and Civico 1993; Sachs 2002; Wolterstorff 2003).

Rabbi Jonathan Sachs (2002) eloquently expressed the need for such healing:

For centuries, Jews knew that they or their children risked being murdered simply because they were Jews. Those tears are written into the very fabric of Jewish memory, which is to say, Jewish identity. How can I let go of that pain when it is written into my very soul? And yet I must. For the sake of my children and theirs, not yet born. I cannot build their future on the hatreds of the past.... The duty I owe my ancestors who died because of their faith is to build a world in which people no longer die because of their faith. (190)

As builders of families and local communities, women often play a uniquely important role in promoting the kind of consciousness Sachs describes and the intergroup reconciliation that can prevent violence or heal the survivors of violent conflict. Yet women are all too often excluded from the governmental arenas in which security arrangements are decided. In 2000, the UN Security Council acknowledged this problem and called for concrete steps to rectify it (Conaway and Sen 2005). This should be an important consideration in America's new foreign policy.

Organized religion has been and continues to be marred by sexism, homophobia, and xenophobia. The traditional equation of women with childbearing drives a cumulative growth in population that is not sustainable and imperils the earth's ecology. Related to this is the notion that sex is inseparable from procreation, a religious basis for the rejection of homosexuality (Scanzoni and Mollenkott 1994). But not all who believe in God hold these views, and it is a mistake of many on the secular left to overlook the struggle between fundamentalists and progressives within each of the world's religions (Lerner 2006; West 1982). The group Opus Dei, for example, interprets Catholicism in a way that legitimizes its right-wing social and political agenda (Walsh 2004), while the Focolare Movement sees the same religious tradition as a call to interreligious dialogue and a global economy of sharing (Gallagher 1998). Rigorous historical scholarship vindicates the progressives, finding that Jesus called for the cancellation of debt (Yoder 1994), for example, and that Muhammad advanced the rights of women (Armstrong 2006; Aslan 2006).

Religion scholar Constance L. Benson (1999) encapsulates why these internal struggles over the authentic meaning of religious traditions matter for the rest of humanity:

> The far-reaching economic, social, and political changes needed to secure a humane future will require far-reaching transformations of consciousness and values. Religious renewal can help bring about the needed consciousness and values, or, in the absence of renewal, the religions of the world can remain part of the problem—continuing to legitimize wealth, patriarchy, and militarism. (215)

Any mass movement that hopes to achieve human security and sustainable global arrangements needs to be as inclusive as possible and welcome every group committed to these goals. Even rich individuals should be included, provided that they are socially responsible, like Warren Buffet. The success of a government for the people will depend on a civil society that celebrates diversity and fully utilizes the unique contributions of every person and group that wants to participate.

This chapter has outlined policy strategies and far-reaching institutional changes that can transform the capitalist state into a government for the people. But what about capitalism itself? Is that economic system the same as a market economy? What can a progressive mass movement do to create an economic system that serves the needs of ordinary people? To these questions I now turn.

APPENDIX 5.1: REFORMING AGRICULTURAL SUBSIDIES

Agricultural subsidies in the United States, which were originally intended to aid struggling family farmers, today mainly benefit big, highly profitable agriculture corporations and their shareholders. Proponents of these subsidies claim that they lower food prices for the American consumer, but to provide a net benefit, the savings would have to be greater than the direct cost of the subsidies to the taxpayer. Even if this were the case, the subsidies impose much greater—indeed unacceptable—indirect and long-term costs on poor farmers in the developing world, the American consumer, and future generations.

First, by making agribusiness more profitable, the subsidies keep more firms and capital producing food in the advanced countries than would otherwise be the case, increasing the global supply of food and reducing its price. Given that the subsidies come out of taxpayers' pockets, this brings little if any net benefit to consumers in the advanced countries, as noted previously, but has serious negative effects on poor countries by reducing the value of their exports and destroying many of their farmers' livelihoods. In the case of the United States and Mexico, this occurred with the North American Free Trade Agreement (NAFTA), which removed Mexican tariffs even while leaving U.S. subsidies in place. NAFTA had the predictable result of impoverishing millions of Mexicans, creating incentives for them to immigrate to the United States, illegally if necessary. Indeed, the Clinton administration expected the treaty to increase illegal immigration and instituted stronger border controls along with the agreement (Chomsky 2007). While the government acted to limit this flow of displaced Mexican farmers and its political fallout, agribusiness welcomed it since it would drive down the already low wages of farm-workers in the United States (Chomsky 1994).

Second, big agriculture is an integral part of an obsolete system that produces poor-quality food in a highly inefficient manner (Kenner 2008). Agribusiness firms produce for national and international markets, increasing both transportation costs and the time between harvesting and eating. The latter requires fruits and vegetables to be harvested before they are ripe and guarantees that they will not be fresh by the time they reach the consumer. The produce contains traces of pesticides, and the animal products contain growth hormones that contribute to obesity, by-products of stress resulting from horrendous animal-raising practices, antibiotics that destroy the human body's intestinal flora, and toxic disinfectants, such as formaldehyde. The system wastes a vast amount of energy and materials on transportation, storage, processing, and packaging. The cereal products and other highly processed food that come out of this system are typically depleted of nutrients and fiber while being laced with preservatives, dyes, and other chemicals.

Third, modern agribusiness is based on unsustainable farming practices, and subsidies create incentives to continue them. Big agriculture's fertilizer and pesticide-intensive, highly mechanized, single-crop farming (monoculture) disrupts local ecosystems, pollutes groundwater, degrades soil fertility, and contributes to soil erosion (Brown 2009). Profit-seeking corporations create these problems and then impose the costs on others, such as the workers, local residents, and consumers who get sick from agricultural chemicals and future generations who will inherit barren land.

Indeed, subsidies to agribusiness are high on the list of America's most dysfunctional policies, simultaneously harming indigent farmers in developing countries, perpetuating a food system that poorly serves existing consumers in advanced countries, and degrading ecosystems on which future generations depend. It is even more remarkable that the staunchest defenders of this corporate welfare are conservative Republicans who continually lecture the entire country about the evils of government handouts and out of control spending. But there is a method to the madness: these same politicians are bankrolled by the very agricultural corporations that profit from the subsidies (Center for Responsive Politics 2011).

A government for the people will immediately eliminate subsidies to agribusiness and use the revenues instead to subsidize small organic food producers serving local markets, consistent with the original purpose of federal farm subsidies. Such a policy would simultaneously benefit all the previously mentioned parties that are harmed by subsidies to big agriculture. One functioning model for sustainable production of healthy food is that of community supported agriculture, where urban consumer cooperatives contract annually with organic farms located near a city. There are dozens of such cooperatives in New York City served by farms in the Hudson Valley that grow a variety of fruits and vegetables (and in some cases meat and dairy products) and ship them fresh every week to a distribution point in the city. The produce for the week is divided equally among the cooperative's shareholders (Just Food 2011).

Consistent with this kind of system, Rynn (2010) suggests that a ring of land around every city should be devoted to producing most of its food supply using sustainable farming methods, thus greatly reducing storage and transportation costs and enabling households to consume produce fresh from the farm.[16] For an eye-opening introduction to modern agribusiness, see the documentary *Food, Inc.* (Kenner 2008).

---

16. In the transition period that will be required to institute such a system of land use, American consumers can substitute food imports from developing countries for much of the food currently being produced by agribusiness. The foreign exchange that developing countries earn from agricultural exports, if invested in their own manufacturing industries, can enable them to become mostly self-sufficient in manufacturing and thus no longer dependent on agricultural exports for foreign exchange.

Thus, Rynn's model of urban areas supported by local food production and manufacturing is a long-term, sustainable arrangement that can be replicated throughout the world, reducing economic globalization and its attendant transportation costs, long-term environmental costs, and adverse effects on local employment and capital accumulation. This would limit trade to goods and services for which urban areas have true comparative advantage, that is, as defined by Adam Smith and David Ricardo. By contrast with today's neoliberals, who abuse the concepts of the classical economists to legitimize the self-serving power of multinational corporations, Smith and Ricardo viewed trade as increasing overall efficiency only when it meets the economic needs of local and national communities (Korten 2001).

CHAPTER 6

Markets without Capitalism

INTRODUCTION

Capitalism gives the market economy a bad name. America and the world are sorely in need of a grand vision and coherent theory of life after capitalism and the role of markets in the economic systems of the future. Defining capitalism is a good place to begin. In my definition, it is an economic system with two essential characteristics. First, its basic unit is the firm that buys its factors of production in markets and sells its products in other markets. Second, the firm is owned by persons other than its workers, and the owners directly or indirectly[1] control it and appropriate economic surplus jointly produced by capital and labor. An enterprise is "capitalist" insofar as it possesses *both* these characteristics. By

---

1. The owners of a small business typically exert direct control over the enterprise, while the stockholders of a corporation exert indirect control through the intermediary of a board of directors and a chief executive officer (CEO). To be sure, individual stockholders generally have little or no control over individual corporations (Berle and Means 1991; Micklethwait and Wooldridge 2005). However, stockholders as a social class control all corporations in the more important sense of setting the profit expectations that CEOs must satisfy in order to remain in power. They do this by buying and selling stock in search of profits. If a corporation's profitability declines under a given CEO, stockholders will sell their stock in the company driving down its value. This makes the company vulnerable to a hostile takeover, threatening to unseat the CEO and overturn his policies. While a small capitalist entrepreneur exerts control more directly and has a more long term relationship with his or her business, their goal is generally the same as that of absentee stockholders—to make money. In the case of worker-owned and -controlled enterprises, by contrast, capital accumulation is a means to an end—maintaining the workers' livelihoods—not an end in itself.

comparison, a firm that possess only the first characteristic—buying and selling in markets—is not capitalist if it is owned and controlled by its workers.

The problem with capitalist firms, I would argue, is not their relationships with markets but rather their structures of ownership and control. Virtually all the evils of capitalism stem from the direction of enterprises by or on behalf of people whose primary or sole interest is making money off other people's labor. The ownership of firms by stockholders or bosses is why the rich get richer while the middle class and poor get poorer (Mandel 1982). It is why corporations abandon their workers in search of cheaper labor in a global race to the bottom (Melman 1983). It is why profit-seeking enterprises develop technologies that disregard the health and safety of their employees and customers and the very existence of ecosystems on which life as we know it depends (Klein 2011).[2]

Conversely, worker ownership and control of firms, whether complete or partial, can be expected to impact all these problems at a fundamental level. In this chapter, I discuss a two-pronged strategy for accomplishing this transition to a postcapitalist, market-based economic system. First, thousands of new enterprises fully owned and controlled by workers can be formed immediately by groups of workers acting locally, modeled on Spain's Mondragon cooperatives (Mondragon Cooperative Corporation 2011) and supported by a progressive mass movement.

Second, existing capitalist corporations can be transformed into hybrid enterprises that are jointly owned and controlled by their workers and outside investors, with some involvement of government. Like the first prong, this one can begin locally through worker buyouts of individual corporations financed by unions and other external sources of credit. However, the second prong is essentially a national political project for instituting partial worker ownership and control of all corporations. It would involve national policies, such as formation of worker equity in lieu

---

2. To be sure, some capitalist businesses are socially responsible, and a worker-owned business can in theory be irresponsible under certain conditions, for example, if the enterprise continues to manufacture an inherently destructive product, such as nuclear weapons, cigarettes, or carbon based fuels (in the context of global warming). In general, however, ethical considerations are extraneous to the culture of American capitalism and to the legally defined fiduciary responsibility of corporate boards. By contrast, a worker-owned and -controlled enterprise is under no pressure to satisfy arbitrary, externally imposed profit expectations; cannot be bought or sold in the interests of profit; and is governed democratically by stakeholders who have the most intimate possible relationship to the workplace, its surrounding community and natural environment, and the firm's suppliers, products, and customers. In such an ownership structure, the self-interest of the owners is generally aligned with the long-term needs of the enterprise itself and thus of other stakeholders and the local community and environment.

of the existing corporate income tax and the substitution of government representation on corporate boards in lieu of excessively cumbersome government regulation.

PRODUCER COOPERATIVES: THE MONDRAGON MODEL

One of the best-kept secrets of the twenty-first century is a highly successful organization of worker-owned and -controlled enterprises, the Mondragon Cooperative Corporation, which grew in a few decades from a small workshop to one of the largest manufacturers of appliances and industrial components in Europe.[3] Seymour Melman (2001, 2002), a pioneering American theorist of industrial democracy, identified Mondragon as a model for linking innovation, productivity, and economic democracy. Nembhard and Haynes (2002) believe that cooperative enterprises of this type hold great promise for African American urban redevelopment. The United Steel Workers and the city of Riverside are currently setting up Mondragon-affiliated producer cooperatives in California (Davidson 2009; Gigacz and Ting 2011). I view Mondragon as a viable model for working Americans who want to regain control of their livelihoods from a global capitalist economy that is eroding their wages and job security.

Producer cooperatives date back at least to the utopian socialist experiments of Robert Owen in the 1820s. Father Jose Maria Arizmendi, a pastor in Spain's Basque region, studied the successes and failures of these early cooperatives and the writings of both Karl Marx and Catholic social teaching. In 1943, responding to the poverty and unemployment in his community, Arizmendi started a small technical school administered on democratic principles that became Mondragon University and expanded over the years to meet the educational needs of producer cooperatives.

After the war, a number of his students designed a small kerosene stove and began a manufacturing operation that became the first Mondragon cooperative. The enterprise was successful, and they consulted their pastor for advice about how to expand and organize on a larger scale. Arizmendi had studied how workers previously lost control of their cooperatives when they raised capital from outside investors. He advised his students to form their own cooperative bank to raise the funds they

---

3. Information in this section is drawn from Davidson (2009), MacCleod (1997), Melman (2001, 2002), and Mondragon Cooperative Corporation (2011).

needed. They did, and the bank expanded alongside an increasing number of industrial cooperatives, providing interest-bearing accounts for the local community and capital for existing and new Mondragon enterprises. This three-part cooperative model—production, education, and finance—is one of the keys to Mondragon's success. Producers need the innovation provided by education and training to succeed in a global marketplace. To retain control and internal democracy, they also need worker ownership of capital.

The other major reason for Mondragon's success is its internal organizational structure. Individual cooperatives are limited to about 500 members to ensure meaningful direct democracy. Worker-owners each have one vote and elect their managing director (and the managing director of the entire corporation) by a majority vote. A co-op's key decisions are made by a governing board drawn from the workers themselves; the managing director participates in these meetings but has little influence over them and is expected to carry out their decisions.

Matters of compensation are decided democratically, and the highest-paid manager or expert earns on average no more than five times the compensation of the lowest-paid worker, compared to a more than 200 to 1 ratio of average CEO to worker pay in recent years in the United States (Mishel 2006). A worker-owner cannot sell her shares as long as she belongs to a Mondragon enterprise; rather, she sells them back to the co-op on leaving, at which point she collects capital gains and (if retiring) a pension. A person is first admitted to the co-op by agreement of the existing members, after working for a brief period as a nonmember, and once admitted cannot be laid off.

If a struggling co-op cannot support all its members during a given period of time, some are sent back to school for retraining or absorbed by other co-ops. Failure of Mondragon enterprises is extremely rare, with only four cases out of the 260 that have been created in 50 years, compared with an approximately 70 percent failure rate within 10 years for start-ups in the United States (Shane 2008). In the unlikely event that a Mondragon enterprise goes out of business, its workers are absorbed by other cooperatives.

Mondragon is a living refutation of the capitalist notion that workers will slack off without top-down management and the threat of job loss and that they are incapable of organizing production by themselves. With the leanest possible administrative hierarchies and with workplaces that are dynamic learning environments, its cooperatives exceed the levels of innovation and productivity of conventional firms. This accounts for their extraordinary success—more than $20 billion in annual sales today and enrollment of some 100,000 worker-owners in 260 enterprises spanning 40 countries (Mondragon Cooperative Corporation 2011). Mondragon is to economic democracy today what the United States was to political democracy in 1776, and Arizmendi is what Locke and Montesquieu were to the founding fathers. To renew itself and lead the world in the field of democracy once more, America needs to build on this pioneering Spanish model as it once built on English parliamentary traditions.

TRANSFORMING CAPITALIST CORPORATIONS[4]

While Mondragon provides a fully developed and tested model of worker ownership and control and can be implemented in the United States with little or no modification, there is no such obvious and ready-made solution to the problem of existing capitalist corporations. Employee stock ownership plans, for example, create worker equity in their corporations but divorce this ownership from control, which remains in the hands of external stockholders typically having a short-term profit agenda. Similarly, employee pension funds, which are diversified across many corporations, cannot give workers control over their own workplaces and livelihoods. The result is that a worker with equity in an employee stock ownership plan or pension fund can still be laid off by a profit-seeking corporation in favor of a cheaper worker abroad. The small amount of stock that the worker retains after termination, needless to say, is scant consolation for loss of their livelihood.

Nor is the converse—worker control divorced from ownership—any more viable in the long term. To be sure, workplace democracy typically increases productivity by eliminating unnecessary administrative overhead and tapping the creativity and intelligence of workers, consistent with the Mondragon model. But while such experiments may have greater-than-average long-term profit potential, top managers typically pull the plug on them when they enter periods of unprofitability and/or when rival, conventionally managed divisions outmaneuver the innovators in the corporation's internal politics. Such was the fate of the Saturn Corporation, a promising worker-controlled and largely autonomous enterprise created by General Motors in 1985 but terminated 20 years

---

4. This section was written in collaboration with Olivier Mathey, a financial professional with expertise in capital markets and corporate taxation. Dr. Mathey also wrote the discussion of technical issues raised by the proposal that appears in Appendix 6.1.

later. Similarly, Germany's system of codetermination, which gives workers partial control but not ownership, left workers vulnerable to capital flight.[5] Unless backed by substantial worker equity and representation on corporate boards, workplace democracy is insecure and usually temporary.

Going beyond the precedents just discussed, the kind of postcapitalist economic system we propose here combines worker ownership with control. Further, it involves two innovations at the level of national policy. First, substantial worker equity would be instituted in exchange for abolition of the corporate income tax.[6] To minimize political resistance to the new proposal, it could be enacted as an option that existing shareholders and top management could forgo or choose to adopt. If widespread loopholes are first eliminated from existing tax law, however, the proposed system would be more advantageous to existing owners and managers than the corporate income tax. Some would still be hell-bent on retaining the status quo, of course, but their position would become increasingly untenable as firms adopting worker ownership and control began to outperform them in the marketplace.

As with the Mondragon model, workers would not be permitted to sell their equity except back to the corporation on retirement. The worker equity part of this grand bargain would appeal to Democrats in Congress, while Republicans would like the tax elimination part, making bipartisan support feasible. Worker ownership and control, as with Mondragon, would increase the level of innovation and productivity of firms. When coupled with elimination of the corporate income tax, American corporations would be well positioned to compete in the global economy without resorting to low-wage labor.

The second national innovation is also a bipartisan grand bargain: government representation on corporate boards in exchange for simplification of onerous regulations. The Federal Reserve would purchase perhaps 10 percent of corporate stock and appoint a member of each corporation's board. Having access to all internal corporate information, the

---

5. Reflecting the country's long social democratic and labor traditions, German law prohibits capitalists from shutting down factories without agreement by workers. As neoliberalism and the American-led race to the bottom spread to Germany, however, capitalists circumvented these traditions by establishing new factories in lower-wage parts of Europe.

6. Based on existing corporate tax rates, that would mean issuing about 30 percent of a corporation's equity to the workers. A higher percentage of worker equity could be achieved with external financing by the Federal Reserve. As discussed in this chapter's appendix, new shares issued to workers would not dilute the value of existing equity, since the workers' shares would not be traded in the stock market.

government director would serve as watchdog for the public interest. He or she would be a salaried civil servant insulated from the forces of crony capitalism.[7] To be sure, wielding only one vote, the government director would prevail in board decisions only as part of a majority coalition of directors representing both labor and capital. But the government director would often hold the swing vote and, having access to the inner workings of the boardroom, would bring an unprecedented degree of transparency to corporate decision making.

This proposed arrangement may be a uniquely effective solution to America's problem of crony capitalism. The interlocking and incestuous nature of corporate boards and their monopoly of inside information enable directors to advance their own interests at the expense of legitimate stakeholders. CEOs carry out these corrupt agendas and receive obscenely lavish compensation packages in return. To be sure, they must also seek to satisfy the profit expectations of shareholders, but this balancing act means that CEOs serve two masters, diluting their commitment to stockholders' interests in violation of their fiduciary responsibilities. And if the system works so poorly even for the owners, where does that leave other stakeholders, including workers, customers, and a general public with an interest in ecological stability? The presence of worker and government representatives on corporate boards would be an antidote to such corruption.

The purpose of having a government representative on corporate boards is not to eliminate regulation but to advance the public interest in the halls of corporate power in ways that existing regulatory regimes cannot. The limitations of the latter stem from the adversarial or potentially adversarial relationship between the regulatory agencies and the companies they regulate. An agency makes rules on behalf of the public, and profit-seeking companies seek to circumvent the rules, requiring the agency to make more complicated rules, in a vicious circle.[8] Having a

---

7. Many will object to expanding the power of the Federal Reserve in this way. Alternatively, the public directors could be appointed by a public agency independent of the Fed, whose director could be elected by the people or appointed by the president. In my opinion, the question of who appoints the public directors is less important than the terms of their appointment. The revolving door between corporate and government office—a system of legalized corruption—should be shut by a rule that no person who was employed in private industry is eligible to serve as a publicly appointed director in that industry, and no person serving as a director can be privately employed later in the same industry. Under these rules, only individuals willing to forgo private gain in order to work for the public interest would agree to serve as publicly appointed directors.
8. Corporations generally prevail in this conflict by getting elected officials to appoint industry representatives to top positions in the agencies, part of what social scientists call "regulatory capture." But politics is an ongoing process, and corporate control of the agencies is never complete or secure, especially when elections change the party in power.

government representative on every corporate board would help break this vicious circle by promoting corporate policies that are informed by the public interest from the outset. The result should be a significant shrinkage of the red tape and paperwork generated by the current, more adversarial regulatory process.

In one sector of the U.S. economy—banking and finance—government representation on corporate boards can not only streamline but also virtually replace traditional regulation, such as the Dodd-Frank law. The intent of this law was to prevent the kind of excessively risky lending and derivative making that created the 2008–2009 financial crisis. But no set of general rules—however complex—can adequately accomplish this, especially in a sector being continually remade by innovation, much of it intended precisely to circumvent regulation. By contrast, the presence of a Federal Reserve employee in corporate boardrooms would enable government to continually monitor risk taking in a simple and effective manner. Further, the entire cohort of these government directors, meeting among themselves, would have a unique capacity to access systemic risk—precisely the kind of knowledge that government needs to prevent financial crises but that is not currently available to external regulators.

The reforms of corporate ownership and governance that we propose here are a uniquely American way of bringing the U.S. economy up to speed with institutional innovations that give some European and Asian firms competitive edges in the world economy, such as German co-determination and the kind of government-corporate partnerships developed in Japan, China, and elsewhere. Important details—such as the exact percentages of worker, government, and outside investor equity—remain to be worked out and will be determined through the political process. (For a discussion of technical issues raised by this proposal, see Appendix 6.1.) As discussed in Chapter 8, the progressive movement can exert pressure on Beltway and corporate elites by organizing an exodus of consumer and investor dollars from the capitalist economy into the emerging economy of Mondragon-type producer cooperatives as well as corporations that are bought out by their workers.

In summary, the progressive movement should be creative and politically pragmatic in promoting worker ownership and control. Its bottom line, however, is the need for at least substantial worker ownership and control, along with some minimal government stake and involvement in existing capitalist corporations. The goal is to fashion an economic system that preserves the advantages of free markets but that works for all Americans, not only for the rich. The present chapter has provided a conceptual framework and strategies for advancing this agenda. But more is involved in securing a sustainable, prosperous, and just future. I turn now to the question of how the United States can create a first-rate public education system for the twenty-first century.

APPENDIX 6.1: BEYOND CAPITALISM—THE NEW CORPORATE MODEL

By Olivier Mathey, PhD

Under the program described above for instituting worker ownership and control of corporations, U.S. C-corporations would be exempted from federal tax obligation in perpetuity provided they freely granted 35 percent of their total stock currently outstanding to the federal government, more specifically the Federal Reserve, together with the promise to grant 35 percent of all future stock issuance as well, to avoid diluting the government's interest while retaining the tax benefit. This arrangement should be looked on favorably by the market, as technically 35 percent of all profits ought to go to taxes, dubious foreign shelters such as the Double Irish and Dutch Sandwich notwithstanding. It is very apparent that, given the obvious fact that these structures only mean to avoid taxation and have no other business purposes, they are technically already illegal under IRS regulations, even if said provisions of the tax code are currently not specifically brought to bear thanks to the generosity of corporate sponsors vis-à-vis the Congress in what amounts to legal bribes. Similarly, withholding taxes on income earned by foreign corporations in the United States ought to be raised to 35 percent as well in order not to entice domestic companies to relocate overseas, as Tyco did a few years back, but these are minor technical details. All in all, freedom from taxation would unleash immense creative forces within corporations, hitherto focused on tax avoidance with all the appertaining personnel and time required, with the added benefit of much greater productivity, so that one might credibly argue that no revenue would be forfeited by the government in practical fact, in spite of the apparent loss of corporate income tax, as higher payroll taxes and dividend payments to the Fed would more than substitute for current corporate levies. A true free lunch indeed. Moreover, corporations in the program would be allowed to repatriate funds held overseas free of tax as well, which may in itself be the source of significant economic activity in the future within the United States The question of states corporate taxes could be dealt with simply, with each individual state within the Union piggybacking on the federal model, in exchange for a further [2] percent capital stake, whose proceeds would be dynamically apportioned by the Fed to the states, depending on the level of actual business conducted by a given corporate entity in a given state on a turnover basis in a given year.

Once in possession of 35 percent of the capital stock of a given C-corporation, the government would then issue four synthetic securities for each share it owns. The first component is the voting right, entitling its bearer to elect the board of directors and opine on corporate matters. The second, the dividend stub, would be the right to receive the dividend if any; the third, called prime, would entitle the bearer to the first [25] percent of the share's appreciation over the next [10] years, while the fourth security, the score, would receive all capital appreciation, if any, beyond [25] percent at the [10]-year mark. Actual upside participation thresholds would vary by industry. The government would then sell the first three securities (voting right, dividend stub, and prime) on 25 percent of the 35 percent stock it owns to longtime employees of the corporation making less than $[100,000] total compensation and in nonexecutive positions, in order to ensure that board cronyism could have no sway over or control on this important portion of the capital base. Such sale to longtime workers would be heavily subsidized to encourage widespread ownership and could be financed at 0 percent interest rate with the Federal Reserve with only a modicum down payment on a nonrecourse basis. Needless to say, said securities would not be freely negotiable but could only be surrendered back to the government, at then prevailing rates. To discourage churning, there would be a minimum [one]-year window between purchases and sales, and there would be concentration limits to make sure no individual or category of eligible workers benefit disproportionately from the program.

Dividends and capital gains paid to the employees under the program would be tax exempt as a further incentive, and it is certain that both the government with its 10 percent remaining voting rights and the newly empowered workers with their 25 percent voting rights would actively militate so that the dividends in question amount to a sizable, albeit sustainable, proportion of net take-home income in very short order if not from the start. One would think that remaining market shareholders would not mind a generalized policy of relatively high payouts across all corporations—far from it. Note that, after research and development, typical corporate cash outlays comprise shares buyback, acquisitions, and dividends, and the former two have a rather checkered history in practice. As CNBC's Jim Cramer has amply demonstrated, virtually all corporations buying back shares exhibit a marked tendency to carry out their purchases closer to market tops than bottoms, thus in effect impoverishing remaining shareholders. Acquisitions, on the other hand, while sometimes a propos as exemplified by Oracle, which grew into the software giant it is through a series of well-timed mergers, more often than not prove simply disastrous, on the line of the fabled AOL-Time Warner hookup. By contrast, no company has ever gone wrong paying a high while sustainable dividend, which also acts as a better protection of share value in times of severe market downturns, as again Jim Cramer has shown. "Sustainable" traditionally has corresponded to about half of after-tax profits and could therefore be safely enhanced in a corporate tax-free environment.

Before we go on exploring the advantages of such a system, let us consider the example of a company already paying high dividends, such as a utility. Let us hypothesize that there are 73 million shares outstanding, paying a yearly dividend of $1.20 each before conversion to tax-free status, and that the company employs 4,600 people. Conversion to tax-free status would then correspond to a new tally of 112.3 MM shares, the original 73 MM and another 39.3 MM, amounting to 35 percent of the new total, granted to the government in exchange for freedom from tax. Assuming no increase in dividend total outlays, each share would now pay $0.78 in dividend per annum. The government would sell primes, dividend, and voting rights on 28 MM shares of the 39.3 MM it owns, which is an average 6,100 certificates per worker on average, paying $4,760 in dividends annually. The purchase price in the case of a natural high yielder would be such that the shares yield at least [10] percent in tax-free dividend per annum, so therefore $47,600 in this instance, and could be financed over [10] years at a [0] percent interest rate after a means-tested down payment. Workers making less than $[20,000] a year would need no down payment, whereas workers closer to the $[100,000] limit would need to put down [20] percent of the purchase price, so that a low-paid worker would be able to finance his or her shares over [10] years from the tax-free dividend at no cost out of pocket while exercising voting rights and participating in the appreciation upside represented by the prime right away and thereby accumulating valuable assets for the long haul, such as retirement.

If the company pays no dividends, there would be a moratorium on loan repayment until the company in question does start paying out a dividend, when improved results warrant such an outlay, or at the Fed's and workers-owners' behest. The price and yield of the discounted shares would be fixed, depending on the growth potential of the industry a particular company is involved in. The payoff would have to be higher in low-growth sectors with poor capital improvement perspectives, such as electric utilities, and could be lower (i.e., shares would be less severely discounted) in high-tech, high-growth areas of the economy.

Note that the Fed's partial ownership essentially would entail automatic auditing of the companies on an annual basis and regulation mainly via suasion, as opposed to heavy, undiscriminating pieces of legal mumbo-jumbo, such as Sarbanes-Oxley or Dodd-Frank, well meaning but in consequential and burdensome in their implementations in an endless, wasteful, and ultimately futile game of cat and mouse between regulator and regulated. Fraud control would be much alleviated with the Fed and workers participating in all corporate decisions (which should make another Enron or WorldCom impossible), including executive compensation, which thereby could be brought down to earth: American CEOs are compensated at such superior levels as compared to their peers on an international level that there cannot be a market explanation for such disparity: cronyism and lack of democracy at the board level is the only possible answer.

Since the Fed would know all essential facts of every major corporations from within, it would now be possible to gauge and monitor systemic risk across all market participants on a real-time basis, as opposed to arm's-length and delayed, ex post, specific requests or subpoena from without, thereby alleviating if not eliminating the so-called too-big-to-fail risk, as the government instantly could implement its will through persuasion and democratic processes on every relevant board if it detected a worrisome global trend, such as, for instance, excessive leverage within the banking industry or concentration of particularly dubious assets, with the participation of the longtime workers block and socially minded possible allies, such as pension plans, quite a few of which being known as activists in their own rights, such as CalPERS. Lighter regulation in turn would make all companies more nimble, proactive, and faster in their decision making, therefore more profitable and responsive to changing market forces. In every poll of business leaders, excessive regulation is always mentioned as the greatest impediment to greater business activity and hiring.

Other advantages of the reform would include, pell-mell, pollution control since the Fed would represent the public on the polluters' boards and would see to it that the standards are strictly adhered to. Labor-management relationships would be greatly improved since in effect the Fed and workers together would almost control management, with the same natural allies as noted earlier, while retaining the crucial majority input of market participants on every board, thereby avoiding the well-known mishaps of state capitalism or "dirigisme." This should bring about greater worker participation and suggestions for research and development, a higher morale, and greater productivity and therefore higher profits and dividends ceteris paribus. Smooth labor-management relations and collective decision making are renowned to be at the core of the old Japanese Miracle, and for good reasons.

Moreover, under our proposal, the famous conflict between the short-term interest of most market shareholders versus the long-term interest of the company itself that is so detrimental to the unfettered capitalist setup would be resolved since both the Fed and the workers would be long-term oriented. No takeover leveraged buyout or merger could be carried out without the workers' consent, which points to greater stability, peace of mind, and democracy in boardrooms. The deleterious collusion between boards and managements so endemic in the traditional capitalist model would also disappear because of the emergence of a strong, equity-rich, prolabor bloc. Debt levels would be more easily controlled with the Fed at the source of the indebtedness as a board member rather than as an outside, after-the-fact macroscopic monitor, with the only tools of short-term interest rates and the money supply size. It should also be easier to get industry to work together on alternative energy programs and other projects that are vital to the nation but whose short-term profitability is uncertain and therefore unappealing to unreformed capitalists. The government would also save untold billions in weapons and other procurement programs since it would now have the inside story on true weapons development costs. Currently, defense contractors' after-tax margins are more than double average industry figures, 25 percent return compared to around 10 percent for industry as a whole.

An important remark is now in order. Our proposal smacks of the "wage-earners' funds" idea put forward by Meiner and Palme in Sweden in the early 1980s. The idea was to use part of a company's profit to buy shares of said company in the open market so that, in due time, these shares could be represented on the board of the company by the workers who, in a second phase, would be left with total control. But there are crucial differences. The "wage-earners' fund" idea is dangerous because it could entice a company to shun growth and instead make itself barely profitable to avoid such progressive takeover. Moreover, buying the shares in the open market could drive their prices to unrealistic levels, which would actually work out to the advantage of capitalist owners or speculators, not the workers. Lastly, the workers themselves would not personally have a say in management. Rather, some "Big Brother" fund substitutes for them, a situation akin to that of the many pension funds in the United States, effectively owned by the workers and controlling

40 percent of the equity outstanding but potentially acting very much like any other capitalist entity, independently of direct labor concern and consideration. This explains why the idea actually met with lukewarm approval among Swedish workers at the time and was actually shelved. Our blueprint calls for direct worker ownership and would actually spur growth, not inhibit it. Moreover, this feature also addresses the major criticism leveled at German-style comanagement (Mitbestimmung). Under German corporate law, a supervisory council (Aufsichtsrat) names and oversees the managerial board (Vorstand), and a 1952 law (BetrVG 1952, revised in 2004) provides that workers in companies with an established Betriebsrat, or works council (11 percent of German companies in practice), have a third of the seats on said Aufsichtsrat. But this disposition essentially allows the other two-thirds representing the shareholders to elect the Vorstand at will. Not good. To remedy this flaw in the case of large companies, a 1976 law calls for parity between workers and shareholders on the Aufsichtsrat, but its president (Vorsitzer) must be a shareholder, and he can cast a tie-breaking vote. Furthermore, management representatives on the Aufsichtsrat, although allied with shareholders, are considered representatives of the workers, further diluting the rank and file. Therefore, in practice, some workers do indeed get Vorstand representation, but it is at no expense and to no financial benefit to them, and because they are generally such a small minority of most managerial boards (Volkswagen being a notable exception), they do not value their board memberships much. It is just a gimmick, as argued long ago by Deppe et al. (1973).

As the proponents of Venezuelan Cogestión argue, this merely makes the workers complicit in their own exploitation. The same comment applies to French ESOPs [employee stock ownership plans] (decree of 1946 and law of 1967), which call for two worker representatives on the board (somewhat more for state-controlled companies) and shares in at most 5 percent of capital. Not so here: workers would ultimately control 25 percent of the shares on a leveraged basis meant to increase their return and free market interests another 65 percent, and the state retains 10 percent. Not only would workers be strong enough for blocking minority rights, but the permanent alliance of the state representative and the workers, together with natural allies such as pension plans, could essentially de facto "nationalize" the company, on a temporary basis at least, while maintaining a strong private sector involvement, unlike Venezuelan Cogestión, which essentially refers to shared management between the workers and the state, frequently after eminent domain expropriation of private sector interests. On that account, Cogestión is a variation on the tired theme of state capitalism that has failed around the world.

CHAPTER 7

Unleashing Minds and Brains

INTRODUCTION

In its Jeffersonian origins, the primary goal of public education in the United States was to equip citizens to participate in democratic governance. As voting rights were extended to poor whites, African Americans, and women, education played a central role in their empowerment. While continuing to pay lip service to this civic function of education, most Americans today view school primarily as the source of skills and credentials needed for individual, private success (Turner 2011). This development reflects the eclipse of democracy itself in the age of global capitalism.

In this mercenary and competitive environment, which America's ruling elites have played no small part in creating, standardized tests of individual performance on verbal and mathematical skills have become the dominant measures of educational success. School districts are increasingly firing teachers and awarding merit pay on the basis of such test scores, notwithstanding that some of the most capable and dedicated personnel in public education work in inner-city schools where low test scores reflect a surrounding culture of poverty.[1] Meanwhile, with education becoming a competition among individuals for test scores, schools

---

1. In New York City, where I live, the Department of Education in theory takes account of the socio-economic status and prior academic skill level of students in its evaluation of teachers. In practice, the schools it is closing because of low test scores—in most cases over the objections of the schools' stakeholders—are disproportionately located in poor, minority communities (Cramer 2011; Grassroots Education Movement 2011).

are increasingly unable to satisfy basic human needs for community and meaning, an indispensable requirement for overcoming gangs, drugs, and violence.

While the goals of education have narrowed in the age of global capitalism, the demands placed on teachers and schools have paradoxically never been more far reaching. Educators are required to deliver higher test scores while *simultaneously* picking up the pieces of a competitive social system that erodes family and local community. Such contradictory expectations, combined with insufficient resources, build failure into public education, creating a culture of blaming that prevents politicians, administrators, teachers, parents, and students from working productively and cooperatively to solve real problems (Comer et al. 1999; James et al. 2010).

As will be discussed in this chapter, the use of test scores to reward and punish educators, far from promoting the academic excellence school reformers claim to want, has very deleterious effects on instruction. Further, and most ironically, it corrupts the very data the reformers imagine to be so reliable. When teacher job loss and merit pay are determined by measurable academic outcomes, an epidemic of teaching to the test instead of the learning needs of children is inevitable. Test scores then go up, but that only means students are getting more testlike instruction, not that they are actually learning more (Koretz 2008; Ravitch 2011). When the federal government stigmatizes and punishes schools or states that do not produce better and better data, state education departments across the country dumb down tests in order to raise their scores, further corrupting the data (Koss 2009; Ravitch 2011).

Indeed, the entire school reform and "accountability" movement is pervaded by the simplistic and misguided notion that academic performance can be improved by collecting "hard data" on student outcomes and then using it to get rid of "bad teachers" and "failing schools" and to award merit pay and grants for "excellence." In reality, the neoliberal reformers who demand high-stakes data are imposing on public schools a corporate culture that has already failed miserably in the private sector (Compton and Weiner 2008; D'Agostino 2012c). That failure runs much deeper than the accounting scandals that brought down companies like Enron and World-Com. More fundamentally, it reflects capitalism's preoccupation with maximizing short-term profit, measured in the hard data of monetary units. Profits go up, but the data may have little to do with the production of wealth, reflecting instead a pervasive externalizing of costs and neglect of long-term investment (Melman 1983; D'Agostino 2012c).[2] Similarly, the gross domestic product goes up even while the quality of life goes down (Cobb, Halstead, and Rowe 1995).[3]

Nor can the inherent limitations of incentive schemes be rectified by creating better incentive schemes, a logical truth systematically ignored by school reformers. One notable example of this fallacy in action is value-added assessment, a method of statistical modeling that aims to disentangle the effects of class size, prior student performance, teacher effectiveness, and other variables on student test scores (D'Agostino 2012c).[4] Such systems—which have recently been adopted by Chicago, New York City, and Louisiana (Dillon 2010)—are intended to isolate and measure teacher effectiveness for purposes of rewarding and punishing teachers (Hanushek and Hoxby 2005b). But if incentives to teach to the test were corrupting education when teacher effectiveness was being poorly measured, improving the measurement will only corrupt it more. I am reminded of Inspector Clouseau's line in the *Pink Panther*, "It is because of my methods that I have so often failed where others have succeeded."

A similar school reform fiasco was devised by Secretary of Education Arne Duncan, a professional basketball player who "reformed" the Chicago school system before bringing his methods to Washington. Duncan's replacement for No Child Left Behind, a now discredited and defunct bipartisan school reform scheme based on state test scores, was a new system of rewards and punishments to be based on better

---

2. "Externalizing" means imposition of costs on parties other than the buyers and sellers of a product, such as workers injured in an unsafe workplace or future generations saddled with the ecological consequences of profitable but unsustainable technologies. The adverse consequences of preoccupation with corporate bottom lines and student test scores is explained by Campbell's Law, which holds that the use of quantitative indicators for high-stakes decision making corrupts both the data and the social process that the indicators are meant to monitor (Campbell 1976, cited in Koss 2009). Another example is the failure of the New York City Police Department to police itself, which occurs because the office in charge of investigating misconduct is under pressure to ignore it in order to produce good data for Mayor Bloomberg (Rashbaum, Goldstein, and Baker 2011). This flows inexorably from the management-by-numbers paradigm that Bloomberg brought to city hall from his successful career providing data to Wall Street traders (Purnick 2009).

3. Indeed, the country's supposedly good economic performance under Ronald Reagan reflected just such data inflation, driven by deregulation that permitted corporations to externalize more of their costs, increased military spending that produced no real wealth, and a stimulus from unsustainable tax cuts and budget deficits that would have to be paid for by future tax increases.

4. Proponents of value-added models include Eric Hanushek (Hanushek and Hoxby 2005a), an economist who also advocates the rewarding and punishing of teachers (Hanuskek and Hoxby 2005b) and questions the importance of class size in student learning (Rothstein and Mishel 2002). The latter issue is discussed later in this chapter.

assessments (Dillon 2011). To be sure, America needs better assessments, such as greater use of essay questions and reduced reliance on multiple-choice tests. But if states are required to show improvements on new and better high-stakes assessments in order to win federal grant money or waivers from impossible federal mandates, which is precisely Duncan's policy, they will certainly dumb down their new assessment rubrics, just as they previously dumbed down their multiple-choice tests. And if they are forced to adopt rigorous rubrics, those who evaluate student work will be pressured to apply the rubrics in a less-than-rigorous manner.

Similarly, if student scores on essays are going to have high-stakes consequences for schools and teachers, the latter will have incentives to teach to the rubric. Indeed, high school teachers in New York City have reported to me that their principals are pushing them to do just that for the English Language Arts Regents Exam, a state test. As a result, students are being trained to mine a work of literature for suitable material to be used on this test. In these schools, literature reading and essay writing are being taught as purely mechanical skills, even to the extent of making students memorize algorithms that are useful in satisfying various essay scoring criteria.

This has little in common with genuine education, which typically requires reflecting on a literary work on the author's terms and writing essays that express the student's own thoughts, activities that may or may not produce high scores on someone else's rubric. The latter may be even less relevant in the case of a highly creative and original essay.[5] Far from promoting such "out-of-the-box" thinking, high-stakes tests teach students to think *in* the box of the test maker's scoring criteria. By inculcating this pernicious habit of mind, high-stakes tests are creating a nation of "in-the-box" people who are incapable of independent and creative thought and thus are interchangeable with machines (Sacks 2001). Good teachers know all this. But Arne Duncan, Michael Bloomberg, and other neoliberal reformers—whatever their intentions—are driving such teachers out of the profession and tying the hands of those who remain (Ravitch 2010).

---

5. Indeed, it is the rubric that must be measured against such work, not the work against the rubric. This kind of critical perspective on rubrics does in fact prevail in schools and countries that use student assessment solely as a source of information for educators. In such settings, the discrepancy between an outstanding student essay and the mediocre evaluation it receives on a rubric opens an important conversation among teachers about what, exactly, they are trying to accomplish in the classroom. This leads to improvements in both the rubric and classroom instruction, just the opposite of the corruption of both measurement and instruction that occurs when rubrics are used as part of an incentive scheme.

Better assessments are necessary but not sufficient for unleashing the minds of America's youth. A fundamentally new paradigm is needed, one that does not empower businessmen, lawyers, politicians, and basketball players to determine what teachers do in classrooms, which is exactly what management-by-numbers systems do (see page 70, footnote 13). Genuine educational renewal demands that every teacher be treated as a professional whose sole job is to educate the student in front of her based on her best judgment about the student's learning needs, not to produce data to please power holders.

The only accountability that should matter is the kind that arises among stakeholders. For example, schools in which teachers observe one another's lessons in an entirely constructive spirit create a culture in which every teacher takes pride in their work—no teacher wants to be judged ineffective by colleagues—while putting the focus on improving instruction, not blaming anyone. Similarly, schools that elicit students' feedback on their educational experiences and in which parents are actively involved bring out the best in every teacher. Such stakeholder-driven accountability is part of a new school governance paradigm, which, along with adequate funding, is an essential requirement for unleashing the minds and brains of all stakeholders in America's schools.

COLLABORATIVE SCHOOL GOVERNANCE: PRACTICING WHAT WE PREACH

All parents know that the deepest and most enduring lessons children learn stem not from what they are told but from what they observe. A parent who smokes cigarettes and then lectures a son or daughter about the evils of smoking will send two messages. The first—about the parent's own lack of integrity—will be more powerful than the intended message, about the evils of smoking. Children are just as observant of adults in schools as they are at home.

If a school wants its students to be excited about learning, it must create an environment in which its teachers can be excited about learning, regarding both their subject matter and their pedagogy. Most of those who go into the teaching profession do so because they were excited about learning when *they* were in school and want to re-create that experience for the next generation. Instead of encountering a work environment where supervisors value and cultivate such unalienated learning, however, teachers are increasingly micromanaged or manipulated with rewards and punishments like laboratory rats, all in the name of "school reform" and "accountability." Far from promoting excitement, that kind of environment actively kills it. Schools of the future must discard this failed paradigm and commit to giving teachers considerable latitude as to what they teach, how they teach it, and how they assess student learning.

If we want students to learn to think for themselves, schools must be environments in which teachers who think for themselves are valued, not punished. In America today, however, schools are expected to whip children into shape to compete in a capitalist society, with success in this preparation measured by standardized test scores. As long as such notions of education prevail, schools will be little dictatorships that punish independent thought, creativity, and indeed intelligence itself.

In any dictatorship, even a benevolent one, directives flow down from the top, and the information flowing up is filtered by the leader's agenda, precluding genuine dialogue and collaboration. Rather than tapping the creativity and intelligence of the entire staff and student body, a school organized in this way is limited by an information and decision bottleneck in the principal's office. Under a malevolent dictator—a "principal from hell"—it is only a matter of time before the school fails. Such a principal may be removed before running "his" school completely into the ground but only after great damage is done to the lives of students and teachers, damage for which restitution is never offered (except in court settlements).

When an entire school system is taken over by a dictator, as New York City schools were in 2002, the potential for damage is incomparably greater. Mayor Michael Bloomberg hired corporate management guru and former General Electric CEO Jack Welch to train principals for his brave new world of school reform (Casey 2006; Hoffman 2005). Welch knew absolutely nothing about teaching or managing schools; his main occupational skill was making money for himself and his shareholders. Placing such a person in charge of training principals was in itself an extraordinary display of contempt for principals, teachers, and the work that goes on in schools.

The mayor and his corporate consultant viewed the source of the school system's problems to be the teachers' union and the "bad teachers" it protected. Thus, school reform in their minds consisted primarily of training principals to break the union and remove "low performers." A commitment to recognizing, valuing, and cultivating the creativity and intelligence of every staff member—the essence of being a collabora-tive principal—was now equated with being "soft" on "incompetence." Not content with the existing supply of principals from hell, Welch created a "Leadership Academy" to mass produce them. That is not what Bloomberg and Welch imagined they were doing, of course, but the road to hell is indeed paved with good intentions.

Welch indoctrinated prospective New York City principals with the management paradigm he had honed at GE—identify your highest and lowest performers, reward the former, and fire the latter (Casey 2006; Hoffman 2005). Even if this had worked in industry—which is not the case[6]—there was no reason to believe that it would be a good way to manage teachers, and it was indeed a disaster. I have written in more detail about Mayor Bloomberg's failed experiment to improve New York City public schools (D'Agostino 2009b). Suffice it to say here that this fiasco is a model of how *not* to create quality schools. If America wants every *student* to feel that they can succeed, it needs schools in which every *teacher* can succeed. This is not to say that schools—or any other organizations—should turn a blind eye to incompetence. The point is rather that cultivating fear of failure is a counterproductive way to motivate competence. Experiments by B. F. Skinner (1965) showed this to be so even in the case of laboratory rats, whose learning is impaired by stress when their mistakes are punished.

So what is a better alternative? There is no more powerful way of building competence in a teacher than having them coteach with a master teacher so that apprentice and master can observe one another's performance and the latter can model exemplary practices. Interacting with a more competent colleague whose role is entirely constructive provides exactly the right combination of challenge and support to promote optimal staff development. If a school or school district is serious about improving teacher quality, that is the way to do it. It is more expensive than other approaches, but this kind of mentoring is the most reliable path to excellence in the long run. It is hard to imagine how anyone who meets existing requirements for becoming a teacher and is motivated to enter the profession in the first place, when provided with this kind of quality training, could fail to become a satisfactory teacher.

The upshot of this analysis is that public schools should be controlled collaboratively by their stakeholders—principals, teachers, parents, and students—not power holders in city halls, state education departments, and the federal Department of Education. The proper role of politicians and school district officials is not to monitor test scores and dispense consequences from Mount Olympus but to provide the resources teachers

6. There is little evidence these methods worked at G.E., where Welch increased profits through predatory financial strategies that had nothing to do with producing wealth or the skillful management of people. These strategies included dodging environmental regulations, overbilling the Department of Defense, abandoning U.S. based manufacturing in favor of cheaper labor abroad, and abandoning manufacturing altogether in favor of acquiring lucrative financial service companies (O'Boyle 1998). It is a scathing commentary on American state capitalism that a person with such a resume was even considered, much less hired, to train school principals.

need to do their jobs. How well they do their jobs—the so-called accountability problem—is a matter best left to the stakeholders, including teachers themselves.

There is nothing outlandish about stakeholder-driven accountability, except to neoliberal elites who imagine that they are uniquely qualified to rule the world. In fact, universities have for centuries monitored and maintained the quality of their own work through a process of peer review, and the result has been an outpouring of knowledge in science and the humanities that has immeasurably enhanced human existence.[7] The apprenticeship system of labor unions, rooted in the medieval guilds, has a similarly long history of successful quality control by peers.

The kind of stakeholder governance I am advocating is already practiced in many public schools, both in the United States and abroad. The Coalition of Essential Schools (2011), with members throughout the United States, is a noteworthy example. Before the Bloomberg era, New York City hosted an entire district of small, collaboratively governed, "alternative" high schools that were highly successful at reducing dropout rates and preparing inner-city youth for college (Meier 2009; Hantzopoulos and Tyner-Mullings 2012).[8] I taught at one of these schools, whose success was celebrated in the film *Homeless to Harvard* (Levin 2003), and know their strengths and weaknesses from personal experience. Putting that experience to work, I helped design a small, innovative public school and drafted the planning documents (D'Agostino 2009a).

The school design I helped create featured a collaborative governance structure, including a strong union chapter, student council, parent association, and community partner.[9] With all these stakeholders feeling a sense of shared ownership of the school, the principal's role is that of

---

7. The only contribution of government and corporate elites, apart from the constructive one of providing resources, has been to corrupt knowledge by enlisting academics to legitimize the elites' own power. Noam Chomsky's voluminous political writings (Ward 2011), for example, expose the role of American political scientists in legitimizing state capitalism. Richard Lewontin (1991) made a similar critique of sociobiologists, and Constance L. Benson (1999) showed how seminal thinkers in modern Christian ethics legitimized the power structure of imperial Germany.
8. Some of these schools still exist but became an endangered species under Bloomberg's top-down management regime. Less bureaucratic and more responsive to the needs of individual students than their traditional counterparts, the alternative high schools have many of the qualities parents seek in charter schools. Unlike the latter, however, they operate under the same union contract and serve special needs students to at least the same extent (Meier 2009).
9. In New York City and elsewhere, small collaborative public schools frequently form partnerships with local institutions—such as universities, businesses, or community organizations—that support the work of the school in some way, such as providing tutoring or internships. This kind of partnering is one way that the Mondragon-type cooperatives discussed in the previous chapter can form mutually beneficial relationships with schools.

coordinator, not boss. Such a governing structure simultaneously makes the principal's job easier and empowers all the other stakeholders. Problems continually arise, of course, but the norm is to acknowledge them honestly and work collaboratively for creative solutions, not to single out individuals for blame and punishment. Those who are serious about improving public education should begin by studying innovative schools of this sort, which have a long record of success (Hantzopoulos and Tyner-Mullings 2012), not untested management-by-numbers schemes devised by businessmen and economists.

FISCAL EQUITY FOR PUBLIC SCHOOLS

Providing a quality education for every child in America will require an end to the shameful system of educational apartheid that adequately funds public schools in affluent suburbs while underfunding schools for the poor and lower middle class (Kozol 1991, 2005; Mayer 2011). To achieve educational parity, disadvantaged children need more resources, not fewer, than their more affluent peers (Adler 2010).[10] These funds should be spent in four areas: (1) building and maintenance of adequate facilities, (2) smaller class sizes, (3) improved teacher training, and (4) programs that are essential to optimal brain performance. To help ensure that public resources are actually used in these ways, all public schools, districts, and boards of education should be independently audited at regular intervals with a clear and understandable report made public after each audit.

A comparison of the facilities of America's affluent and poor school districts reveals a highly visible aspect of fiscal injustice. In Illinois, a three-to-one discrepancy in spending per student is reflected in the quality and level of maintenance of facilities (Black 2011). Many schools serving the poor lack adequate libraries, science laboratories, and/or facilities for athletics and the arts. Half of public school principals surveyed in New York City in 2008 reported overcrowding issues (Horowitz 2009), a statistic that is unthinkable in affluent suburban districts. Jonathan Kozol (2005) found similar neglect in dozens of schools

---

10. Eric Hanushek and other school reformers who say that resources do not matter will not have an iota of credibility until they advocate slashing the budgets of *their* children's schools and using that money to equalize spending for the children of the poor. After all, if resources do not matter, such equalization would not hurt anyone. It would be a cost-free way of generating sorely needed goodwill among the poor, who believe—however foolishly, as the reformers would have it—that large discrepancies in public school funding are an ugly and intolerable injustice.

he visited in various parts of the country. In the digital age, large discrepancies in the quality and availability of computing facilities, software, interactive whiteboards, and other instructional technologies are another troubling example of inequitable access to facilities. Correcting these injustices will require a massive investment in underfunded schools.

Numerous peer-reviewed articles, government reports, and other studies have established the importance of small class sizes for a quality education (Class Size Matters 2011). One of the leading dissenters from this literature is neoliberal economist Eric Hanushek, who is employed by the Hoover Institution, a right-wing think tank bankrolled by big corporations. Hanushek has testified repeatedly as an expert witness against school districts and other plaintiffs seeking to rectify inequitable public school funding through the courts (Adler 2010). He has produced a number of clever arguments why class size does not matter that have been discredited by experts (Krueger and Whitmore 2001; Mishel and Rothstein 2002). As every stakeholder in education knows, dismissing class size as unimportant is simply absurd (see Chapter 3, footnote 10). Ruling against one of Hanushek's clients, a judge opined, "Only a fool would find that money does not matter in education" (Adler 2010). And yet a man with a PhD in economics cannot be such a fool. Rather, Hanushek's pseudo-scientific theories are a thinly veiled legitimation of inequality and a vicious attack on the poor.[11]

In a recent survey of elementary school teachers, only 25 percent of those who serve the poor had class sizes of eighteen or fewer, compared with 62 percent of those who serve middle-class or affluent students (Adler 2010). As noted in Chapter 3, poor students are academically disadvantaged in a number of ways and are therefore in greater need of individual attention than affluent students. To rectify this discrepancy, all general education elementary school class sizes in poor districts should be eighteen or fewer, which will require an increase in funding to pay for expanded teaching staffs. In order to attract qualified teachers to work in poor neighborhoods with academically needy children, especially in shortage areas such as mathematics, science, and English as a second language, equitable compensation for all teachers is essential. This will require additional funding to bring the salaries of teachers in many poor districts up to the level of those in affluent districts.

---

11. Indeed, this is just another legitimation of wealth and power of the sort exposed by Chomsky, Lewontin, and Benson mentioned previously (footnote 7).

In addition to facilities and class sizes, the third area requiring increased funding is teacher training. It is common in the United States for new teachers to be given undesirable and difficult teaching assignments that would tax even experienced teachers while being required to devote extra time to staff development programs that often do not address the kind of problems they encounter in the classroom. The inevitable result is a high rate of burnout and dropout from the profession among new teachers. The kind of mentoring system discussed in the previous section can help solve these problems and is effective where it is already practiced. It should be the norm in school systems throughout the country. The additional cost of paying mentors is a necessary investment in upgrading the effectiveness of teachers. This is especially important in schools that serve the poor, which face special challenges.

The fourth area requiring increased funding encompasses programs necessary for optimal brain functioning, which are typically neglected in schools that serve the poor. While improvements in school governance, facilities, class size, and teacher training shape the macrocosm in which learning occurs, it is also necessary to attend to the microcosm—the human brain—which is the basis of all learning. The three most important factors at this level are physical activity, nutrition, and rest.[12]

Athletic activity develops brain fitness and mind-body integration, while the visual and performing arts develop right-brain and sensorimotor skills as well as creativity and aesthetic appreciation. These disciplines should be valued at least as highly as mathematics, language arts, and other traditional left-brain subjects. It is the common experience of schools with strong programs in athletics and the arts that many students who struggle with the academic curricula excel in these bodily-kinesthetic curricula and vice versa. Every school should be committed to educating the whole person, which means providing every student ample opportunities to excel at what they do best while challenging and supporting them to develop aptitudes that do not come easily to them. The rich and upper middle class send their children to well-funded private and suburban public schools that generally provide such an education. It is the birthright of every child regardless of class.

The second factor on which brain performance depends is nutrition. Reflecting an increased awareness of its importance, many schools are

---

12. This assumes that fresh air, clean water, and an environment free of toxins and other health hazards exists in every school, which is unfortunately not the case in many poor districts (Kozol 1991, 2005). Such conditions are an intolerable scandal in a country as rich as the United States, and rectifying them is an urgent moral imperative.

revolutionizing the offerings of their vending machines and cafeteria menus (New York Coalition for Healthy School Food 2011). Highly processed foods that are low in nutrients and fiber while containing refined carbohydrates, trans fats, and chemical additives are a menace not only to health in general but to the brain in particular. Also important but less widely known, the typical modern diet—based largely on grains and the meat and dairy products of grain-fed animals—contains an excessive amount of omega-6 fatty acids relative to omega-3 fatty acids (Simopoulos and Robinson 1999). The latter are derived primarily from green plants, the meat and dairy products of pasture-fed animals, and fish.[13] There is a large body of peer-reviewed research on the importance of omega-3 fatty acids for optimal brain function and the consequences of omega-3 deficiencies including depression, attention deficit disorders, and hyperactivity (Simopoulos and Robinson 1999).

Ensuring that every citizen has access to a quality diet informed by nutritional science should be one of the highest priorities of every government. That will require the kind of transformation of America's agricultural and food system discussed in Chapter 5 (Appendix 5.1). Short of this, every effort must be made to provide healthy food for the nation's schoolchildren. Here again, money is a decisive factor; affluent children have access to healthy food to a much greater extent than poor children, one of the many shameful facts associated with child poverty in America. The diet provided in vending machines and cafeterias can help rectify this imbalance, and adequate funding to that end must be made available in urban school systems.

Finally, proper rest is an essential prerequisite of optimal brain function and thus of teacher and student performance. Sleep disorders are common in the United States and deprive many students of the energy and alertness needed to perform well in school. To be sure, the amount of sleep students get at night is beyond the control of educators. Some innovative schools, however, have set aside time in their schedules for the group practice of meditation, which provides deeper rest than sleep, combined with a higher level of alertness than occurs during normal

_____

13. Humans are well adapted to a high omega-3 diet because we evolved over a period of several million years eating primarily the meat of animals that lived on green plants (or algae) while shifting to an omega-6 diet based on agriculture only very recently. A fatty acid–balanced vegetarian diet would contain walnuts, flaxseed oil, and canola oil—concentrated sources of omega-3—as well as non–omega-6 carbohydrates such as potatoes and yams, thus reducing reliance on grains. Artemis Simopolous, author of numerous peer-reviewed articles on the health effects of omega-3 fatty acids, traces a range of health disorders to the grain-based diet (Simopoulos and Robinson 1999).

waking activity (David Lynch Foundation 2011). The success of these programs is consistent with peer-reviewed research showing that meditation reduces insomnia and the effects of stress while improving academic performance and general well-being.[14]

PUBLIC SCHOOLS AND THE MIDDLE CLASS REVOLUTION

This chapter has outlined what it will take to fully unleash the minds and brains of America's youth and other school stakeholders. It will mean replacing standardized-test-based incentive schemes with school-based accountability and instituting collaborative school governance that involves all stakeholders. In addition, it will mean providing for every child the kind of education that is currently offered only in well-funded private and public schools. Such an education requires properly maintained facilities, including well-equipped classrooms, libraries, laboratories, art rooms, and athletic facilities. It requires small class sizes, time and resources for collaborative teacher training and professional development, and equitable pay for teachers. Finally, a quality education includes first-rate programs in physical education and the arts, healthy food, and innovative health and wellness programs of proven effectiveness.

Jonathan Kozol (1991, 2005) poses the question: What kind of society tolerates such a scandalous discrepancy in school funding that children of the rich and upper middle class receive all or many of these things while children of the poor receive few if any? And why is this question itself not on the country's political agenda? On the rare occasions that rich and powerful people are confronted with such questions, they typically respond that it will do no good to "throw money" at the problems of America's public schools (Adler 2010). But these same elites would not even *consider* sending their own children to schools as badly funded as those that serve the poor. The progressive movement should relentlessly expose the cynicism and hypocrisy of this position, which pervades the neoliberal school reform movement.

---

14. The most extensive body of peer-reviewed research on this subject has been conducted on the Transcendental Meditation (TM) technique taught by Maharishi Mahesh Yogi. The deep rest and heightened alertness experienced during TM has been measured in terms of oxygen consumption—an index of metabolic activity—and EEG (brain wave) patterns. Statistical studies have been conducted comparing practitioners of TM with non-TM control groups on a wide range of health and wellness indicators. A bibliography of peer-reviewed research appears on the TM Web site (Maharishi Foundation USA 2011).

But there is more at issue here than cynicism and hypocrisy; the rich and powerful also have objective economic reasons for not wanting to talk about money in connection with public education. Providing a first-rate education to every child in America would require a revolution in the country's fiscal priorities, which currently serve the purposes of these same elites. It would mean diverting hundreds of billions of dollars every year from military programs, prisons, and tax breaks for corporations and the rich into all the unmet needs described in this chapter, which are the needs of the poor and lower middle class. Rather than acquiesce in such a revolution, the rich and powerful use test scores as a stick to beat inner-city teachers, making scapegoats of the middle-class workers who struggle day after day to salvage human lives from the wreckage of American state capitalism.

The upshot of this analysis is that the middle class itself must lead the revolution against plutocracy and state capitalism, joined by the minority of the rich and majority of the poor who will support such far-reaching change. There are a number of synergistic political strategies through which the progressive movement can accomplish this, and I discuss these in the next chapter. Suffice it to say here that the schools themselves are part of the solution whenever they become places where political transformation occurs (Anyon 2005; Teachers Unite 2011). This has nothing to do with "politicizing" schools in the sense of indoctrinating children with right- or left-wing ideology. Rather, it means reinventing the original Jeffersonian concept of school as preparation for citizenship in a democracy. That involves talking about how power is organized in America and how it should be organized. Liberal and conservative teachers will give opposing answers to such questions. Students need to hear both sides of this debate, form their own opinions, and learn to present their ideas—backed by evidence—orally and in writing.

Nor can such lessons be confined to the classroom. It is not enough to study the Constitution and read in textbooks how American democracy supposedly works. Schools need to become places where students *experience* democracy. That means asking why their school does not have solar panels on the roof and agitating to get them installed. It means social studies classes in which students go out into the community and investigate injustices they find there. It means science classes in which students take water samples from the local river or aquifer and measure pollution levels. It means English classes in which students write informed letters to politicians and businessmen about climate change, poverty, and water pollution; propose policy solutions; and ask the power holders what they are going to do to on behalf of justice and saving the planet. It means reading their replies and being able to evaluate them. This is what democracy looks like.

None of this will be on the standardized tests, and teachers who are forced to maximize test scores will have little time for any of it. Liberating schools from the tyranny of test preparation is part of what is needed to liberate America from state capitalism. To be sure, students also need to know about the French Revolution, what goes on in cells, and how to solve equations. What else they need to know is currently under discussion by state education departments in the United States that are collaborating on the development of common core curriculum and learning standards (Hansel and Durban 2010). This is a positive development for a number of reasons and will bring the United States up to speed with advanced industrial democracies in the rest of the world (Darling-Hammond 2010).[15] But assessments of student learning in relation to such standards should be for the use of educators in improving instruction, not for the use of power holders in rewarding and punishing educators.

The status quo in American public education reflects the power relationships and fiscal priorities of state capitalism. Authentic educational renewal will therefore require a transformation of that system. Students, teachers, and schools can and should be protagonists in that transformation (Anyon 2005; Teachers Unite 2011) but are currently impeded by the tyranny of test preparation and authoritarian school governance. The progressive movement can strike a blow against that tyranny by supporting teachers in their struggle for professional autonomy against the school reform juggernaut. In so doing, it will unleash the people who can unleash the minds and brains of America's youth. What else can the progressive movement do to achieve the policy and institutional reforms outlined in this book? To that crucially important question I now turn.

---

15. The standards being developed are specific enough to guide the creation of textbooks and enable schools of education to provide teachers with knowledge they can actually use in their classrooms. On the other hand, they are general enough to give teachers latitude about what and how they teach. There is some debate about how much instructional time should devoted to the core curriculum, with estimates ranging from two-thirds to 85 percent. I favor two-thirds, which allows ample time for student-chosen electives and the kind of real-world projects and inquiries discussed previously.

CHAPTER 8

Renewing Democracy

INTRODUCTION

Democracy is more than elections. The Soviet Union held elections, but there was only one party to vote for, and it also controlled the media. Using different and more subtle methods, America's capitalist elite today monopolizes power just as surely as the communist leaders before them. Instead of banning opposition parties, the rich and corporate CEOs subvert the electoral system itself so that they get what they want regardless of which party is elected. Aided and abetted by the Supreme Court, they perpetuate a system in which candidates and parties depend on privately purchased television advertisements and therefore on contributions from corporations and rich individuals to pay for the ads.[1] Ordinary people can also make campaign contributions, of course, but no one can compete with the rich when it comes to bankrolling politicians, political organizations, and think tanks. Raymond Smith (2010) has cataloged many other undemocratic features of America's political system, such as the Electoral College, winner-take-all congressional elections, and a Senate that disproportionately represents conservative rural voters.

Similarly, on freedom of the press, there is much less than meets the eye. Newspapers, general circulation magazines, and broadcast television are heavily dependent on big corporate advertisers and shape their content accordingly, virtually ruling out sustained and far-reaching criticism

---

1. In its 2010 Citizens United decision, the Supreme Court interpreted the First Amendment's right of free speech to encompass unlimited political spending by corporations and other special interests (Common Cause 2011b).

of the corporate elite (Bagdikian 2004). Most media enterprises of all kinds are themselves subsidiaries of a few giant corporations like Disney, Time Warner, and Rupert Murdoch's News Corporation, with CEOs controlling hiring from the top. This exerts a conservative bias on media content that trumps the liberal bias of professional journalists (Bagdikian 2004), as bosses generally trump their subordinates.[2]

Journalists who have to compete for access to "news" lose out if they are too critical of the power holders who make the news, rendering the mass media largely a conduit of corporate and government propaganda (Herman and Chomsky 2002) . Finally, some of the most important decisions of all are made in Pentagon offices and corporate boardrooms behind a veil of secrecy that "freedom of the press" cannot penetrate. While there is some legitimate need for confidentiality, control of information by powerful people breeds abuse of power.[3] Based on past abuses, like the multiyear, systematic deception of Congress and the American public about the course of the Vietnam War (Ellsberg 2003), the public would be well advised to assume the worst.

The upshot of this analysis is that America's political-economic system is democratic in its outward forms—contested elections and freedom of the press from overt control by the state—but effectively disenfranchises the 99 percent, as the Occupy movement has aptly labeled the combined middle and lower classes. Given this plutocracy, how can progressive movements leverage the people power of mass protests into far-reaching institutional and policy change? I propose four strategies for accomplishing this: (1) transformation of electoral politics, (2) internal education, (3) mobilization to support and build street protests, and (4) linkages with unions and worker ownership and control initiatives. Every individual who wants to contribute to progressive change brings a unique mix of personal gifts and resources, prior relationships, and affiliations to this menu of strategic areas and can choose accordingly how to connect with and contribute to the movement.

I am a scholar, for example, and spend most of my time reading, thinking, writing, and teaching. Since these are the things I do best and am

---

2. This top-down control of media content becomes apparent whenever journalists seriously challenge corporate power. For example, CBS censored a *60 Minutes* exposé of the cigarette industry featuring whistle-blower Jeffrey Wigand, an incident dramatized in the film *The Insider* (Mann 1999). Conservative complaints that the media are against them are valid only in the realm of some cultural and social issues.

3. As discussed on page 135, the abuses of corporate boardroom secrecy can be greatly reduced, without violating legitimate confidentiality needs, by having a public official on every corporate board.

most passionate about, internal education is the strategic area where I can make the best contribution. I recognize that internal education will not accomplish anything unless it is combined with electoral action, mass mobilization, and worker initiatives. While internal education is lame without these other activities, however, the latter are blind if undertaken by confused and uniformed people, who therefore need education. In this chapter, I aim to explain why each of these four strategic areas is necessary to get from a mass movement to a government for the people and postcapitalist economic system.

TRANSFORMING THE POLITICAL SYSTEM

Notwithstanding the stranglehold of corporations and the rich on electoral politics, some elections do make a difference. Since presidents appoint the executive branch officials who make public policy as well as the Supreme Court justices and federal judges who interpret the law, it matters who is sitting in the White House. Also, when unusually courageous local, state, or national elected officials take on corporate interests, progressives must rally to their side and be sure they get reelected. A popular mass movement should not abandon electoral and Washington Beltway politics but needs to be very selective in its involvements.

Much more of the movement's scarce time and resources should be spent promoting fundamental institutional and policy reforms—worker ownership and control of corporations, downsizing of the national security state, and job-creating public investment in a green infrastructure and urban public schools. Such fundamental reforms, discussed in the previous three chapters, should be the central demands of any progressive mass movement aiming to create a sustainable, peaceful and just future. The movement should frame this agenda using the discourse of government responsibility, human security, and a green New Deal, concepts with broad appeal across most of the political spectrum. Movement activists can create and disseminate a voter guide with report cards on these priorities for all candidates, and target electoral action to those who can significantly advance or impede the progressive agenda.

Without this kind of focus on and clarity about goals, street protests will have little impact on the quotidian realm of public policies, laws, and institutions. The policy agenda outlined in this book can actually create the kind of future protesters want, providing benchmarks of real social progress. Indeed, it identifies the objective results sufficient for protestors to declare victory and return to their normal routines in a world transformed by their actions. I am not suggesting, of course, that the movement should exclude every other policy issue, but a core agenda is needed that possesses two characteristics. First, it must be coherently designed to actually produce the results everyone wants, results that are encompassed in the concept of "human security." Second, it must appeal to and energize a large majority. The agenda I am proposing meets both of these criteria. It can be the movement's concrete alternative both to right-wing populism and the institutionalized conservatism of the state capitalist elite.

Assuming broad consensus on the policy agenda I have indicated, systemic political change will be needed to achieve it. First, electoral system reform is needed to break the power of money over American politics. The Fair Elections Now Act sponsored by Senator Dick Durban, for example, would use public matching funds to level the playing field between big and small campaign donors (Common Cause 2011a). Another important reform in this area is the DISCLOSE Act, which was passed by the House in 2010 but repeatedly blocked by a Republican-led filibuster. This legislation would require the names of big donors to be disclosed on campaign ads and prohibit companies with conflicts of interest or significant foreign ownership from spending any money to influence federal elections (Common Cause 2011a).

Second, enacting the movement's policy agenda into law will require constitutional change. For example, Common Cause is promoting a constitutional amendment that would overturn the Citizens United decision (Common Cause 2011b), reestablishing limits on corporate political contributions.

Domination of the electoral system, however, is by no means the only form of power that the rich and big corporations use to suppress American democracy. Indeed, the country's political system is undemocratic in so many ways (Smith 2010) that piecemeal legislation and constitutional amendments are not a feasible path to the kind of robust democracy the country needs. The root of the problem is that the growth of corporate power and the unprecedented concentration of wealth associated with it have outstripped America's eighteenth-century constitutional arrangements, which were created under entirely different circumstances. In addition, television and information technologies have created new possibilities for direct democracy that Madison and Hamilton could never have imagined. In fact, the founders actually considered this alternative to representative democracy and rejected it not on principle but only because it was not feasible under existing conditions (Hamilton, Madison, and Jay 2011).

If not by constitutional amendments, then, how can such fundamental change be effected at the national level? For conservatives, most of whom consider the 1787 constitution to be divinely inspired, even the question is scandalous. Ironically, however, this very document could never have been enacted by conservatives; the founders were in reality revolutionaries.[4] At the time, they lived under the 1777 Articles of Confederation, a constitution containing provisions for amendment just as the one in force today. Boldly discarding these provisions,[5] they appealed directly to the principle of popular sovereignty, the unique authority of the people to make or unmake constitutions. If the founding fathers could mobilize popular sovereignty in this way in 1787, Americans can do so again today.

The right of revolution cannot be granted or withheld by any constitution, person, or group; it is inherent in the people as a whole and *unalienable*, arising as a corollary of the unalienable rights to life, liberty, and the pursuit of happiness, according to the Declaration of Independence.[6] The 1787 constitution was enacted in the name of the people, and it is the people who retain the unique sovereign authority to set it aside and enact a better one in its place. It does not matter how much conservatives worship the Constitution; they do not have the authority to grant or take away the right of revolution. It does not matter what the Supreme Court says; that institution is a creature of the Constitution, which itself exists only at the pleasure of the people and for as long as they consider it legitimate. It does not even matter what procedures for amendment are written in Article V, since that, too was enacted in the name of the people, who retain the unique sovereign authority to alter or abolish it.

How, then, would such revolutionary change occur? First, while the people have the authority to set aside or abolish the Constitution, it is neither necessary nor prudent to actually do so. Instead, I support an exercise of national direct democracy that would put the policy and institutional reform agenda in this book to a vote of all eligible citizens in a

---

4. By "revolutionary," I mean that the founders did not idealize the past and were willing to break from it. The character of their innovation is a separate question. Many historians view the 1787 constitution as a subversion by self-interested elites of the more robust democracy that existed after the revolution (Beard 2011; Zinn 2003). Whatever the de facto character of the new constitution, however, its legitimacy was firmly rooted in the norm of popular sovereignty, which remains the gold standard for revolutionary political change today.

5. Article XIII of the Articles of Confederation required amendments to be approved by *every state legislature*. The Constitutional Convention of 1787 discarded this provision, deciding that agreement by nine states would be sufficient and that state ratification conventions, rather than the legislatures, would decide on behalf of the states.

6. Jefferson wrote, "Whenever any Form of Government becomes destructive of these ends, it is the Right of the People to alter or to abolish it" (Preamble to the Declaration of Independence).

national referendum.[7] A coherent and well-crafted bill, enacted into law by the people directly, would take its place alongside existing law and legislation, and would be implemented by the executive branch and adjudicated by the courts just like any law enacted by Congress. While the Supreme Court could rule on the act, it would not have the last word since the Court is a creature of the Constitution and is subject to the sovereign people, who are the creator of the Constitution.

The only remaining question is the size of the vote needed to enact a national referendum of this sort. There are no preexisting rules. When the founding fathers enacted an entirely new constitution in 1787, they simply made up the procedures they needed, setting the threshold of approval high enough to ensure that the new system would have sufficient legitimacy to succeed (approval by nine of the 13 states). I believe that a supermajority vote of 60 to 75 percent of registered voters, combined with an outpouring of support in the streets and on the Internet, would be sufficient. If millions of Pakistanis, Tunisians, and Egyptians taking to the streets were able to overthrow their dictatorial governments, mass protests by Americans demanding well-defined policy and institutional reforms supported by a supermajority of citizens could force the hand of the Beltway and corporate elites. Taken as a whole, these reforms— demilitarization, worker ownership and control of enterprises, and a far-reaching program of tax reform and public investment—would go a long way towards replacing state capitalism with a just and sustainable political-economic system and restoring democracy in America.

BUILDING THE PROGRESSIVE MOVEMENT

The kind of political agenda outlined in this book and the mass protests that began gaining traction in America in 2011 are two legs of the four-legged stool I am calling the "progressive movement." Without a coherent political agenda, mass protests have limited effect on institutions and policies, and without masses of people in the streets, political agendas are co-opted and swallowed up by the state capitalist system. The two other legs of the movement are linkages to workers, including

---

7. This proposal is largely modeled on one by Senator Mike Gravel (National Initiative for Democracy 2011), but with two modifications. First, Gravel's call for a constitutional amendment to enact such reform predated the Occupy and related progressive movements. As indicated above, I believe that alteration of the constitution can now be enacted through a direct act of popular sovereignty, which is the path I favor. Second, Gravel envisioned using electronic media for voting on frequent national referenda, which would require a level of data security that may not be technologically possible (O'Brien 2012).

unions and worker ownership and control initiatives, and, finally, internal education. It is helpful to consider all four of these strategic areas in the overall context of movement building.

The protests that began in Wisconsin and the Wall Street area in 2011 are forging new political communities through geographically based relationships and face-to-face communication. At the core of these communities are those who physically occupied Wisconsin's capitol building, Zuccotti Park and numerous other sites and who were and continue to be arrested in civil disobedience actions. Radiating from these local cores are concentric circles of support from those who contribute varying amounts of time or money to the cause or who attend marches and rallies. Overlapping with these local communities and connecting them all are virtual communities whose participants communicate through social media and who support and are energized by the mass protests and their overarching goal of economic justice.

All this face-to-face and digital communication constitutes a revival of what political scientists call "civil society." It was this kind of revival in Eastern Europe and Russia in the 1980s that eventually brought down the Soviet communist system, which was tottering from an internal economic crisis. That occurred even without the benefit of the Internet and modern mobile devices. The spreading digital revolution is accelerating these forces of change worldwide, as seen dramatically in the Arab Spring and the recent toppling of Middle Eastern dictatorships. America's system of state capitalism is next.

The kind of communication and relationship networks I am describing function in two ways. First, they can be used to mobilize mass demonstrations in support of the movement's political agenda and, when necessary, in support of the frontline protestors who occupy sites and practice civil disobedience. Second, they are conduits of political information for what I am calling internal education. While the public is systematically misinformed by right-wing pundits, politicians, think tanks, and the corporate-controlled media, the movement's face-to-face and digital networks can enable its participants who are active in the academic, policy, electoral, and Washington Beltway arenas to communicate what they are learning to street activists and the broader circles of supporters and sympathizers who are connected to the movement digitally.

The totality of these communication and relationship networks can function like a new kind of political organization. Unlike existing political parties, these networks one can bypass the moribund institutions of state capitalism and build a movement capable of challenging them. The constructive agenda is a government for the people that can enact the movement's goals into law and public policy. The main instrument for accomplishing this is the national direct democracy outlined previously, first applied to the urgent policy and institutional reforms outlined in this book, then periodically to other initiatives as an ongoing exercise of popular sovereignty.

Finally, unions and workers forming Mondragon-type cooperatives should be an integral part of these networks. Workers and unions can bring themselves and their members onto the streets for mass protests and provide other organizing resources. The movement as a whole can also rally to the side of public employees under attack by right-wing state governments, as occurred in Wisconsin in 2011; teachers under attack from neoliberal school reformers; and striking private sector unions. Unions and worker cooperatives can participate in the movement's internal education both to inform others about their struggles and to become informed about broader political issues.

In addition, producer cooperatives as well as firms that workers take over through union-sponsored buyouts can reach out to the movement as potential consumers of their goods and services. Following the Mondragon model, credit unions can channel capital from movement depositors to movement enterprises, bypassing Wall Street.[8] Both as consumers and as depositors, members of the movement can thereby withdraw their funds from the state capitalist economy and support the emerging economy of worker-owned and -controlled enterprises. Such a boycott of corporate capitalism, undertaken on a large scale, can give the movement bargaining power to pressure the corporate elite into agreeing to national worker ownership and control, as outlined in Chapter 6. There would be a synergy between this economic initiative and the political initiative to institute worker ownership and control as part of a national referendum.

Even with the physical clearing of Zuccotti Park and other occupied sites by police, and however much popular protests may wax and wane in the coming years, there is no rolling back the renewal of civil society now afoot. The networks and relationships forged in the crucible of the Occupy movement are not going away, and mass mobilization is taking new forms. The progressive movement is awakening a sleeping giant, America's beleaguered middle class. The days are over when that middle

---

8. In addition, corporations bought out by workers can raise some equity capital through a mutual fund that buys their stock and resells it to movement investors in the form of a diversified financial product, also bypassing Wall Street. Rules would have to be established to prevent the rich from gaining control of the mutual fund by buying a majority of its shares. For example, the fund by design might issue only nonvoting shares, with its directors being elected democratically by the worker-owned enterprises that participate.

class believed, respected, and deferred to America's state capitalist elite, and without legitimacy and deference, no political-economic elite can rule (Schell 2004; Sharp 1973).

This was true of the European monarchies that fell in the eighteenth and nineteenth centuries; the colonial, fascist, and communist regimes that fell in the twentieth; and, more recently, the Middle Eastern dictatorships that were swept into the dustbin of history during the Arab Spring. America's political and economic institutions today are every bit as rotten, in their own way, as the French monarchy in the 1780s, Britain's colonial regime in India in the 1940s, the Soviet Union in the 1980s, and Egypt's Mubarak regime in 2011. The days of America's state capitalism are numbered. It is time to build the government for the people and postcapitalist economy that will take its place when it falls.

CONCLUSION: CAN AMERICA LEAD AGAIN?

While a progressive mass movement can draw inspiration from the democratic revolutions that have shaken the halls of power since 1776, these same revolutions are also cautionary tales. Indian independence was marred by Hindu-Muslim violence, and now the tensions between India and Pakistan; Russian democracy by class polarization and continued authoritarianism; and the overthrow of Mubarak by continued poverty, entrenched military power, and the rise of Islamic fundamentalism. What will replace state capitalism in America is as yet undetermined. But the stakes could hardly be higher, not only for the country's middle class but for the world as well.

If a weak or incompetent postcapitalist government emerges in America and effective global leadership does not arise elsewhere, future generations throughout the globe will live in hell. Storms, floods, and droughts will destroy agriculture; social chaos and violence will rage on all sides; and several billion people will die from starvation, dehydration, disease, and political violence. I am not being dramatic. This is a sober, factual description of the expected consequences of irreversible climate change, which is overtaking our planet even as you are reading this book.

A government for the people in the United States and a socially responsible postcapitalist economy is the world's best hope for averting this nightmare. To be sure, no one country can or should dominate the world of the twenty-first century. But the United States, in collaboration with the world's other governments and the United Nations, can help bend the arc of history in the direction of peace, justice, and sustainable prosperity. That is the mission of America's progressive movement.

APPENDIX

Psychology of the Radical Right

INTRODUCTION: AUTHORITARIANISM, MACHISMO, AND RIGHT-WING ATTITUDES

There is a large body of research on the psychology of right-wing attitudes that goes back to the clinical observations of Wilhelm Reich (1961, 1970) in the 1930s and the survey data and depth interviews of *The Authoritarian Personality* (Adorno et al. 1950), one of the great classics of American social science. These early studies—which uncovered a syndrome of repressed rage and sexual needs at the basis of ethnocentrism, anti-Semitism, and social-economic conservatism—are still relevant today, especially for understanding the psychology of religious fundamentalism. Dorothy Dinnerstein (1977) and Nancy Chodorow (1978) launched another important branch of inquiry, uncovering the cultural and psychological sources of the masculine and feminine personality types.

Beginning in the 1980s, important new contributions to this literature came from the emerging fields of psychohistory and political psychology. Alice Miller's (1983) psychobiography of Adolf Hitler traced the fascist personality to its origins in punitive child rearing. Lloyd deMause (1982, 1984) examined child-rearing patterns, their historical evolution, their effects on individual psychology, and the large-scale expression of individual psychopathology in group fantasies and social phenomena, including group conflict, oppression, and war. Myriam Miedzian (2002) explored the link between masculinity and violence, and I did survey research establishing authoritarianism and machismo as strong predictors of militarist policy preferences (D'Agostino 1993, 1995). David Beisel (2009) and Richard Morrock (2010) applied psychohistorical methods in case studies of fascism and militarism. In the discussion that follows, I want to examine the psychology of sacred cows and scapegoats that underpins the right-wing defense of state capitalism in the United States today.[1]

GROUP FANTASY AND ECONOMIC REALITY

Connecting the dots of my research on militarism and my eleven years of experience as a New York City public school teacher, I have a unique window on a national "group fantasy" (deMause 1982) that revolves around sacred cows and scapegoats. In this fantasy, military power, wealth, and the free market are sacred cows, presided over by a priesthood of Pentagon officials, corporate CEOs, and conservative pundits and politicians. The failures of this system in the real world—patently obvious to ordinary Americans under current economic conditions—are blamed on scapegoats: teachers, unions, and government officials.

This ideology, which especially characterized the period from Ronald Reagan through George W. Bush, can be summarized as follows. American military power is a benign force that makes the world safe for freedom and democracy. The free market economy, if only left to itself, would create jobs for every able-bodied person and usher in an age of universal prosperity. But union rules and government regulations are strangling private enterprise. Union pay and benefits are bankrupting state governments and making U.S. corporations uncompetitive. Public school teachers are not preparing American youth to compete in the global economy. "Tax-and-spend" politicians are feeding a ravenous and unproductive public sector with the hard-earned wealth of the middle class. Capital is being siphoned from the engines of economic growth into a dysfunctional, corrupt, and bloated world of earmarks, out-of-control red tape, and entitlement programs that sap ordinary people of their personal responsibility (Armey and Kibbe 2010; Beck 2010).

As psychohistorians have shown (deMause 1982; Morrock 2010), the power of group fantasies derives from unconscious complexes they express. While this set of ideas is no exception, there is another reason it exerts such a strong grip on America's political imagination: it provides a narrative that enables ordinary Americans to make sense of their

---

1. Most of the material that follows was published in an earlier form in the *Journal of Psychohistory* (D'Agostino 2012a) and is reprinted here with permission of the editor.

economic frustrations. As Richard Wolff (2010) notes in his book *Capitalism Hits the Fan*, these frustrations have a basis in reality—the demise of the American dream beginning in the 1970s. It is no coincidence that the group fantasy I have described arose in this historical situation; its first version was articulated by California governor Ronald Reagan, then by President Reagan, the "great communicator" (deMause 1984). In one form or another, it has animated the Republican Party and a broad array of grassroots conservative groups ever since.

In addition to the subjective needs it satisfies, this national group fantasy draws plausibility from another source—it contains important grains of truth about external reality. Urban public schools *are* failing the nation's youth, albeit not for the reasons "school reform" ideologues tout. Some government expenditures *are* squandering the country's resources and depleting the middle class; it is just that this description applies much more to the national security state idealized by conservatives than to the "nanny state" they vilify. Unions *have* increased the costs of production. But for the 25 years after World War II, the rising cost of labor actually spurred productivity by creating incentives for capitalists to invest in machinery. At the same time, union wages and benefits broadly distributed the fruits of industrial progress, creating both middle-class prosperity and the aggregate demand needed to buy the goods and services the country was so efficiently producing.

I would argue that a progressive mass movement in the United States, in order to succeed, must do justice to these truths. It must address the legitimate grievances of ordinary Americans who *are* being ripped off by their political-economic system and reframe their understanding of who is ripping them off, how they are doing so, and what alternative arrangements can achieve peace, justice, and sustainable prosperity. While the bulk of this book is devoted to these questions, in this appendix my focus is on the psychological underpinnings of the sacred cows and scapegoats fantasy described previously.

CAPITALIST POLITICS AND THE PSYCHODYNAMICS OF TRAUMA

Big government and corporations can serve as surrogate objects for the displacement of feelings we had as children toward our big and powerful parents. The fierce political polarization between left and right in the United States today reflects the way different "psychoclasses" relate to these institutions.[2] The sacred cows and scapegoats group fantasy is not an expression of some monolithic national psyche. It is the expression of one psychoclass, what George Lackoff (2002) calls the "strict father" type and what political psychologists call authoritarianism (Adorno et al. 1950; Altemeyer 1981; D'Agostino 1993, 1995; Hewitt 2006).[3] This psycho-class typically exhibits politically conservative policy preferences across several domains—defense and foreign policy, social and moral issues like gay rights and abortion, and economic issues such as taxation and the regulation of markets. Members of Lackoff's "nurturing parent" psycho-class hold opposing, liberal policy preferences in each of these domains. These patterns, which have been confirmed by survey research (Glynn et al. 1999), are statistical generalizations. Individual conservatives and liberals, of course, exhibit endless unique variations.

A person raised in a punitive manner—the defining characteristic of the "strict father" psychoclass—carries around within them a traumatized child seething with rage and resentment. When identifying with this inner child, he or she experiences the father as a tyrant that must be elim-inated or broken free from—the psychological template of conservative attitudes toward government. This same person also has an internalized image of the father they experienced as a small child—awesome and all powerful, always right, free to do whatever he wants, and getting what he wants by threatening to use force or actually using it. Identifying with this inner father may be the psychological basis for sacralizing both military power and the freedom of big corporations to do what they want—"the free market." In this parent-identified state of mind, the typical feeling is not rage and resentment but contempt for anyone who is weak or dependent.

The inner emotional life of a right-wing authoritarian thus oscillates between the two poles of enraged child and punitive parent. When identifying with the traumatized inner child, the person perceives "government" as an out-of-control tyrant that robs them, renders them

---

2. A psychoclass is a human group defined by personality characteristics that arise from a common pattern of child rearing (deMause 1982). Although not using the term "psychoclass," cognitive linguist George Lackoff (2002) analyzed conservatism and liberalism in relation to underlying "strict father" and "nurturant parent" psychological types that correspond closely to the concept of psychoclass. I borrow Lackoff's terms but go beyond cognitive theory by ana-lyzing the etiology and psychodynamics of the "strict father" type.

3. In the following discussion of what I am calling the "strict father" personality and psychody-namics, I draw especially from Miller (1990) and the classical research on authoritarianism (Adorno et al. 1950; Reich 1961, 1970). I also draw from reflection on personal experience, having grown up in a conservative Republican family with a strict father.

powerless, and takes away their freedom. Since this painful material is repressed and unconscious, however, it is not associated with the parental punishment—corporal or verbal—that gave rise to it. The material is not displaced onto the violent arm of government—the national security state—but onto the nurturing arm—the so-called nanny state. This displacement may account for the fury with which right-wing authoritarians attack liberal politicians and the leaders of teachers' and other public service unions, who are perceived as protecting the bad government officials and teachers.

At other times, when identifying with the inner father, this same person idealizes the national security state and big corporations, which must not be restricted in any way. Escaping from the pain, humiliation, and powerlessness of the child, the person now becomes all-powerful and free. Any limits on military power and free markets—say international law or environmental regulations—are perceived as a threat to this inner power and freedom. Spending constraints that apply to every other government program, even Medicare, cannot be applied to military power, which must be compulsively amassed without limit.

While in this father-identified mode, the person feels contempt for the weak, the same contempt the person's father felt for his or her weakness in childhood. This contempt is displaced onto the weak and vulnerable in society—children and those dependent on public services—and onto those who care for them and provide these services, such as public school teachers. This is entirely compatible with idealization of the unusually tough teacher or government official—like the authoritarian math teacher in the movie *Stand and Deliver* or the all-powerful leader needed to remake public education envisioned in *Waiting for Superman*. This complex goes hand in hand with idealization of charter schools—which break the government mold and bring the idealized market competition and free enterprise into education.

PSYCHOCLASSES AND THE SLEEPING GIANT

I find it helpful to think of a psychoclass as a set of concentric circles. At the center are "hard-core" individuals, families, and subcultures that exhibit the characteristics of the group in an extreme form. For example, Christian fundamentalist James Dobson is a hard-core leader of the "strict father" group. While the hard core is a small minority of the population, the psychoclass as a whole encompasses increasing numbers of people as the criteria for inclusion become less and less stringent.

Extreme right-wing authoritarians defend the sacred cows of American state capitalism and attack its scapegoats with great vehemence. A much larger segment of the U.S. population—authoritarian to a lesser but still significant extent—is receptive to these ideologies. Wealthy conservatives, such as the Koch brothers and Rupert Murdoch, bankroll think tanks and media outlets that amplify the ideologies and propagate them as far into the political mainstream as authoritarian attitudes allow, at times creating electoral majorities. It is these ideological conditions that have enabled extreme right-wing pundits and politicians to dominate the Republican Party, win elections, and enact their political agenda into law and public policy.

I like to think of the American middle class as a sleeping giant. The 2011 Wisconsin uprising against the state's right-wing politicians and in support of its public employees provided a glimpse of what could happen on a national scale if this giant were to awaken. The Occupy protests later that year triggered what may be just such a national movement. Progressive movements of this sort, if directed toward a well-designed set of policy goals, can topple America's plutocracy and state capitalist system and rebuild the country's political economy on just and sustainable foundations.

In order to succeed, such a movement must frame its political agenda using a discourse that resonates with the majority of Americans, not only those near the core of the "nurturing parent" psychoclass. One of the themes of this popular discourse, I would argue, should be *responsibility*. Government and corporations—parent surrogates in the national psyche—have responsibilities. With great power comes great responsibility. What Harry Truman said about himself applies to every power holder—"the buck stops here." This meshes with the existing movement for corporate social responsibility. It also meshes with the widespread mood in the United States today that government has a responsibility to create jobs.

Formulated in psychological terms, the agenda of policy and institutional reforms presented in this book can be summarized as follows. The national security state—surrogate for parental violence—must be downsized, while the parts of government that provide for human needs—surrogate for the nurturing parent—must be built up. The hard core of the strict father psychoclass, of course, is fiercely resisting any such policy agenda. But it is by no means inevitable that the ideology generated by that small group will capture a majority of the American middle class. A progressive mass movement with competent leadership can win over the middle class. To do so, the movement's policy agenda must be rendered morally compelling to the electorate with a discourse of government and corporate responsibility.

KINDER AND GENTLER PEOPLE

In addition to framing its political agenda using a winning discourse, a progressive movement needs to be aware of and intervene in the culture of parenting that shapes the personalities of future generations. One way of doing this is to support classes in humane parenting for school-aged boys and girls (Miedzian 2002). These classes, which focus on the developmental needs of babies, have a number of beneficial effects. They bring out the nurturing side of boys, an important antidote to machismo and the violence frequently associated with it. By making young people aware of all the work, energy, time, and money involved in raising a child properly, they reduce teenage pregnancy. Finally, and most important in the present context, these classes go a long way toward breaking the cycle of punitive parenting.

In the absence of countervailing cultural norms, adults who were raised in a punitive manner tend to raise their own children the same way. However, ideas about nurturing fathers and humane parenting have been slowly penetrating popular culture for decades and are helping to break this cycle. To be sure, there is a backlash against such ideas in the strict father subculture, as seen in James Dobson's Focus on the Family organization or the promotion of corporal punishment by Michael Pearl and other fundamentalists (Eckholm 2011). Indeed, there is a culture war over parenting that parallels the ideological war between right and the left on larger political issues. Progressive people need to understand the importance of this culture war for the mental health of future generations and weigh in on the side of humane parenting. Supporting humane parenting classes in schools is a powerful way of doing this.

Bibliography

Abrahamian, Ervand. 1982. *Iran between Revolutions*. Princeton, NJ: Princeton University Press.

Adler, Moshe. 2010. *Economics for the Rest of Us: Debunking the Science That Makes Life Dismal*. New York: New Press. http://monetary.org/wp-content/uploads/2011/09/32-page-brochure.pdf

Adorno Theodore W., E. Frenkel-Brunswick, D. J. Levinson, and R. N. Sanford. 1950. *The Authoritarian Personality*. New York: Harper and Row.

Altemeyer, Bob. 1981. *Right-Wing Authoritarianism*. Winnipeg: University of Manitoba Press.

American Monetary Institute. 2011. "Introduction to Monetary Reform." http://www.monetary.org/intro-to-monetary-reform

Anyon, Jean. 2005. *Radical Possibilities: Public Policy, Urban Education, and a New Social Movement*. New York: Routledge.

Armey, Dick, and Matt Kibbe. 2010. *Give Us Liberty: A Tea Party Manifesto*. New York: HarperCollins.

Armstrong, Karen. 2006. *Muhammad: A Prophet for Our Time*. New York: HarperOne.

Aronowitz, Stanley. 2005. *Just around The Corner: The Paradox of the Jobless Recovery*. Philadelphia: Temple University Press.

Aslan, Reza. 2006. *No God but God: The Origins, Evolution, and Future of Islam*. New York: Random House Trade Paperbacks.

Bagdikian, B. H. (2004). *The Media Monopoly*. Boston: Beacon Press.

Baker, Eva L., Paul E. Barton, Linda Darling-Hammond, Edward Haertel, Helen F. Ladd, Robert L. Linn, Diane Ravitch, Richard Rothstein, Richard J. Shavelson, and Lorrie A. Shepard. 2010. "Problems with the Use of

Student Test Scores to Evaluate Teachers." Economic Policy Institute Briefing Paper #278. http://epi.3cdn.net/724cd9a1eb91c40ff0_hwm6iij90 .pdf

Baker, Peter. 2010. "Arms Treaty with Russia Headed for Ratification." *New York Times*, December 21. http://www.nytimes.com/2010/12/22/world/ europe/22start.html?scp=6&sq=

Banks, Erik. 2007. *Finance: The Basics*. New York: Routledge.

Beard, Charles A. 2011. *An Economic Interpretation of the Constitution of the United States*. Clark, NJ: The Lawbook Exchange.

Beck, Glenn. 2009. *Arguing with Idiots: How to Stop Small Minds and Big Government*. New York: Threshold Editions and Mercury Radio Arts.

Beck, Glenn. 2010. *Broke: The Plan to Restore Our Trust, Truth, Treasure*. New York: Threshold Editions and Mercury Radio Arts.

Beisel, David. 2009. *The Suicidal Embrace: Hitler, the Allies, and the Origins of the Second World War*. 2nd ed. Nyack, NY: Circumstantial Productions.

Beljac, Marko. 2011. "The Case for Minimum Deterrence." Nuclear Resonances blog. http://scisec.net/?p=154

Bell, Daniel. 1973. *The Coming of Post-Industrial Society: A Venture in Social Fore-casting*. New York: Basic Books.

Bennett, John T. 2011. "Sen. Kyl: Obama's Goal for Nuclear Weapon-Free World Is 'Loopy' " The Hill, April 12. http://thehill.com/homenews/ administration/155459-kyl-obamas-goal-for-a-nuclear-weapons-free-world -is-loopy

Benson, Constance L. 1999. *God and Caesar: Troeltsch's Social Teaching as Legiti-mation*. New Brunswick, NJ: Transaction.

Berle, Adolph A., and Gardiner C. Means. 1991. *The Modern Corporation and Private Property*. New Brunswick, NJ: Transaction.

Berliner, David C. and Bruce J. Biddle. 1995. *The Manufactured Crisis: Myths, Fraud, and the Attack on America's Public Schools*. Reading, MA: Addison-Wesley.

Berliner, David C., and Bruce J. Biddle. 1996. "Making Molehills Out of Mole-hills: Reply to Lawrence Stedman's Review of 'The Manufactured Crisis.' " *Education Policy Analysis Archives* 4, no. 3 (February 26).

Bilmes, Linda J., and Joseph E. Stiglitz. 2008. *The Three Trillion Dollar War: The True Cost of the Iraq Conflict*. New York: Norton.

Black, Lisa. 2011. "Spending Gap between State's Rich, Poor Schools Is Vast." *Chicago Tribune*, November 7.

Bluestone, Barry, and Bennett Harrison. 1984. *The Deindustrialization of America: Plant Closings, Community Abandonment, and the Dismantling of Basic Industry*. New York: Basic Books.

Bowles, Samuel and Howard Gintis. 2011. "Beyond the Educational Frontier: The Great American Dream Freeze," in Richard Arum et al. ed., *The Struc-ture of Schooling: Readings in the Sociology of Education*. Thousand Oaks, CA: Sage Publishers.

Brecher, Jeremy, Brendan Smith, and Tim Costello. 2009. "Global Labor's For-
    gotten Plan to Fight the Great Depression." Znet, March 18. http://www
    .zcommunications.org/global-labor-s-forgotten-plan-to-fight-the-great
    -depression-by-jeremy-brecher

Breen, Michael. 2010. "U.S. Security Umbrella Bolsters Korea's Growth." *Korea
    Times*, March 5.

Brennan, James F. 2009. "New York City Public School Improvement before and
    after Mayoral Control." In *NYC Schools under Bloomberg and Klein: What
    Parents, Teachers, and Policymakers Need to Know*, ed. Ravitch et al. New York:
    Lulu. http://www.lulu.com/product/paperback/nyc-schools-under-bloom
    bergklein-what-parents-teachers-and-policymakers-need-to-know/4970767

Brown, Lester R. 2009. *Plan B 4.0: Mobilizing to Save Civilization*. New York:
    Norton.

Bunzl, Martin. 2004. "Counterfactual History: A User's Guide." *The American
    Historical Review*, Vol. 109, No. 3, June. http://www.historycooperative.org
    /journals/ahr/109.3/bunzl.html

Burroughs, John. 1998. *The Legality of Threat or Use of Nuclear Weapons: A Guide to
    the Historic Opinion of the International Court of Justice*. Piscataway, NJ: Trans-
    action.

Burroughs, John, Jacqueline Cabasso, Felicity Hill, Andrew Lichterman, Jennifer
    Nordstrom, Michael Spies, and Peter Weiss. 2007. *Nuclear Disorder or
    Cooperative Security? An Assessment of the Final Report of the Weapons of Mass
    Destruction Commission and Its Implications for U.S. Policy*. New York: Lawyers'
    Committee on Nuclear Policy.

Butler, Smedley D. 2003. *War Is a Racket*. Port Townsend, WA: Feral House.

Cabasso, Jacqueline. 2007a. "Nuclear Weapons Research and Development." In
    *Nuclear Disorder or Cooperative Security? An Assessment of the Final Report of the
    Weapons of Mass Destruction Commission and Its Implications for U.S. Policy*, ed.
    John Burroughs, Jacqueline Cabasso, Felicity Hill, Andrew Lichterman,
    Jennifer Nordstrom, Michael Spies, and Peter Weiss. New York: Lawyers'
    Committee on Nuclear Policy.

Cabasso, Jacqueline. 2007b. "Redefining Security in Human Terms." In *Nuclear
    Disorder or Cooperative Security? An Assessment of the Final Report of the Weap-
    ons of Mass Destruction Commission and Its Implications for U.S. Policy*, ed. John
    Burroughs, Jacqueline Cabasso, Felicity Hill, Andrew Lichterman, Jennifer
    Nordstrom, Michael Spies, and Peter Weiss. New York: Lawyers' Commit-
    tee on Nuclear Policy.

Caldeira, Ken, and James F. Kasting. 1992. "The Life Span of the Biosphere
    Revisited." *Nature* 360 (December).

Calmes, Jackie. 2010. "Obama Is Against a Compromise on Bush Tax Cuts." *New
    York Times*, September 7.

Campbell, Donald T. 1976. "Assessing the Impact of Planned Social Change."
    Public Affairs Center, Dartmouth College, Hanover, NH. http://www.eric
    .ed.gov/PDFS/ED303512.pdf

Caro, Robert. 1975. *The Power Broker: Robert Moses and the Fall of New York*. New York: Vintage.

Casey, Leo. 2006. "Leading the Race to the Bottom. Tweed's Leadership Academy and Jack Welch." EdWize, January 6. http://www.edwize.org/leading-the-race-to-the-bottom-tweeds-leadership-academy-and-jack-welch

Cassata, Donna. 2011. Defense Hawks Insist on Sparing Military from Cuts." Associated Press, November 22. http://www.google.com/hostednews/ap/article/ALeqM5h_1qxgk61pOM1cVrl3CG1j8xUicg?docId=40f5508ae702460b9c1b0eb342de6358

Center for Responsive Politics. 2011. "Agribusiness." OpenSecrets.org http://www.opensecrets.org/industries/indus.php

Center for Research on Education Outcomes. 2009. "Multiple Choice: Charter School Performance in 16 States." http://credo.stanford.edu/reports/MULTIPLE_CHOICE_CREDO.pdf

Chernus, Ira. 1989. *Dr. Strangegod: On the Symbolic Meaning of Nuclear Weapons*. Columbia: University of South Carolina Press.

Chomsky, Noam. 1994. "The Clinton Vision: Update." *Z Magazine*, January.

Chomsky, Noam. 2003. *Hegemony or Survival: America's Quest for Global Dominance*. New York: Henry Holt.

Chomsky, Noam. 2006. *Failed States: The Abuse of Power and the Assault on Democracy*. New York: Holt Paperbacks.

Chomsky, Noam. 2007. "Starving the Poor." *Khaleej Times*, May 15. http://www.chomsky.info/articles/20070515.htm

Chomsky, Noam. 2008. "It's the Oil, Stupid!" *Khaleej Times*, July 8. http://www.khaleejtimes.com/DisplayArticleNew.asp?col=&section=opinion&xfile=data/opinion/2008/July/opinion_July32.xml

Chomsky, Noam, and Edward S. Herman. 1979. *The Washington Connection and Third World Fascism*. Boston: South End Press.

Chodorow, Nancy. 1978. *The Reproduction of Mothering: Psychoanalysis and the Sociology of Gender*. Berkeley: University of California Press.

Chullikatt, Francis. 2011. "The Nuclear Question: The Church's Teachings and the Current State of Affairs." Text of Archbishop Francis Chullikat's speech on nuclear disarmament, July 5. *National Catholic Reporter*, July 5. http://ncronline.org/news/peace/text-archbishop-francis-chullikat%E2%80%99s-speech-nuclear-disarmament

Civico, Aldo. 2010. "La experiencia estrella de Palermo," in Bernardo Kliksberg, ed. *Inseguridad Ciudadana. ¿Como Mejorarla?* Buenos Aires: Pearson Education.

Civico, Aldo. 2012. "We are Illegal but not Illegitimate: Modes of Policing in Medellin." *Political and Legal Anthropology Review* 35, No 1.

Clark, Colin. 1940. Conditions of Economic Progress. London: Macmillan and Company.

Class Size Matters. 2011. "Research Studies Showing the Benefits of Class Size Reduction." http://www.classsizematters.org/research-and-links-2

Coalition of Essential Schools. 2011. "About CES." http://www.essentialschools.org

Cobb, Clifford, Ted Halstead, and Jonathan Rowe. 1995. "If the GDP Is Up, Why Is America Down?" *Atlantic Monthly*, October. http://www.theatlantic.com/past/politics/ecbig/gdp.htm

Cobb, Clifford W., and Phillipe Diaz. 2009. *Why Global Poverty?* New York: Robert Schalkenbach Foundation.

Cohen, Benjamin J. 2001. "Bretton Woods System." *Routledge Encyclopedia of International Political Economy*. http://www.polsci.ucsb.edu/faculty/cohen/inpress/bretton.html

Collins, Randall. 2011. "Functional and Conflict Theories of Educational Stratification," in Richard Arum et al. ed., *The Structure of Schooling: Readings in the Sociology of Education*. Thousand Oaks, CA: Sage Publishers.

Comer, James P., et al., eds. 1999. *Child by Child: The Comer Process for Change in Education*. New York: Teachers College Press.

Common Cause. 2011a. "A Constitutional Amendment to Reverse Citizens United." http://www.commoncause.org/site/pp.asp?c=dkLNK1MQIwG&b=7840855

Common Cause. 2011b. "Money in Politics." http://www.commoncause.org/site/pp.asp?c=dkLNK1MQIwG&b=4764307

Compton, Mary, and Lois Weiner. 2008. *The Global Assault on Teaching, Teachers, and Their Unions*. New York: Palgrave Macmillan.

Conaway, Camille Pampell, and Anjalina Sen. 2005. *Beyond Conflict Prevention: How Women Prevent Violence and Build Sustainable Peace*. New York: Global Action to Prevent War and Women's International League for Peace and Freedom.

Congressional Research Service. 2010. "Cost of Major U.S. Wars." http://www.fas.org/sgp/crs/natsec/RS22926.pdf

Cramer, Philissa. 2011. "Judge Rejects UFT-NAACP Claims, Allows Co-Locations, Closures." Gotham Schools, July 21. http://gothamschools.org/2011/07/21/judge-rejects-uft-naacp-claims-allows-co-locations-closures

Cullen, Louis M. 2003. *A History of Japan, 1582–1941: Internal and External Worlds*. New York: Cambridge University Press.

Daily Kos. 2012. "No Surprise: Oakland Police Chief Lied to Discredit Occupy Oakland." Daily Kos, January 14. http://www.dailykos.com/story/2012/01/14/1054602/-No-Surprise-Oakland-Police-Chief-Lied-to-Discredit-Occupy-Oakland-

D'Agostino, Brian. 1993. "Self Perception and National Security Policy." Doctoral diss., Columbia University). Ann Arbor, MI: University Microfilms International.

D'Agostino, Brian. 1995. "Self-Images of Hawks and Doves: A Control Systems Model of Militarism." *Political Psychology* 16, no. 2: 259–95.

D'Agostino, Brian. 2009a. "Design for an Innovative Public School." http://brian.bendag.com/education.php

D'Agostino, Brian. 2009b. "Holding Mayor Bloomberg Accountable." NYC Rubber Room Reporter, October 28. http://nycrubberroomreporter.blogspot.com/2009/10/holding-mayor-bloomberg-accountable-by.html

D'Agostino, Brian. 2012a. "Scapegoats and Sacred Cows: The Ideology of American State Capitalism." *Journal of Psychohistory* 39, no. 3.

D'Agostino, Brian. 2012b. 'Waiting for Superman': Neglecting Children and Scapegoating Teachers. *Journal of Psychohistory*, forthcoming.

D'Agostino, Brian. 2012c. "Beyond the Welch Paradigm: Why Value Added Assessment in not a Path to Educational Quality." Unpublished paper.

Dame, Frederick William. 2001. *History of Switzerland*. Lewiston, NY: Edwin Mellen Press.

Darling-Hammond, Linda. 2010. "Soaring Systems: High Flyers All Have Equitable Funding, Shared Curriculum, and Quality Teaching." *American Educator* 34, no. 4.

David Lynch Foundation. 2011. "Our Work: Schools." http://www.davidlynch foundation.org/schools.html

Davidson, Karl. 2009. "One Worker, One Vote: US Steelworkers to Experiment with Factory Ownership, Mondragon Style." International Labor Rights Forum. http://www.laborrights.org/freedom-at-work/news/12198

Deller, Nicole, Arjun Makhijani, and John Burroughs. 2003. *Rule of Power or Rule of Law? An Assessment of U.S. Policies and Actions Regarding Security-Related Treaties*. New York: Apex Press.

deMause, Lloyd. 1982. *Foundations of Psychohistory*. New York: Creative Roots, Inc.

deMause, Lloyd. 1984. *Reagan's America*. New York: Creative Roots Press.

Deming, W. Edwards. 1984. *Out of the Crisis*. Cambridge, MA. M.I.T. Press.

Deming, W. Edwards. 2000. *The New Economics for Industry, Government, Education*.2nd ed. Cambridge, MA: MIT Press.

Deppe, F., et al. 1973. *Kritik der Mitbestimmung*. Frankfurt: Suhrkamp Verlag.

Diaz, Phillipe. 2010. *The End of Poverty? Think Again*. Canoga Park, CA: Cinema Libre Studio. http://www.cinemalibrestudio.com

Dillon, Sam. 2010. "Method to Grade Teachers Provokes Battles." *New York Times*, August 31. http://www.nytimes.com/2010/09/01/education/01teacher.html

Dillon, Sam. 2011. "Obama to Waive Parts of No Child Left Behind." *New York Times*, September 22. http://www.nytimes.com/2011/09/23/education/23educ.html

Dinnerstein, D. 1977. *The Mermaid and the Minotaur: Sexual Arrangements and Human Malaise*. New York: Harper and Row.

Domhoff, G. William. 2011. "Wealth, Income, and Power." http://sociology.ucsc.edu/whorulesamerica/power/wealth.html

Dudek, Bernard, Rachel Milton, Lance Hori, and Alex Flaster. 2006. *Inside 9/11*. Chicago, IL: Tower Productions for National Geographic Channel

Dumas, Lloyd Jeffry. 1986. *The Overburdened Economy: Uncovering the Causes of Chronic Unemployment, Inflation, and National Decline*. Berkeley: University of California Press.

Duncan, Greg J., and Richard J. Murnane. 2011. *Whither Opportunity? Rising Inequality, Schools, and Children's Life Chances*. New York: Russell Sage Foundation.

Eckholm, Eric. 2011. "Preaching Virtue of Spanking, Even as Deaths Fuel Debate." *New York Times*, November 6. http://www.nytimes.com/2011/11/07/us/deaths-put-focus-on-pastors-advocacy-of-spanking.html?_r=1&emc=eta1

Eisenhower, Dwight D. 1953. "The Chance for Peace." Address to the American Society of Newspaper Editors, April 16, 1953. http://www.information clearinghouse.info/article9743.htm

Ellsberg, Daniel. 2003. *Secrets: A Memoir of Vietnam and the Pentagon Papers.* London: Penguin.

Falk, Richard A., Samuel S. Kim, and Saul H. Mendlovitz, eds. 1991. *The United Nations and a Just World Order.* Boulder, CO: Westview Press.

Ferguson, Charles. 2010. Inside Job. Culver City, CA: Sony Pictures Classics.

Fitzgerald, A. Ernest. 1989. *The Pentagonists: An Insider's View of Waste, Mismanagement and Fraud in Defense Spending.* New York: Houghton Mifflin.

Fitzgerald, Frances. 2001. *Way Out There in the Blue: Reagan, Star Wars and the End of the Cold War.* New York: Simon and Schuster.

Freeman, Marsha. 2009. "The True History of the U.S. Fusion Program—and Who Tried to Kill It." *21st Century Science and Technology*, 15–29.

Friedman, Milton. 1962. *Capitalism and Freedom.* Chicago: University of Chicago Press.

Freidman, Milton, and Anna Jacobson Schwartz. 1963. *Monetary History of the United States.* Princeton, NJ: Princeton University Press.

Fusfeld, Daniel R. 1988. In *Economics: Principles of Political Economy.* Boston: Scott, Foresman.

Gaddis, John Lewis. 2005. *The Cold War: A New History.* New York: Penguin Press.

Gallagher, Jim. 1998. *Woman's Work: Story of the Focolare Movement and Its Founder.* Hyde Park, NY: New City Press.

Gast, Scott. 2010. "Maryland Launches Genuine Progress Indicator." *Yes! Magazine*, April 2. http://www.yesmagazine.org/new-economy/maryland-launches-genuine-progress-indicator

Gates, Robert. 2011. "Defense Secretary Robert Gates on Military Spending Cuts." *PBS NewsHour* interview, January 6.

Gelbspan, Ross. 2004. *Boiling Point: How Politicians, Big Oil and Coal, Journalists, and Activists Have Fueled the Climate Crisis—And What We Can Do to Avert Disaster.* New York: Basic Books.

George, Henry. 2006. *Progress and Poverty.* New York: Cosimo Classics.

Gigacz, Stefan, and Helen Ting. 2011. "California City's Mondragon Plan Moves Forward." desarrollo.net, August 23.

Giordano, Mary Ann. 2011. If Teaching Improves, Bloomberg Says Large Classes Are Fine by Him. The New York Times, December 2. http://www.nytimes.com/schoolbook/2011/12/02/bloomberg-says-large-classes-are-fine-by-him/?scp=4&sq=bloomberg%20m.i.t%20speech&st=cse

Global Action to Prevent War and Armed Conflict. 2008. "Preventing Armed Violence and Ending War: The Global Action to Prevent War Program

Statement, 2008–2010." http://www.globalactionpw.org/wp/wp-content/uploads/program-statement-2008.pdf

Global Teach-In. 2012. Building a New Economy and New Wealth. http://www.globalteachin.com/

Glynn, Carroll J., Susan Herbst, Robert Shapiro, and Garrett O'Keefe. 1999. *Public Opinion*. Westview Press.

Goldstein, Fred. 2008. *Low Wage Capitalism: Colossus with Feet of Clay*. New York: World View Forum.

Goldstein, Joshua S., and Jon C. Pevehouse. 2011. *International Relations*. 10th ed. New York: Longman.

Gordon, Robert J., ed. 1986. *The American Business Cycle: Continuity and Change*. Cambridge, MA: National Bureau of Economic Research.

Grassroots Education Movement. 2010. *The Truth about Charter Schools in New York City*. New York: Grassroots Education Movement. http://www.waitingforsupermantruth.org/?page_id=408

Grassroots Education Movement. 2011. *The Inconvenient Truth behind* Waiting for Superman (DVD). New York: Grassroots Education Movement and Real Reform Studios Production. http://www.waitingforsupermantruth.org/

Greenhut, Steven. 2009. *How Public Employee Unions Are Raiding Treasuries, Controlling Our Lives, and Bankrupting the Nation*. Santa Ana, CA: The Forum Press.

Greenspan, Alan. 2008. *The Age of Turbulence: Adventures in a New World*. New York: Penguin.

Grubb, W. Norton. 2009. *The Money Myth: School Resources, Outcomes, and Equity*. New York: Russell Sage Foundation.

Hamilton, Alexander, James Madison, and John Jay. 2011. *The Federalist Papers*. New York: Soho Books.

Hansel, Lisa, and Jennifer Durban. 2010. "Common Core Curriculum: An Idea Whose Time Has Come." *American Educator* 34, no. 4

Hantzopoulos, Maria and Alia R. Tyner-Mullings. 2012. *Critical Small Schools: Beyond Privatization in New York City Urban Educational Reform*. Charlotte, NC: Information Age Publishing.

Hanushek, Eric A. 2002. *Teacher Quality*. Stanford, CA: Hoover Institution Press. http://edpro.stanford.edu/hanushek/admin/pages/files/uploads/Teacher%20quality.Evers-Izumi.pdf

Hanushek, Eric A., and Caroline B. Hoxby. 2005a. "Developing Value Added Measure for Teachers and Schools." In *Reforming Education in Arkansas*, by Koret Task Force. Stanford, CA: Hoover Institution Press.

Hanushek, Eric A., and Caroline M. Hoxby. 2005b. "Rewarding Teachers." In *Reforming Education in Arkansas*, by Koret Task Force. Stanford, CA: Hoover Institution Press.

Harrington, Michael. 1962. *The Other America: Poverty in the United States*. New York: Macmillan.

Hartung, William D. 1994. *And Weapons for All: How America's Multibillion Dollar Arms Trade Warps our Foreign Policy and Subverts Democracy at Home*. New York: HarperCollins.

Hartung, William D. 2002. "The Role of the Arms Lobby in the Bush Administration's Radical Reversal of Two Decades of U.S. Nuclear Policy, a World Policy Institute Special Report (May 2002)." New York: World Policy Institute.

Hartung, William D. 2010. *Prophets of War: Lockheed Martin and the Making of the Military-Industrial Complex*. New York: Nation Books.

Harvey, Fiona. 2011. "World Headed for Irreversible Climate Change in Five Years, IEA Warns." *The Guardian*, November 9. http://www.guardian.co .uk/environment/2011/nov/09/fossil-fuel-infrastructure-climate-change?CMP =EMCENVEML1631

Hawthorne, Fran. 2008. *Pension Dumping: The Reasons, the Wreckage, the Stakes for Wall Street*. New York: Bloomberg Press.

Heilbroner, Robert L. 1985. *The Nature and Logic of Capitalism*. New York: Norton.

Herman, Edward S., and Noam Chomsky. 2002. *Manufacturing Consent: The Political Economy of the Mass Media*. New York: Pantheon.

Hess, Frederick M. 2006. *Tough Love for Schools: Essays on Competition, Accountability, and Excellence*.

Hewitt, William F. 2006. "Lakoff and Frank—Looking at the Contemporary American Right." *Journal of Psychohistory* 34, no. 2: 163–70.

Hilsman, Roger. 1992. *George Bush vs. Saddam Hussein: Military Success! Political Failure?* Novato, CA: Presidio.

Hiltermann, Joost. 2003. "America Didn't Seem to Mind Poison Gas." *International Herald Tribune*, January 17.

Hoffman, Mary. 2005. "Jack Welch Is My Daddy." Independent Community of Educators, March 8. http://ice-uft.org/daddy.htm

Horowitz, Emily. 2009. "School Overcrowding: What Principals Say." In *NYC Schools under Bloomberg and Klein: What Parents, Teachers, and Policymakers Need to Know*, ed. Ravitch et al. New York: Lulu. http://www.lulu.com/ product/paperback/nyc-schools-under-bloombergklein-what-parents-teachers -and-policymakers-need-to-know/4970767

Ikle, Fred C., et al. 1988. *Discriminate Deterrence: Report of the Commission on Integrated Long-Term Strategy*. Washington, DC: U.S. Government Printing Office.

James, Michael, et al. 2010. *Education's Highest Aim*. Hyde Park, NY: New City Press.

Jervis, Robert. 2005. *American Foreign Policy in a New Era*. New York, Routledge.

Johnson, Chalmers. 2004. *Blowback: The Costs and Consequences of the American Empire*. 2nd ed. New York: Henry Holt.

Johnson, William. 2012. "Confessions of a Bad Teacher." *The New York Times*, March 3. http://www.nytimes.com/2012/03/04/opinion/sunday/confessions -of-a-bad-teacher.html?_r=1&src=rechp

Just Food. 2011. "What Is CSA?" http://www.justfood.org/csa

Karan, Dan. 2002. "Democracy and Housing in Community Development, in *From Community Economic Development and Ethnic Entrepreneurship to Economic Democracy: The Cooperative Alternative*. Umea, Sweden: Partnership for Multiethnic Inclusion.

Kaufmann, J. E., et al. 2011. *The Maginot Line: History and Guide*. Barnsley: Pen and Sword.

Kaya, Yoichi, and Keiichi Yokobori. 1997. *Environment, Energy, and Economy: Strategies for Sustainability*. Tokyo: United Nations University Press.

Kennedy, Paul M. 1989. *The Rise and Fall of the Great Powers: Economic Change, and Military Conflict from 1500 to 2000*. New York: Vintage Books.

Kenner, Robert. 2008. *Food, Inc.* Beverly Hills, CA: Magnolia Pictures Participant Media.

Keynes, John Maynard. 2010. *The General Theory of Employment, Interest, and Money*. Whitefish, MT: Kessinger Publishing.

King, Jamilah. 2011. "Thousands Protest Wisconsin Gov. Scott Walker's Anti-Union Attack." *Colorlines*, February 17. http://colorlines.com/archives/2011/02/thousands_protest_wisconsin_gov_scott_ walkers_anti-union _attack.html

Kissinger, Henry. 1969. *Nuclear Weapons and Foreign Policy*. New York: Norton.

Klare, Michael. 2002. *Resource Wars: The New Landscape of Global Conflict*. New York: Holt Paperbacks.

Klein, Joel I. 2007. *Statement in Tough Choices or Tough Times: The Report of the New Commission on the Skills of the American Workforce*. San Francisco: Wiley.

Klein, Naomi. 2011. "Capitalism vs. the Climate." *The Nation*, November 28.

Knopp, Sarah. 2008. "Charter Schools and the Attack on Public Education." *International Socialist Review*, issue 62, November–December. http://www .isreview.org/issues/62/feat-charterschools.shtml

Koretz, Daniel. 2008. *Measuring Up: What Educational Testing Really Tells Us*. Cambridge, MA: Harvard University Press.

Korten, David C. 2001. *When Corporations Rule the World*. 2nd ed. San Francisco: Berrett Koehler Publishers and Kumarian Press.

Koss, Steve. 2009. "Test Score Inflation: Campbell's Law at Work." In *NYC Schools Under Bloomberg and Klein: What Parents, Teachers, and Policymakers Need to Know*, ed. Ravitch et al. New York: Lulu. http://www.lulu.com/product/paperback/nyc-schools-under-bloombergklein-what-parents -teachers-and-policymakers-need-to-know/4970767

Kozol, Jonathan. 1991. *Savage Inequalities: Children in America's Schools*. New York: HarperCollins.

Kozol, Jonathan. 2005. *The Shame of the Nation: The Restoration of Apartheid Schooling in America*. New York: Crown Publishing Group.

Kramer, Andrew E. 2008. "Deals with Iraq Are Set to Bring Oil Giants Back." *New York Times*, June 19.

Krueger, Alan, and Diane Whitmore. 2001. "Would Smaller Class Sizes Help Close the Black-White Achievement Gap?" Princeton University working paper 451.

Krugman, Paul. 2009. "How Did Economists Get It So Wrong?" *New York Times Magazine*, September 2. http://www.nytimes.com/2009/09/06/magazine/06Economic-t.html?pagewanted=all

Krugman, Paul. 2011a. "Making Things in America." *New York Times*, May 20. http://www.nytimes.com/2011/05/20/opinion/20krugman.html?emc=eta1

Krugman, Paul. 2011b. "Things to Tax." *New York Times*, November 27.

Lackoff, George. 2002. *Moral Politics: How Liberals and Conservatives Think*. Chicago: University of Chicago Press.

Laursen, Eric. 2010. "Back to Reaganomics." *The Independent*, December 15.

Lederach, John Paul. 1995. *Preparing for Peace: Conflict Transformation across Cultures*. Syracuse, NY: Syracuse University Press.

Lederach, John Paul. 2005. *The Moral Imagination: The Art and Soul of Building Peace*. New York: Oxford University Press.

Lerner, Michael. 2006. *The Left Hand of God: Taking Back Our Country from the Religious Right*. New York: HarperOne.

Levin, Peter. 2003. *Homeless to Harvard: The Liz Murray Story*. Lifetime Television.

Lewis, Jeffrey G. 2008. "Minimum Deterrence." *Bulletin of the Atomic Scientists*, July/August.

Lewontin, R. C. 1991. *Biology as Ideology: The Doctrine of DNA*. New York: Harper Perennial.

Lifton, Robert J. 1979. *The Broken Connection: On Death and the Continuity of Life*. New York, Simon and Schuster.

Lifton, Robert J., and Eric Markusen. 1990. *The Genocidal Mentality: Nazi Holocaust and Nuclear Threat*. New York: Basic Books.

Lifton, Robert J., and Richard Falk. 1982. *Indefensible Weapons: The Political and Psychological Case Against Nuclear Weapons*. New York: Basic Books.

Lloyd, Marion. 2002. "Soviets Close to Using A-Bomb in 1962 Crisis, Forum Is Told." *Boston Globe*, October 13. http://www.latinamericanstudies.org/cold-war/sovietsbomb.htm

Lockhart, Paul. 2009. *Mathematician's Lament: How School Cheats Us Out of Our Most Fascinating and Imaginative Art Form*. New York: Bellevue Literary Press.

Luhby, Tami. 2011. "Who Are the 1 Percent?" CNN, October 29. http://money.cnn.com/2011/10/20/news/economy/occupy_wall_street_income/index.htm

Lupica, Mike. 2011. "Newt Gingrich's 'Get a Job after You Take a Bath' Comment Reeks of Hypocrisy." *Daily News*, November 21. http://www.nydailynews.com/news/politics/newt-gingrich-a-job-a-bath-comment-reeks-hypocrisy-article-1.980460

MacLeod, Greg. 1997. *From Mondragon to America: Experiments in Community Economic Development*. Sydney, Nova Scotia: Cape Bretton University Press.

Maharishi Foundation USA. 2011. "Top Hundred Published Studies.: http://
    www.tm.org/research-on-meditation

Mandel, Ernest. 1982. *Introduction to Marxism*. London: Pluto Press.

Mandel, Ernest. 1986. *The Meaning of the Second World War*. New York: Random
    House.

Mann, Michael. 1999. *The Insider*. Burbank, CA: Touchstone Pictures.

Maslow, Abraham H. 1987. *Motivation and Personality*. New York: HarperCollins.

Matgouranis, Christopher. 2010. "The Underemployed College Graduate."
    Center for College Affordability and Productivity, October 18. http://
    centerforcollegeaffordability.org/archives/1761

Mayer, Janet Grossbach. 2011. *As Bad as They Say? Three Decades of Teaching in the
    Bronx*. New York: Fordham University Press.

McCaffery, Daniel F., J. R. Lockwood, Daniel M. Koretz, and Laura S.
    Hamilton. 2003. *Evaluating Value-Added Models for Teacher Accountability*.
    Santa Monica, CA: RAND Corporation.

McCaffery, Ed. 2010. "It's Unfair, and There's a Better Way." *Wall Street
    Journal*, September 20.

Mearsheimer, John J. 2010. "Why Is Europe Peaceful Today?" *European Political
    Science* 9.

Meier, Deborah. 2009. "New York City Schools: Then and Now." In *NYC
    Schools Under Bloomberg and Klein: What Parents, Teachers, and Policymakers
    Need to Know*, ed. Ravitch et al. New York: Lulu. http://www.lulu.com/
    product/paperback/nyc-schools-under-bloombergklein-what-parents
    -teachers-and-policymakers-need-to-know/4970767

Melman, Seymour. 1956. *Dynamic Factors in Industrial Productivity*. Oxford:
    Blackwell.

Melman, Seymour. 1983. *Profits without Production*. New York: Alfred A. Knopf.

Melman, Seymour. 1989. *The Demilitarized Society*. Nottingham: Spokesman
    Books.

Melman, Seymour. 2001. *After Capitalism: From Managerialism to Workplace
    Democracy*. New York: Alfred A. Knopf.

Melman, Seymour. 2002. "Mondragon: A Model for Linking Innovation,
    Productivity and Economic Democracy." In *From Community Economic
    Development and Ethnic Entrepreneurship to Economic Democracy: The
    Cooperative Alternative*. Umea: Partnership for Multiethnic Inclusion.

Mendlovitz, Saul. 1999. "Prospects for Abolishing War: A Proposal for the
    Twenty-First Century." *Rutgers Law Review* 52.

Micklethwait, John, and Adrian Wooldridge. 2005. *The Company: A Short History
    of a Revolutionary Idea*. New York: Modern Library.

Miedzian, Myriam. 2002. *Boys Will Be Boys: Breaking the Link between Masculinity
    and Violence*. Herndon, VA: Lantern Books.

Miller, Alice. 1983. *For Your Own Good: Hidden Cruelty in Childrearing and the
    Roots of Violence*. Translated by H. Hannum and H. Hannum. New York:
    Farrar, Straus and Giroux.

Miller, Julie A. 1991. "Report Questioning 'Crisis' in Education Triggers an Uproar." *Education Week*, October 9. http://www.edweek.org/ew/articles/1991/10/09/06crisis.h11.html

Min, David. 2011a. "Faulty Conclusions Based on Shoddy Foundations." Center for American Progress, February. http://www.americanprogress.org/issues/2011/02/pdf/pinto.pdf

Min, David. 2011b. "Why Wallison Is Wrong about the Genesis of the U.S. Housing Crisis." Center for American Progress, July 12. http://www.americanprogress.org/issues/2011/07/wallison.html

Mishel, Lawrence. 2006. "CEO to Worker Pay Imbalance Grows." Economic Policy Institute, June 21. http://www.epi.org/publication/webfeatures_snapshots_20060621

Mishel, Lawrence. 2011. "Regulatory Uncertainty: A Phony Explanation for Our Jobs Problem." Economic Policy Institute, September 27. http://www.epi.org/publication/regulatory-uncertainty-phony-explanation

Mishel, Lawrence, and Richard Rothstein, eds. 2002. *The Class Size Debate*. Washington, DC: Economic Policy Institute.

Møller, Bjørn. 1996. "Common Security and Non-Offensive Defence as Guidelines for Defence Planning and Arms Control?" *International Journal of Peace Studies* 1 (July). http://www.gmu.edu/programs/icar/ijps/vol1_2/Moeller.htm

Mondragon Cooperative Corporation. 2011. "Who We Are." http://www.mcc.es/ENG.aspx

Moore, Mike. 2008. *Twilight War: The Folly of U.S. Space Dominance*. Oakland, CA: The Independent Institute.

Morrock, Richard. 2010. *The Psychology of Genocide and Violent Oppression: A Study of Mass Cruelty from Nazi Germany to Rwanda*. Jefferson, North NC: McFarland.

Moxley, Charles J., Jr. 2011. "Obama's Nuclear Posture Review: An Ambitious Program for Nuclear Arms Control but a Retreat from the Objective of Nuclear Disarmament." *Fordham International Law Journal* 34. http://lcnp.org/wcourt/FordhamMoxleyFinal.pdf

Moxley, Charles J., Jr., John Burroughs, and Jonathan Granoff. 2011. "Nuclear Weapons and Compliance with International Humanitarian Law and the Nuclear Non-Proliferation Treaty." *Fordham International Law Journal* 34. http://lcnp.org/wcourt/Fordhamfinaljoint.pdf

National Bureau of Economic Research. 2011. "U.S. Business Cycle Expansions and Contractions." http://www.nber.org/cycles/cyclesmain.html

National Center on Education and the Economy. 1990. *America's Choice: High Skills or Low Wages*. Washington, DC: National Center on Education and the Economy.

National Center on Education and the Economy. 2007. *Tough Choices or Tough Times: The Report of the New Commission on the Skills of the American Workforce*. San Francisco: Wiley.

National Commission on Excellence in Education. 1983. *A Nation at Risk: The Imperative for Education Reform*. Washington, DC: U.S. Department of Education. http://www2.ed.gov/pubs/NatAtRisk/index.html

National Initiative for Democracy. 2011. "What Is the National Initiative for Democracy?" http://ni4d.us/national_initiative

Nembhard, Jessica Gordon, and Curtis Haynes Jr. 2002. "Using Mondragon as a Model for African American Urban Redevelopment." In *From Community Economic Development and Ethnic Entrepreneurship to Economic Democracy: The Cooperative Alternative*. Umea: Partnership for Multiethnic Inclusion.

Newman, Andy. 2011. "Occupy Protestors Reach Two-Month Milestone." *New York Times*, November 18. http://cityroom.blogs.nytimes.com/2011/11/17/protesters-and-officers-clash-near-wall-street/?hp

New York Coalition for Healthy School Food. 2011. "Create Change." http://www.healthylunches.org/createchange.htm

Noguera, Pedro. 2008. "Making School Matter: Providing Support to At-Risk Students and Reducing the Dropout Rate." Paper presented to the New York State Governor's Summit on Student Engagement and Dropout Prevention, October 10.

Nordhaus, William D. 2012. "Why the Global Warming Skeptics Are Wrong." *New York Review of Books*, March 22. http://www.nybooks.com/articles/archives/2012/mar/22/why-global-warming-skeptics-are-wrong/

Nozick, Robert. 1974. *Anarchy, State, and Utopia*. Oxford: Basil Blackwell.

O'Boyle, Thomas. 1998. *At Any Cost: Jack Welch, General Electric, and the Pursuit of Profit*. New York: Vintage Books.

O'Brien, Miles. 2012. "Internet Voting: Will Democracy or Hackers Win?" *PBS NewsHour*, February 16. http://www.pbs.org/newshour/bb/politics/jan-june12/internetvoting_02-16.html

Olson, Mancur. 1971. *The Logic of Collective Action: Public Goods and the Theory of Groups*. Cambridge, MA: Harvard University Press.

Organization for Economic Cooperation and Development. 2010. "PISA 2009 Results: Executive Summary." http://www.oecd.org/dataoecd/34/60/46619703.pdf

Orme-Johnson D. W., et al. 1988. "International Peace Project in the Middle East: The Effect of the Maharishi Technology of the Unified Field." *Journal of Conflict Resolution* 32: 776–812.

Parenti, Michael. 2002. *The Terrorism Trap: September 11 and Beyond*. San Francisco: City Lights Publishers.

Pepin, Jacques. 2011. *The Origin of AIDS*. Cambridge: Cambridge University Press.

Pintacuda, Ennio and Aldo Civico. 1993. *La Scelta*. Casale Monferrato, Italy: Piemme.

Pollin, Robert, and Heidi Garrett-Peltier. 2010. "The U.S. Employment Effects of Military and Domestic Spending Priorities: An Updated Analysis." Political Economy Research Institute. http://www.peri.umass.edu/236/hash/9b5e62a1aa9f65f4d22f799a612f6021/publication/382

Preble, Christopher. 2011. "Of Course: Paul Ryan's Budget Avoids Cuts to Military Spending." *Opposing Views*, April 6. http://www.opposingviews.com/i/of-course-paul-ryan%E2%80%99s-budget-avoids-cuts-to-military-spending

Purnick, Joyce. 2009. *Mike Bloomberg: Money, Power, Politics*. New York: Public Affairs.

Raa, Thijs ten. 2005. *The Economics of Input-Output Analysis*. New York: Cambridge University Press.

Rachwal, Paul. 2008. "Ford, Chrysler Cut Advertising Costs while Toyota and GM Boost Spending." *Left Lane News*, June 13. http://www.leftlanenews .com/ford-chrysler-cut-advertising-costs-while-toyota-and-gm-boost-it.html

Rashbaum, William K., Joseph Goldstein, and Al Baker. 2011. "Experts Say N.Y. Police Dept. Isn't Policing Itself." *New York Times*, November 2. http:// www.nytimes.com/2011/11/03/nyregion/experts-say-ny-police-dept-isnt -policing-itself.html?_r=1&hp

Ravitch, Diane. 2010. *The Death and Life of the Great American School System: How Testing and Choice Are Undermining Education*. New York: Basic Books.

Ravitch, Diane. 2011. "School 'Reform': A Failing Grade." *New York Review of Books*, September 29. http://www.nybooks.com/articles/archives/2011/sep/ 29/school-reform-failing-grade

Ravitch, Diane. 2012. "Schools We Can Envy." *New York Review of Books*, March 8.

Reich, Wilhelm. 1961. *Character Analysis*. Translated by V. R. Carfagno. New York: Farrar, Straus and Giroux.

Reich, Wilhelm. 1970. *The Mass Psychology of Fascism*, Translated by V. R. Carfagno. New York: Farrar, Straus and Giroux.

Reinert, Erik. 2008. *How Rich Countries Got Rich and Why Poor Countries Stay Poor*. New York: PublicAffairs Books.

Renzulli, Linda A. and Vincent J. Roscigno. 2011. "Charter Schools and the Public Good," in Richard Arum et al. ed., *The Structure of Schooling: Readings in the Sociology of Education*. Thousand Oaks, CA: Sage Publishers.

Richardson, Katherine, Will Steffen, Hans Joachim Schellnhuber, et al. 2009. *Climate Change: Global Risks, Challenges, and Decisions*. Copenhagen: University of Copenhagen. http://climatecongress.ku.dk/pdf/synthesisreport/

Romer, Christina D. 2011. "Needed: Plain Talk about the Dollar." *New York Times*, May 21. http://www.nytimes.com/2011/05/22/business/economy/ 22view.html?emc=eta1

Romer, Christina D. 2012. "Do Manufacturers Need Special Treatment?" *New York Times*, February 4. http://www.nytimes.com/2012/02/05/business/do -manufacturers-need-special-treatment-economic-view.html?_r=1&hp

Romm, Joseph. 2010. "Exxon Mobil Paid No Federal Income Tax in 2009. Climate Progress blog. http://climateprogress.org/2010/04/06/exxon -mobil-paid-no-federal-income-tax-in-2009

Rothstein, Richard, and Lawrence Mishel, eds. 2002. *The Class Size Debate*. Washington, DC: Economic Policy Institute.

Rothstein, Jesse. 2010. "Teacher Quality in Educational Production: Tracking, Decay, and Student Achievement." *Quarterly Journal of Economics* 125, no. 1: 175–214. http://www.nber.org/papers/w14442

Rothstein, Jesse. 2011. "Review of 'Learning about Teaching': Initial Findings from the Measures of Effective Teaching Project." National Education Policy Center. http://nepc.colorado.edu/thinktank/review-learning-about-teaching

Rui, Ning and Erling E. Boe. 2012. "Who teaches in American charter schools? Findings from secondary analysis of the 1999–2000 Schools and Staffing Survey." *International Journal of Research & Method in Education* 10.

Rynn, Jon. 2010. *Manufacturing Green Prosperity: The Power to Rebuild the American Middle Class*. New York: Praeger.

Sachs, Jonathan. 2002. *The Dignity of Difference: How to Avoid the Clash of Civilizations*. New York: Continuum.

Sacks, Peter. 2001. *Standardized Minds: The High Price of America's Testing Culture and What We Can Do to Change It*. Cambridge, MA: Da Capo Press.

Salary.com. 2011. "Salary Wizard." http://www.salary.com/salary/index.asp

Santelli, Rick. 2009. "President Obama, Are You Listening." Video and transcript of comments on CNBC, February 19. http://www.rightpundits.com/?p=2921

Scanzoni Letha Dawson and Virginia Ramey Mollenkott. 1994. *Is the Homosexual My Neighbor? A Positive Christian Response*. New York: HarperOne.

Schell, Jonathan. 2004. *The Unconquerable World: Power, Nonviolence, and the Will of the People*. New York: Holt Paperbacks.

Schelling, Thomas C. 1981. *The Strategy of Conflict*. Cambridge, MA. Harvard University Press.

Semple, Kirk. 2011. "Bridge Repairs by a Company Tied to Beijing." *New York Times*, August 10. http://www.nytimes.com/2011/08/11/nyregion/china-construction-co-involved-in-new-yorks-public-works.html?_r=1&emc=eta1

Shane, Scott A. 2008. *The Illusions of Entrepreneurship: The Costly Myths That Entrepreneurs, Investors and Policy Makers Live By*. New Haven, CT: Yale University Press.

Sharp, Gene. 1973. *The Politics of Nonviolent Action*. Boston: Porter Sargent Publishers.

Simopoulos, Artemis P., and Jo Robinson. 1999. *The Omega Diet: The Lifesaving Nutritional Program Based on the Diet of the Island of Crete*. New York: Harper Paperbacks.

Skinner, B. F. 1965. *Science and Human Behavior*. New York: Free Press.

Smith, Chris. 2011. "Bloomberg's One Percent Solution." *New York*, November 28.

Smith, Raymond A. 2010. *Importing Democracy: Ideas from Around the World to Reform and Revitalize American Politics and Government*. Santa Barbara, CA: Praeger.

Spiro, David E. 1999. *The Hidden Hand of American Hegemony: Petrodollar Recycling and International Markets*. Ithaca, NY: Cornell University Press.

Stearns, Peter N., Michael Adas, Stuart B. Schwartz, and Marc Jason Gilbert. 2011. *World Civilizations: The Global Experience*. 6th ed. Upper Saddle River, NJ: Longman.

Stedman, Lawrence C. 1996a. "Respecting the Evidence: The Achievement Crisis Remains Real." *Education Policy Analysis Archives* 4, no. 7 (April 4).

Stedman, Lawrence C. 1996b. "Review of 'The Manufactured Crisis.' " *Education Policy Analysis Archives* 4, no. 1 (January 23).

Stelter, Brian, and Tim Arango. 2010. "News Corp. Reels in a Top Educator." *New York Times*, November 9. http://mediadecoder.blogs.nytimes.com /2010/11/09/news-corp-reels-in-a-top-educator

Stiglitz, Joseph E. 2003. *Globalization and its Discontents*. New York: Norton.

Stiglitz, Joseph E. 2007. *Making Globalization Work*. New York: Norton.

Stiglitz, Joseph E. 2010. *Freefall: America, Free Markets, and the Sinking of the World Economy*. New York: Norton.

Stiglitz, Joseph E., and Carl E. Walsh. 2006. *Economics*. 4th ed. New York: Norton.

Stockholm International Peace Research Institute. 2011. "Military Expenditures Database." http://www.sipri.org/databases/milex

Stolberg, Sheryl Gay, and Helene Cooper. 2009. "Obama Adds Troops, but Maps Exit Plan." *New York Times*, December 1.

Strozier, Charles B., David M. Terman, James W. Jones, and Katherine A. Boyd. 2010. *The Fundamentalist Mindset: Psychological Perspectives on Religion, Violence, and History*. New York: Oxford University Press.

Tavernise, Sabrina. 2011. "U.S. Poverty Rate, at 15 Percent, Is Highest since 1993." *New York Times*, September 13.

Tax Policy Center. 2011. "Distribution by Income Class of All Returns, Taxable Returns, Itemized Returns, and Tax Liability at 1999 Rates and 1999 Law and 1999 Income Levels." http://www.taxpolicycenter.org/taxfacts/ displayafact.cfm?Docid=217

Teachers Unite. 2011. "Mission Statement." http://teachersunite.net/node/335

Toffler, Alvin. 1984. *The Third Wave*. New York: Bantam.

Toussaint, Eric. 2009. "Complete Transcript of 'The End of Poverty?' In *Why Global Poverty?*, ed. Clifford W. Cobb and Phillipe Diaz. New York: Robert Schalkenbach Foundation.

Trip, Gabriel. 2011. "Teachers Wonder: Why the Heapings of Scorn?" *New York Times*, March 3. http://www.nytimes.com/2011/03/03/education/ 03teacher.html?scp=1&sq=teachers%20scorn&st=cse

Turner, Ralph. 2011. "Sponsored and Contest Mobility and the School System," in Richard Arum et al. ed., *The Structure of Schooling: Readings in the Sociology of Education*. Thousand Oaks, CA:Sage Publishers.

Uchitelle, Louis. 2006. *The Disposable American: Layoffs and Their Consequences*. New York: Alfred A. Knopf.

UNICEF. 1999. "Iraq Surveys Show 'Humanitarian Emergency.' " *Newsline*, August 12.

United Nations. 1945. "Charter of the United Nations." http://www.un.org/en/ documents/charter

United Nations. 2007. "Model Nuclear Weapons Convention: Convention on the Prohibition of the Development, Testing, Production, Stockpiling, Transfer, Use and Threat of Use of Nuclear Weapons and on Their

Elimination." United Nations General Assembly. http://inesap.org/sites/default/files/inesap_old/mNWC_2007_Unversion_English_N0821377.pdf

United Nations. 2011. "Millennium Development Goals." http://www.un.org/millenniumgoals

United Nations International Law Commission. 1950. "Principles of International Law Recognized in the Charter of the Nürnberg Tribunal and in the Judgment of the Tribunal." United Nations. http://untreaty.un.org/ilc/texts/instruments/english/draft%20articles/7_1_1950.pdf

U.S. Bureau of Economic Analysis. 2011. http://www.bea.gov/iTable/iTable.cfm?ReqID=9&step=1

U.S. Bureau of Labor Statistics. 2010. "International Comparisons of Manufacturing Productivity and Unit Labor Cost Trends/" http://www.bls.gov/fls/#tables

U.S. Census Bureau. 2010. *Current Population Survey, 1960 to 2010. Annual Social and Economic Supplements*. Washington, DC: U.S. Government Printing Office.

U.S. Department of Defense. 2000. "Joint Vision 2020." http://www.fs.fed.us

U.S. Department of Defense. 2009. "Active Duty Military Personnel Strengths by Regional Area and by Country (309A)," September 30, 2009. http://siadapp.dmdc.osd.mil/personnel/MILITARY/history/hst0909.pdf

U.S. Department of Education. 2011. "Institute of Education Sciences, National Center for Education Statistics, International Activities Program." http://nces.ed.gov/surveys/international

U.S. Department of Health and Human Services. 2011. "The 2011 HHS Poverty Guidelines." http://aspe.hhs.gov/poverty/11poverty.shtml

U.S. Department of State. 2010. "Treaty between the United States of America and the Russian Federation on Measures for the Further Reduction and Limitation of Strategic Arms." April 8. http://www.state.gov/documents/organization/140035.pdf

U.S. Energy Information Administration. 2011. http://www.eia.doe.gov/errormsg.html?v=http://www.eia.doe.gov:80/emeu/cabs/topworldtables1_2.htm

U.S. Office of Management and Budget. 2011. "Budget of the United States Government, Fiscal Year 2012, Summary Tables." http://www.whitehouse.gov/sites/default/files/omb/budget/fy2012/assets/tables.pdf

U.S. Office of Personnel Management. 2007. "Federal Civilian Workforce Statistics: The Fact Book, 2007 Edition." http://www.opm.gov/feddata/factbook/2007/2007FACTBOOK.pdf

U.S. Social Security Administration. 2011. Measures of Central Tendency for Wage Data. http://www.ssa.gov/oact/cola/central.html

U.S. Small Business Administration. 2011. "How Important Are Small Businesses to the U.S. Economy?" http://www.sba.gov/advocacy/7495/8420

Varoufakis, Yanis. 1998. *Foundations of Economics: A Beginner's Companion*. New York: Routledge.

Wallace, Deborah, and Rodrick Wallace. 2001. *A Plague on Your Houses: How New York Was Burned Down and National Public Health Crumbled*. Brooklyn, NY: Verso.

Wallison, Peter. 2011. "Government-Sponsored Meltdown." *Wall Street Journal*, July 12. http://online.wsj.com/article/SB10001424052702304760604576423670655568418.html

Walsh, Michael. 2004. *Opus Dei: An Investigation into the Powerful Secretive Society within the Catholic Church*. New York: HarperOne.

Ward, Dana. 2011. "Chomsky Bibliography." Anarchy Archives. http://dwardmac.pitzer.edu/Anarchist_Archives/chomsky/chomskybiblio.html

Weiss, Peter. 2011. Taking the Law Seriously: The Imperative Need for a Nuclear Weapons Convention. *Fordham International Law Journal* 34. http://lcnp.org/wcourt/Weiss_FinaltoAuthor.pdf

Welch, Jack with Suzie Welch. 2005. *Winning*. New York: HarperBusiness.

West, Cornel. 1982. *Prophesy Deliverance: An Afro-American Revolutionary Christianity*. Philadelphia, PA: The Westminster Press.

Winerip, Michael. 2012. "Hard-Working Teachers, Sabotaged When Student Test Scores Slip." *The New York Times*, March 4. http://www.nytimes.com/2012/03/05/nyregion/in-brooklyn-hard-working-teachers-sabotaged-when-student-test-scores-slip.html

Wheeler, Winslow T. 2011. "What Is the Defense Budget?" Center for Defense Information, February 11. http://www.cdi.org/program/document.cfm?documentid=4641&programID=37&from_page=../friendlyversion/printversion.cfm

Wolfe, Nathan. 2011. *The Viral Storm: The Dawn of a New Pandemic Age*. New York: Macmillan.

Wolff, Richard D. 2010. *Capitalism Hits the Fan: The Global Economic Meltdown and What to Do about It*. Northampton, MA: Olive Branch Press.

Wolterstorff, Eric. 2003. A Speculative Model of How Groups Respond to Threats. Dissertation, Union Institute and University. http://shiftingculture.com/monograph.php

World Bank. 2011. "Gini Index." http://data.worldbank.org/indicator/SI.POV.GINI

Wright, Ronald. 2004. *A Short History of Progress*. Cambridge, MA: Da Capo Press.

Yoder, John Howard. 1994. *The Politics of Jesus*. 2nd ed. Grand Rapids, MI: W. B. Eerdmans.

Young-Smith, Barron. 2010. "START to Finish? The Fate of Obama's Nuclear Treaty." *The New Republic*, November 13. http://www.tnr.com/article/politics/79148/start-treaty-obama-kyl-nuclear

Zinn, Howard. 2003. *A People's History of the United States*. New York: HarperCollins.

Index

About the Author

BRIAN D'AGOSTINO teaches political economy and history at the Harry Van Arsdale Jr. Center for Labor Studies, Empire State College. He previously taught political science at Adelphi University and City University of New York, and worked for eleven years as a New York City public school teacher. He holds a PhD from Columbia University and is the author of numerous publications on public affairs and political psychology including the peer-reviewed article "Self-Images of Hawks and Doves."